FREUD IN ZION

The History of Psychoanalysis Series

Professor Brett Kahr and Professor Peter L. Rudnytsky (Series Editors)
Published and distributed by Karnac Books

Other titles in the Series

FREUD IN ZION

Psychoanalysis and the Making of Modern Jewish Identity

Eran J. Rolnik

KARNAC

First published in Hebrew in 2007 by
Am Oved Books, Tel Aviv, Israel

First published in English in 2012 by
Karnac Books Ltd
118 Finchley Road, London NW3 5HT

Cover: *Construction day in a Kibbutz*, Palestine 1936.
Photographer: Rudi Weissenstein

Translated by Haim Watzman

British Library Cataloguing in Publication Data

A C.I.P. for this book is available from the British Library

ISBN 978 1 78049 053 3

Edited, designed and produced by The Studio Publishing Services Ltd
www.publishingservicesuk.co.uk
e-mail: studio@publishingservicesuk.co.uk

www.karnacbooks.com

CONTENTS

ABOUT THE AUTHOR

Eran J. Rolnik is a psychiatrist, psychoanalyst, and historian. He teaches at Tel Aviv University and at the Max Eitingon Institute for Psychoanalysis in Jerusalem. He works in Tel Aviv in private practice.

A vast outpouring of scholarly literature has been devoted to the question of Freud's Jewish identity and its bearings on the history of psychoanalysis, as well as to the Jewish origins of psychoanalysis. There has likewise been no shortage of valuable studies on the reception of psychoanalysis in specific countries, including the USA, France, and Russia, but also more far-flung outposts, from India to Mexico. But, until the present book by Eran J. Rolnik, no one has illuminated either what the author terms "the Jewish signifier" of psychoanalysis or its contours as "a multi-dimensional cultural–historical artefact of modernity" by turning the tables and investigating the impact of psychoanalysis itself on (in the words of his subtitle) "the making of modern Jewish identity".

Central to Rolnik's project is the ambiguity encapsulated in his evocative title, *Freud in Zion*. For "Zion" differs from other place names in referring equivocally to either a "metaphysical condition" or a "geographical location", or to both at once; and when Rolnik speaks of "Freud in Zion," he thus encompasses everything from (1) "the appearance of the Zionist version of the European 'New Man', and its connection to the Freudian view of man", through (2) "the migration, following the rise of the Nazis in Germany, of psychoanalysis out of

Central Europe", to (3) "the consolidation of psychoanalytic discourse in the Yishuv following the arrival of immigrant analysts and the founding of the Institute of Psychoanalysis in Jerusalem"—these being the "three broad contexts" delineated by Rolnik in the six concise yet densely packed chapters of his book.

If *Freud in Zion* stands out on account of the uniqueness of its conception, its author is, by virtue of his interdisciplinary training and cross-cultural perspectives, singularly well qualified for his task. Trained in both psychiatry and history, Eran Rolnik is himself a translator of Freud, a practicing psychoanalyst, and a member of the Scientific Committee of the Israel Psychoanalytic Society. Originally published to a chorus of acclaim in Hebrew in 2007, *Freud in Zion*, fluently translated by Haim Watzman, can, in this considerably revised and streamlined version, reach the international audience it assuredly deserves.

Much of what makes *Freud in Zion* so compelling is Rolnik's capacity to bring out the connections that make poetry of history. Not only was Vienna the birthplace of both Zionism and psychoanalysis, but Freud and Theodor Herzl lived literally "a few doors from each other on the same street". More significantly, the Vienna that was home to both the "father of psychoanalysis" and the "prophet of the Jewish state" itself "lay at the frontier between the Occident and the Orient". As a crossroads between East and West, Vienna—also, of course, a cauldron of anti-Semitism—is, thereby, the uncanny twin of Jerusalem, although the traditional contrast between Jews from Eastern Europe (*Ostjuden*) and those from Western Europe came to be redefined as that between "Jews who had come from Europe and the Old Yishuv—the Jews who had lived in Palestine before the Zionist influx". Along the same lines, Rolnik makes the excellent point that "Athens and Rome, not Jerusalem, inspired Freud's phantasmagoric world", and it was only to the classical cities that "he would make pilgrimages".

Of the twin foci of Rolnik's mapping of the history of psychoanalysis in what, from 1918 to 1948, was British-ruled Palestine, before becoming the state of Israel in 1948, it is probably as "a chapter in the chronicle of the psychoanalytic movement and idea as it progressed through the twentieth century", rather than for its examination of how Freud's ideas formed "a part of the crystallisation of a distinct Hebrew culture in the Land of Israel", that *Freud in Zion* will initially appeal to most readers. For scholars of psychoanalysis, one of the chief pleasures in the book will be the parade of characters who traverse its pages: Arnold Zweig, Martin Buber, Siegfried Bernfeld, Bertha Pappenheim, Frieda Fromm-Reichmann, Moshe Wulff, David Eder, Dorian-Isador Feigenbaum, Felix Boehm, Otto Fenichel, Heinz Kohut, Kurt Lewin, and Gershom Scholem, to name a handful, many of whom might be well known in other connections, but who are all depicted here in a new light.

Apart from Freud himself, however, no actor plays a more prominent role in Rolnik's historical drama than does Max Eitingon. Although Eitingon remains the most shadowy member of the "Secret Committee", renowned chiefly for the munificence of his purse and his unswerving loyalty to Freud, Rolnik observes that Eitingon's labours in Berlin in the 1920s—including his founding of the Psychoanalytic Polyclinic and his crafting of the tripartite training scheme that still bears his name—have obscured his other outstanding achievement, the establishment of the psychoanalytic institute and society in Jerusalem, following his altogether unexpected emigration to Palestine in 1933.

On a personal level, as Rolnik notes, "Eitingon's decision to move to Palestine was the first sign his agenda was not equal to Freud's". Freud, moreover, was never an unequivocal supporter of "the Jewish people's national aspirations", and this, too, contributed to the cooling in his attitude toward his "Zionist disciple". During the protracted efforts to establish a chair in psychoanalysis at the Hebrew University, which did not come to fruition until 1977 with the appointment of Joseph Sandler, Eitingon was astonished to discover that Moshe Wulff believed that he had Freud's backing; and this was indeed the case, though Freud concealed his contacts with a member of the university board of trustees from Eitingon. But the cruellest blow came only after Freud's death, when, at Anna Freud's behest, Eitingon asked Arnold Zweig, who also lived in Palestine but shared Freud's critical attitude toward "the Zionist project", for his letters from Freud so that copies could be made. Among these was one dated 10 February 1937, justly termed by Rolnik a "wicked letter", in which Freud disparaged both Eitingon and his second wife Mira in the most callous fashion. Notwithstanding this evidence of Freud's disdain, Eitingon magnanimously wrote to Zweig,

I do not care what generations to come will think of this letter. Then, like now, I suffice myself with the fact that we loved this exceptional man. He also erred when he doubted Mira's love for him. But that, too, is of no importance compared to the fact that he was there and was worthy of our love.

Like Eitingon, who was born in Mogilew, White Russia, Wulff, born in Odessa, spoke Russian as his first language. (Wulff, incidentally, as Rolnik points out, enjoys the distinction of being cited both by Freud in *Totem and Taboo* and by Winnicott in his paper on transitional objects.) Indeed, all of the founders of the Palestine Psychoanalytic Society were physicians, and the "great majority had resided, at one point or another, in Russia or the Soviet Union". The latter fact highlights a further valuable dimension of Rolnik's book, that is, his tracing of the indebtedness of Zionism to the grand experiments of socialism and communism, and how the utopian aspirations of the latter were inevitably in tension with Freud's intractable pessimism about the human condition, although "his Zionist readers preferred to bridge the gap between these different perceptions of man by a selective reading of psychoanalytic theory". As Rolnik writes in his epilogue, "unlike the Zionists, Freud never rejected the Jew of the Exile, and, unlike the socialists, he never rejected the bourgeois life. He did not pretend to be designing a 'new man,' much less a 'new Jew'". For the analysts who came to Palestine in 1933 or 1938 "under catastrophic circumstances", however, this emigration "was in effect a repeat trauma, since it involved early memories of abandonment and loss of identity", since so many of them had "spent their childhoods in the eastern provinces of the Austro-Hungarian empire or Czarist Russia", and "more than 1.25 million Jews left Russia during the decade preceding the First World War".

With respect to the history of psychoanalysis, Rolnik reminds the reader that Eitingon, who codified the rules of training that have indelibly shaped psychoanalysis as an institution, himself underwent nothing more than an "ambulatory" analysis with Freud, during which, "twice a week, for a month and a half, Eitingon accompanied the professor for a night-time walk through the streets of Vienna", and this was "the first 'training analysis' in the history of the movement". The Berlin Institute, as is well known, was "both innovative and conservative": innovative in its establishment of the Polyclinic that brought analytic treatment to hundreds of people who could otherwise never have afforded it, as well as in the deployment by Fenichel and others of psychoanalysis as a "socio-critical theory", but conservative in its uncompromising fealty to Freud. It is, therefore, not surprising that Eitingon and his colleagues in Jerusalem took pride in re-creating a "Little Berlin", and that the bylaws of the Jerusalem Institute "contained an unusually draconian provision aimed at ensuring that none would use the name of Freud's theory in vain", which was enforced by the requirement that "any member who wished to give a public lecture on any topic relating to psychoanalysis was to inform the Institute's governing committee in advance and receive the committee's consent".

Readers will draw their own conclusions about the implications of these facts set forth by Rolnik; indeed, different readers are bound to accentuate their favourite threads in his exceptionally rich and variegated tapestry. At its centre lies the tragedy of the disintegration of the Berlin Psychoanalytic Institute with the ascendancy of the Third Reich, and its mutation in 1936 into the German Institute for Psychological Research and Psychotherapy, better known as the Goering Institute. Rolnik recounts the harrowing story of the arrest in October 1935 of Edith Jacobson, and he poignantly notes that, after Felix Boehm and Carl Müller-Braunschweig succeeded Eitingon at the helm, "a locked cupboard at the Institute, referred to as the 'poison cabinet', held the one remaining copy of Freud's works". He renders the verdict that "German psychoanalysts did not display unusual resilience in standing up to the regime's demands", contrasting their pusillanimity with the hardiness displayed by the German Society of Art Historians, which, as late as 1938, resisted the directive of the Ministry of Education that it expel its Jewish members.

Those who may be insufficiently acquainted with the history and culture of Israel have an opportunity to learn from Rolnik some basic vocabulary—*Yishuv, aliyot, halutz*—as well as to profit from his expertise on a range of fascinating topics, including the many strands of Zionist thought, translations of Freud into Hebrew, the reception of *Moses and Monotheism*, the debates over "Oedipus at the Kibbutz", psychoanalytic criticism of modern Hebrew literature, and how the analytic pioneers in this modern welfare state successfully lobbied to be exempted from "having to record the full names of their patients on their invoices and annual tax reports—a precedent-setting decision that benefits psychoanalysts in Israel to this day".

From his extensive trawling in both published sources and in unpublished letters and documents, Rolnik brings forth material that might come as a revelation even to seasoned scholars of psychoanalysis. In addition to Freud's "wicked" letter to Arnold Zweig about Eitingon, I would single out a hitherto overlooked 1951 article in a Hebrew journal by Chaim Bloch, a student of Hasidism and Kabbalah, who reported having met Freud twenty-five years earlier—that is, circa 1925—in order to ask him to furnish an introduction to a book Bloch had written. In the course of their conversation, it emerged that "Freud already had in hand a manuscript that included the thesis that Moses, the great prophet of the Jews, was an Egyptian who was murdered by the Israelites". As Rolnik emphasises, "if true, this is evidence that *Moses and Monotheism*, the composition of which has always been dated to the years 1933–1938, was, in fact, written almost ten years earlier".

Although Bloch was himself a vociferous opponent of Zionism who, in all likelihood, never set foot in Palestine, his encounter with the founder of psychoanalysis none the less sheds a revealing light on Rolnik's thesis concerning the "inherent tension", indeed the "contradiction in terms", that underlies the purported "affinity" claimed by the early Zionists for Freud's theories. Freud adamantly informed Bloch that "he was repelled by the idea that we are chosen and superior to other nations", and adduced the writings not only of Herzl but also of Herzl's partner in the founding of the Zionist movement, Max Nordau, to support his own conviction, in Rolnik's paraphrase, "that the Holy Scriptures are a pile of superstitions and traditions from Egypt". For his part, the orthodox Bloch pleaded with Freud not to publish his study of Moses and the Torah, which, according to his 1951 article, he called "abominable sacrifices to the antisemitic demon". Not surprisingly, the disagreement became heated, and the meeting ended with Freud saying to Bloch as he strode from the room, "I won't write the introduction to your book and I don't want to see you again". When the two men ran into each other on the street a few years later, Freud had forgotten their earlier conversation. Upon being reminded of it by Bloch, Freud replied, "I remember your insolence, and I don't want to see you again", as he turned away.

For Freud biographers, his interactions with Bloch will be reminiscent of more famous occasions—including those with Breuer and Ferenczi—when Freud literally gave the cold shoulder to men who, unlike Bloch, had once been of great emotional importance to him but with whom he had had a falling out. From Rolnik's historical and cultural perspective, however, it is rather emblematic of the agon that is the great theme of his book. No less pertinent in this connection is the response, published in 1942, by the poet Shin Shalom to the appearance of the Hebrew translation of *The Psychopathology of Everyday Life*. Under the title "Freud's repressed Judaism", Shalom indicted Freud as, in Rolnik's summary, a representative of "the generation of assimilation, who hoped to find a solution for his own ills in the obliteration of his Jewish self". As the "central piece of evidence" for his premise that "a repressed Jewish experience lay behind Freud's doctrines", moreover, Shalom adduced "one of the examples Freud offered in his book, a conversation with a young Jewish friend about the 'social state of the people that we are both sons of'".

Shalom's already convincing case becomes even stronger once we realise that his prime exhibit is the notorious *aliquis* analysis in Chapter Two of the *Psychopathology*, which is indubitably autobiographical, even though Freud ascribes it to a fictitious interlocutor. How telling it is that Freud could give voice to his "repressed Judaism" only in this disavowed form! To quote Shalom directly:

> The generational cry of the anguished Jewish nation that was compelled to repress and conceal its birth and its explicit name, its desire and its mission, in order to give in to the forceful gentile reality of the world and all that is in it is what gave rise to the crushing and broad wings of this theory. Herzl, a member of Freud's generation and a party to his fate at first, was in fact the great discoverer and great redeemer of that repressed fundamental experience that Freud himself, originator of the theory of repression, could not comprehend.

If, as Eran Rolnik aphoristically condenses his lesson in the epilogue, "Zionism . . . may not have agreed with Freud's theory, but very badly needed it", it is equally the merit of his formidable contribution to psychoanalytic scholarship to have shown the converse to be true as well.

Professor Peter L. Rudnytsky
Series Co-Editor
Gainesville, Florida

For Nili

PREFACE

Some time ago, while translating Freud into Hebrew, I encountered a passage that struck me as both outrageous and intriguing. In the course of his discussion of the possible effects of inborn tendencies on the direction in which the ego develops, Freud claimed that it does not imply any mystical overvaluation of heredity to think it is credible that the psychological peculiarities of families, races, and nations, even in their attitudes toward psychoanalysis, are already laid down for the ego even before it has come into existence (Freud, 1937c).

Freud tracked, with both pleasure and suspicion, the rapid acceptance of psychoanalysis in different countries. But in the century since he wrote his "On the history of the psychoanalytic movement" (Freud 1914d), psychoanalytic historiography has come a long way beyond the polemical constraints, cultural prejudices, and partisan agendas so characteristic of its early days. The history of psychoanalysis is now usually looked on as a case study that can cast light on the anatomy and evolution of intellectual, scientific, and social ideas in general, and not just on its own turf. The most successful works in this field have focused not only on the evolution of psychoanalysis as an institution-alised form of therapy but, more importantly, on the discipline as a multi-dimensional cultural–historical artefact of modernity. The study of the reception of psychoanalysis and of the emergence of particular psychoanalytic cultures illuminates the theoretical diversity of psychoanalysis, but, even more so, the history of the political and cultural milieus in which psychoanalysis took root. Russian revolutionaries, American psychiatrists, Bloomsbury Circle writers, and French existentialists—these as well as other more or less heterogeneous groups developed their own versions of Freud. So did Jewish intellectuals and pioneers of the *Yishuv*—the Jewish community in Palestine under the British Mandate.

While Freud's teachings gained footholds in many countries almost as soon as he first published them in Vienna, the institutionalisation of psychoanalysis as a form of treatment was accomplished to a large extent by migrant German-speaking psychoanalysts in the 1930s and 1940s. In fact, during just seven years, from 1932 to 1939, the majority of Central European psychoanalysts emigrated out of what was commonly and somewhat ambiguously called the "German cultural sphere" (*Deutsche Kulturkreis*). Like the movement out of Germany and Central Europe of intellectuals, scholars, and scientists in other fields of knowledge, the psychoanalytic exodus had tremendous consequences for both clinical theory and the politics of the psychoanalytic movement, as well as for the growth of the local psychoanalytic communities into which the emigrants were absorbed. The encounter with the brutally anti-Semitic Nazi regime and the flight to countries with different intellectual and scientific traditions, along with Freud's death in 1939, took psychoanalysis into its post-Freudian era.

Freud in Zion looks at the reception of psychoanalysis, in its various guises, before, during, and following the immigration of German-speaking Freudians to Mandatory Palestine. I survey a period stretching from approximately 1905 to roughly 1950. As in other parts of the world, psychoanalysis was not accepted straightforwardly and without incident by the Yishuv. My task as a historian is to offer an account of the local reception of psychoanalysis as a specific case and to interpret it while being careful to avoid reductive cultural determinism, let alone an essentialist Lamarckian line of reasoning of the kind to which Freud himself was prone in his later years. I first look at the points of entry through which psychoanalysis entered Zionist and modern Hebrew culture. Then, I show that, despite the affinity that early Zionists claimed to have for Freud's theories, there was an inherent tension, at times even an evident contradiction in terms.

History is not written on a blank slate, and many friends and scholars have contributed to this study and facilitated its author's intellectual development. The influence that is most complex and difficult to decode, but most interesting from the point of view of a psychoanalyst who is also a historian, is that of my parents, Rivka and Amos Rolnik, to whom I am in great debt. I also wish to thank Dan Dinar, who has been a source of support and inspiration from the time I first added the study of history to my clinical work. I owe special gratitude to the late Rafael Moses, who mentored me with wisdom and generosity during the first stages of this study.

My book is based on unpublished letters and documents. The directors of the Freud Museum in London and of the Freud Collection in the Manuscript Division of the Library of Congress in Washington, Michael Molnar, the late Kurt Eissler, and Harold Blum were of great assistance in the first stages of my research, when it looked as if the story of psychoanalysis in Israel would forever remain locked up in archives. In a section below, I provide a key to the archives and manuscript collections that appear in the book for these unpublished sources.

Special thanks go to the Israel Psychoanalytic Society for allowing me to examine Max Eitingon's papers even before they were completely sorted and transferred to the Israel State Archives. Historians of psychoanalysis Nellie Thompson of New York, Michael Schröter of Berlin, Riccardo Steiner of London, and the late Lydia Marinelli of Vienna, offered critique and advice, as did Israeli historian Boaz Neuman. I am grateful to Haim Watzman, my English translator, and to Ilana Shamir and Emmanuel Berman, the editors of the Hebrew version of this book, which was published by Am Oved Books in 2007. Equally indispensable for the realisation of this monograph were Karnac's exceptional team headed by Oliver Rathbone; also Peter Rudnytsky and Brett Kahr, the Series Editors.

It is a great pleasure to thank the institutes and funds that have supported my research: the Central Zionist Archives, The Foundation for the Commemoration of Max and Henriette Bodenheimer; the *Neuberger* Memorial *Foundation* for German–Jewish Studies of the Institute for German History at Tel Aviv University; the Leo Baeck Institute of Jerusalem, which awarded me its Jacob Katz Prize; the Axel Springer Foundation of Berlin; the Memorial Foundation for Jewish Culture of New York; the David Herzog Fund in Graz; the

Sigmund Freud Foundation of Frankfurt; the Minerva Foundation of Munich; the Simon Dubnow Institute for Jewish History and Culture at Leipzig University; John Bunzl of the Austrian Institute for International Studies and the Israel–Palestine Project in Vienna; and the Stephan Roth Institute for the Study of Contemporary Anti-semitism and Racism at Tel Aviv University. Above all, I thank Nili, my beloved wife, without whose faith this work would not have been.

Eran Rolnik
Tel Aviv, summer 2011

Archives and manuscript collections

ABS: The Archives of the British Psychoanalytical Society, London.

AEA: The Albert Einstein Archives, The Hebrew University Jerus-alem.

AFC: Anna Freud Collection, The Freud Collection, Washington, DC.

AFM: The Freud Museum and Research Centre, London.

AHA: Ahad Ha'Am (Asher Ginsberg) Archives, (Schwarz Collection in Tel Aviv and in the National Library in Jeruslaem).

AJE: The Aviezer Yellin Archives of Jewish Education in Israel and the Diaspora, Tel Aviv University.

ANYP: The A. A. Brill Library and Archives of the New York Psycho-analytic Institute, New York.

AZA: Stiftung Archive Der Akademie Der Künste. Arnold Zweig Nachlass, Berlin.

BAK: Bundesarchiv, Archiv zur Geschichte der Psychoanalyse, Koblenz.

CZA: Central Zionist Archives, Jerusalem.

ECI: Eitingon Collection, Israel State Archives, Jerusalem.

FCLC: The Freud Collection in the Manuscript Division of the Library of Congress, Washington, DC.

GAL: Gnazim Archives of Hebrew Literature, Tel Aviv.

HNB: Haim Nachman Bialik Archive/Museum, Tel Aviv.

HUA: Hebrew University Archives, Jerusalem.

INL: Israel National Library, Jerusalem.

LBI: Chaim Eitingon Collection, Leo Baeck Institute, New York.

LIR: Lavon Institute for Labour Reseach, Tel-Aviv.
PFC: Paul Federn Collection, The Freud Collection, Washington, DC.
SBC: Siegfried Bernfeld Collection, The Freud Collection, Washington, DC.
SFH: Sigmund Freud Haus, Vienna.
SHA: HaShomer HaTza'ir Archives, Givat Haviva, Israel.
TAC: Tel Aviv City Archives.
YIVO: Institute for Jewish Research Archive, New York.

"Last night I had a vivid dream of Jerusalem. But it was a mixture of Vienna Forest and Berchtesgaden. It seems that my imagination cannot reach any further than that"

(Anna Freud, 1934)

Introduction: a costly dream

> "I certainly do not intend to regurgitate on other nations the grief I had to swallow from the Germans"
>
> (Sigmund Freud, 1922)

Dr Richard Karthaus, neurologist and psychoanalyst, medical officer in the British army and Central European intellectual, was ashamed to be alive. It was September 1945 and he was sitting in his office in the British hospital at Latrun, in the Jerusalem foothills. In Karthaus's pocket was a passport issued by the British Mandate administration in Palestine. Had he only been able to act like those freedom fighters who, at the moment of truth, had turned their guns on themselves or swallowed poison capsules that they always carried with them. He wore a British uniform, and in his thinking he sought to blend all that was good from the teachings of Sigmund Freud and Karl Marx.

He recalled his arrival in Palestine in 1933. A socialist and global authority on war neurosis, Dr Karthaus had been drummed out of the Berlin Psychoanalytic Society after he spoke out against Freud's dualistic theory of drives. He refused to accept the premise that the sexual drive was countered by a death drive. For years he had listened to the dreams of his patients, plumbed their unconscious, and had tried to bring the world of their childhoods into their consciousness. His purpose was to help them identify the cryptic presence of their past and its impact on how they perceived themselves and the world. The Nazi accession to power and his departure from Europe did not dampen the doctor's enthusiasm. When he reached his new home he was ecstatic, barely able to contain his emotions. For a moment, he was tempted to ask himself how a sober man like him, who had attended Freud in person in Vienna and who knew very well the difference between reality and fantasy, had been swept away by the Zionist dream so strongly that he actually settled in the Promised Land.

Karthaus set up his clinic in Haifa, a city where he could treat patients in German so long as the sign outside was in Hebrew. It already seemed to him then that the inhabitants of the Yishuv, the Jewish community in Palestine, loathed him and other German-speaking intellectuals almost more than they loathed the Arabs, the true inhabitants of this country, whose existence, Karthaus lamented, the earlier Jewish settlers had made sure to keep a secret.

Dr Richard Karthaus, a Viennese doctor and Freud's *Schülers-schüler* (student's student), is the protagonist of *Costly Dream* (*Traum ist Teuer*, 1989), the last *roman à clef* written by Arnold Zweig, a German–Jewish novelist and correspondent of Freud's. The novel was inspired by the brief Zionist interlude in Zweig's life, during which he lived on Mount Carmel in Haifa, underwent psychoanalysis with one of Freud's pupil's, and tried to find a place for himself in the Yishuv's cultural and intellectual life.

Zweig's novel is set in Palestine during the war, and portrays Karthaus's gradual disillusionment with the Zionist ideal that he had espoused before going into Palestinian exile. After the end of the Second World War, Zweig, disappointed by Zionism and now an enthusiastic socialist, returned to Europe. He accepted an official invitation to move into the Soviet zone of occupation. There, he was to enjoy two more decades of creative and political activity that guaranteed him a place in the East German literary pantheon.

Seeking, apparently, to conform to the East German official line on Zionism, Zweig's novel maintains a clear distinction between Karthaus, the individual who grows disenchanted with Zionism, and Karthaus, the narrator, who, years later, reflects on his earlier "mistaken" political convictions. When the book finally appeared, in

1962, it had been some seventeen years in the writing. The long gestation was in part due to the Communist censor, who obliged Zweig to rewrite several passages. Even so, *Traum ist Teuer* remained controversial in East Germany—although not because of references to Zionists. What bothered a number of critics was the prominence Zweig gave to Freudian theories. One reviewer deemed Zweig's treatment of the subject naïve, because he "uncritically" accepted Freudian theories and juxtaposed them with Marxist ones (O'Doherty, 2001).

The three decades during which the British ruled Palestine under a League of Nations Mandate, from 1918 to 1948, were formative years for Jewish nationalism and the new Hebrew culture of the Yishuv. They were also the decisive years of the Jewish–Arab conflict (cf. Gorny, 2001; Horowitz & Lissak, 1978; Shafir, 1989; Shapira, 1992). In *Freud in Zion*, I recount, and imbue with historical meaning, one of the less known encounters that occurred on the margins of these dramatic political events and processes—the encounter between psychoanalysis and Jewish society in the Land of Israel.

Psychoanalysis's ability to span cultures and resonate with a wide variety of intellectual traditions and historical memories has attracted the attention of scholars from a number of fields (cf. Damousi, 2005; Decker, 1977; Hale, 1977, 1995; Hartnack, 1990; Hinshelwood, 1995; Hollander, 1990; Miller, 1998; Plotkin, 2001; Timms & Segal, 1988; Turkle, 1992). The interrelationships of events that occur in psychological and mental spaces and those that take place in historical space are elusive. Tracking the migration of an idea and the acceptance of a scientific theory does not allow for the construction of tight causal and chronological sequences. On the one hand, the history of psychoanalysis in the Yishuv and in the state of Israel can be cast as a chapter in the chronicle of the psychoanalytic movement and idea as it progressed through the twentieth century. Alternatively, the local discourse about Freud's ideas can be presented as a part of the crystallisation of a distinct Hebrew culture in the Land of Israel. I seek to integrate both these points of view, and to look at the development of the psychoanalytic discipline in Mandatory Palestine as further evidence that, despite its profound and passionate links to ancient historical times, the modern Jewish settlement in the Land of Israel and the new Hebrew culture that it created are principally a part of modern European history. Freudian theory's penetration of Hebrew culture and the local discourse about psychoanalysis's ideas cannot be understood in detachment from the circumstances that compelled psychoanalysis to move out of the German cultural sphere. Therefore, as with many other episodes in the history of science and ideas, politics imposed, for a time, a common fate, of a sort, between a political–ideological movement, Zionism, and a scientific movement, psychoanalysis.

This book's six chapters cover the three broad contexts through which I view psychoanalysis's formative years in the Land of Israel. The first of these is the appearance of the Zionist version of the European "New Man", and its connection to the Freudian view of man. The second is the migration, following the rise of the Nazis in Germany, of psychoanalysis out of Central Europe. The third is the consolidation of psychoanalytic discourse in the Yishuv following the arrival of immigrant analysts and the founding of the Institute for Psychoanalysis in Jerusalem.

As the capital of a disintegrating empire and the birthplace of the dynamic unconscious, Freud's Vienna stood at several crossroads. It lay at the frontier between the Occident and the Orient: the latter, according to historian Eric Hobsbawm (1997), began at the city's eastern limits. It also stood at the boundary between enlightenment and romanticism, as well as at the leading edge of modernity. Furthermore, it was a focal point of both social democracy and virulent anti-Semitism, and of both psychoanalysis and Jewish nationalism (cf. Beller, 1989; Boyer, 1995; Schorske, 1981; Stanislawski, 2001). How are we to understand the affinity that early Zionists professed to find in Freud's theory?

Zionism's programme was, first and foremost, political, but the movement also encompassed philosophical doctrines, literary writings, and ideas that were more intellectual and theoretical than practically political. The two principal sources of Zionist discourse were modern Western thought and Jewish heritage. Even though it was sometimes viewed as an incarnation of religious ideas or the culmination of a long-term process in Jewish history, Zionist thinking, at the start, was characterised by its pragmatism and its ideological eclecticism. It engaged in an ongoing give and take with dominant ideas of its time that did not have any obvious connection to either nationalism or religious tradition. In engaging with Darwinism, Nietzscheism, socialism, existentialism, and psychoanalysis, Zionist thinking ranged far and wide across the field of modern science and philosophy. These intellectual movements played an important role in the process of secularisation that European Jewish society underwent, and provided (sometimes incompatible) justifications, arguments, and values that were appropriated into the Zionist movement's variegated ideological arsenal.[1] Works by Darwin, Marx, Nietzsche, Spinoza, and Freud were widely discussed and debated within the Jewish community. Zionist discourse deemed especially important those scholarly works that could offer alternatives to the traditional religious explanations for the existential plight of the Jewish people. Such scholarship could serve as a source of legitimacy and authority for the fundamental Zionist demand to gather the world's Jews in their ancestral land, where they could exercise sovereign power over their own society, politics, and culture (cf. Berkowitz, 1993, Golomb, 2004; Myers, 1995; Sand, 2000; Shavit & Reinharz, 2009; Vital, 1975).

Sickness and degeneracy were central tropes in Zionist representations of European Jews. Beginning in the second half of the eighteenth century, the Jews, as an ethnic minority, were referred to in both Jewish and anti-Semitic works as an atrophied and sickly body that required different physical and cultural conditions to "repair" it and restore it to normality. The growing popularisation of the discourse on the "degeneration of civilized nations" coincided with the rise of the Zionist movement, and Zionist thinkers of different schools conceptualised the Jewish problem in medical or psychiatric terms. The field of psychology also played a role in replacing Judaism's theological discourse with Zionism's political discourse. An inseparable component of this healing process was the refurbishing of the Jewish mentality (cf. Hess, 2002; Hirsch, 2009; Pick, 1993). In pitching itself to young Jews, the Zionist revolution often played on eroticism and gender. The Jewish collective's national aspirations were depicted as physical and mental desire. The Hebrew pioneer returning to the land of his forefathers was likened to a small child returning to his mother, his desire for the land like the desire of an infant for his mother's breast. In historical terms, the encounter between the repairers of the body and the healers of the soul, as expressed by the Zionist movement, was nothing less than dramatic.

Among the images out of which Zionism constructed its image of the "New Jew", which was a specifically Jewish version the European icon of the "New Man", those pertaining to sexuality and masculinity played a central role (cf. Biale, 1997; Boyarin, 1997; Bunzl, 1997; Efron, 2001; Elboim-Dror, 1994; Gilman, 1991, 1993a; Gluzman, 1997; Hart,

2000; Neumann, 2011). Some Zionists found in Freud's thought a way of linking between the private and public spheres of human activity, of connecting the desires and inhibitions of the individual to the nation's yearnings and aspirations. Freud's early writings, his historical investigations, and his theory of infantile sexuality seemed ready-made for those who maintained that Jewish memory of the past had a devastating effect on the inhibited and suppressed sexuality of the young Jew, on his tenuous masculinity, and, thus, on his proverbial neuroticism and faintness of will. The appearance of *The Interpretation of Dreams* (Freud, 1900a) offered a way for the symbolic world of the Jewish unconscious to break through the barrier of repression and exhibit its unique ethnic characteristics. This was applied, for example, to the campaign for the revival of the Hebrew language, which was seen as a necessary condition for the people's national rebirth. Later, Freud devoted works to the questions of religion and society. The process whereby the New Jew was constructed, and the politicisation of the collective Jewish psyche, could, thus, invoke both Freud's clinical writings and his works of social theory to facilitate a smooth transition from the psychology of the individual to that of the collective. In its refined analytical version, Freud's Lamarckism made it possible to conceive of the individual psyche as containing, in miniature, the entire history of humanity, whether via the Oedipal family romance of childhood or the world of archaic fantasies that the individual inherited from his forebears.

Freud was well aware of the neo-romantic and ideological interpretations of fundamental psychoanalytic concepts such as "repression" and "the unconscious". Just as he repeatedly fended off attempts to term psychoanalysis a "world-view", he made every effort to prevent the reduction of the psychoanalytic project to the problem of the Jewish people. For this reason, he refrained from mentioning the ethnic origins and religious affiliations of his patients (most of whom were Jews), and stressed at every opportunity the duty of psychoanalysis to uncover the common human elements that lie behind the desires, anxieties, and inhibitions of every human being. Too much attention to Jewish problems, even from a scientific perspective, was liable to relegate psychoanalysis to the margins of the period's intellectual and scientific discourse. Nevertheless, from a historical perspective, we cannot disregard the fact that the Jewish signifier was evident from the field's earliest years and that Judaism was part of Freud's inner world, and part of the self-conception of most of his disciples and opponents. Unsurprisingly, this issue was an important one in the reception given to Freud's ideas by modern Hebrew culture. The repeated attempts to enlist Freud in the Zionist cause also compelled him to address the question of the connection between his Jewish origin and his theories. This question touched from the start on the innermost part of the psychoanalytic project and was seen, even in the field's early years, as subversive of its claims to universality. Freud was unwilling to put at risk the universal claims of his teachings even in his final years, after the *Anschluss* that annexed Austria to the Third Reich and forced him to flee to London, a time when it was more tempting than ever for him to seek the support of his ethnic collective and to take comfort in Jewish solidarity.

Historians of the Zionist movement debate questions such as whether Zionism was a national revival or a colonial movement. If it was indeed a national movement, should it be understood in the context of modern nineteenth-century European nationalism, and, if so, was it an example of Western political nationalism or Eastern cultural–ethnic nationalism? A national or nationalistic movement? Socialist, national, or social–nationalist? An old guard or revolutionary movement? Secular–pragmatic, secular–redemptionist, messianic–religious, or, as has recently been proposed, an exceptional test case of a "modern gnosis" converted into a political theology? Was the pioneering Zionist movement unique among nationalist, socialist, and social–national movements? Did it represent a uniquely Jewish, Zionist, pioneering phenomenon in modern history? (Cf. Avineri, 1981; Funkenstein, 1991; Ohana, 2010; Reinharz & Shapira, 1996; Schweid, 1985; Sternhell, 1998; Vital, 1975, 1982, 1987.)

Some of these issues of meta-historical interpretation useful for understanding of Zionism reverberate in the process by which psychoanalysis found its place in the new Hebrew culture. It would be difficult not to notice, for example, the similarity between the debate over the putative implications of the ethnicity of Freud and his early disciples for their scientific thinking—an issue that has preoccupied the historiography of psychoanalysis nearly from the start—and the debate over the theological origins of Zionism as a political phenomenon. In fact, tracking the process by which Freud's ideas were introduced can cast light on the debate over Zionism's political–theological aspects. It also will provide a guide to the intellectual roots of the conceptual debates that preoccupied psychoanalysis in Israel for many years thereafter. Seen in these terms, the present work, while focusing on the early years of psychoanalysis in pre-state Israel, plumbs the mental and intellectual DNA of Israeli psychoanalysis while also enquiring into the metaphysical and unconscious foundations of Zionism and of modern Hebrew culture. Clinical and theoretical developments most commonly studied within the general context of the evolution of psychoanalytic science here retain their particular historical meaning. However tentative and incomplete the links between history and theory presented here, this narrative of the formative years of psychoanalysis in the Yishuv and Israel seeks to lay the foundation for future endeavours to uncover the deeper historical and intellectual currents underlying contemporary Israeli clinical discourse. Quite often, the true pulse of scientific debates beats far beneath the surface, and must be sought in the realm of political and intellectual history.

For those who saw Freud's teachings as a call for humans to enter into themselves, to return to the "original" and the "authentic" self, Zionism took on therapeutic meaning. Almost immediately, psychoanalysis found enthusiastic followers among champions of Jewish national particularity. In the new discipline, they found a fusion of radicalism and tradition amenable to their ideological ends. Freud's positivist ideas seemed to reconcile Jewish particularism with both the universalism of European Enlightenment and German neo-romanticism, providing scientific support for Zionism's romantic attempt to reconstruct a unified (and unifying) national past. Early attempts made in Vienna by leaders of Jewish youth movements, as well as by analysts such as Siegfried Bernfeld, to reconcile Freud's ideas with both Marxism and the life philosophy (*Lebensphilosophie*) of thinkers such as Martin Buber were an early indication of the convoluted context in which psychoanalysis would gain a footing in Jewish Palestine and, later, in Israel. Moreover, Freudian texts served as an intellectual arena where the East European and Central European intellectual traditions, with their corresponding Zionist self-understandings, could contend and reconcile. As a case in point: as early as 1920, Ernest Jones reported to Freud a conversation with Chaim Weizmann, in which the Zionist leader (who would become Israel's first president) took pride in those "poor Galician immigrants who arrive in Palestine with no clothes but holding Marx's *Capital* in one hand and in the other, Freud's *Interpretation of Dreams*".

The immigrants of the Second and Third Aliyot established the Yishuv's ideological and socio-cultural foundations.[2] The minds of these men and women were cast largely in the mould of the Russian intelligentsia. One of their chief accomplishments was the transformation of the utopian–egalitarian ideas and socialist myths they brought with them from Eastern Europe into concrete schemas for Zionist action in Palestine (cf. Bein, 1952; Ben-Artzi, 1997; Eisenstadt & Noah, 1999; Halpern & Reinharz, 1991; Sternhell, 1998). Psychoanalytic ideas were, thus, already percolating into Zionist thinking and Hebrew culture during the first two decades of the twentieth century. Their principal agents were several Viennese analysts, in particular the youth movement leaders of the first three *aliyot*, or waves of Jewish immigration to the Land of Israel, who had become acquainted with Freudian ideas in their countries of origin. Russian Jewry had been exposed to Freud in the years preceding the revolution of 1917, and German-speaking Jews viewed Freud and his theories as one of the great achievements of secular Jewish integration into Central European culture. The development of the psychoanalytic discourse in the Yishuv was, thus, shaped by the joint action of two historical processes that began in Europe: the appearance of the Zionist revolution's "New Man" at the end of the nineteenth century, and the immigration of German-speaking psychoanalysts and intellectuals to Palestine. While the myth of the "New Man" shaped the forms of Zionist activity and the way in which psychological and social problems were cast, immigrant analysts were looked upon by influential Zionists as potential agents of social progress, responsible for not just healing the mental suffering of individuals, but also that of the Yishuv as a whole.

The Zionist movement, like most national movements, developed an instrumental relationship to the past. It strove to provide its followers with a sense of a collective present and future by constructing of a unitary collective–mythological past. The *halutz* (pioneer), the Jewish immigrant who settled in the Land of Israel and engaged in farming or manual labour, was a newcomer who had freed himself from the chains of an oppressive past and who would, henceforth, determine his own fate. He was portrayed in terms that were simultaneously historical, abstract, and mythic (cf. Wistrich & Ohana, 1995; Zerubavel, 1995). This image contained within it a tension, one that would surface continually throughout the history of the Yishuv and Israel, between the cultural heritage and past of individual immigrants and Zionism's interest in constructing an imaginary collective diasporic Jewish past that pointed teleologically toward a shared future in the Holy Land. From the onset of political Zionism, the need to build a society with a fixed and distinctive identity encouraged the establishment of a "grand narrative", one capable of both embracing and overshadowing manifold historical memories, cultural identities, and ethnic sensibilities that might still linger beneath the surface. In ensuring that the association between personal suffering and the plight of the Jewish collective would not remain within metaphorical boundaries, a scientific connection had to be found between the private and the public, between the sickness of the individual and that of the collective. It is hardly surprising, then, that the first of Freud's essays to be translated into Hebrew was *Group Psychology and the Analysis of the Ego* (1921c), published in 1928.

The encounter between the pioneers and Freud's immigrant disciples was notable for both its enthusiasm and the misunderstanding it engendered. The immigrants made several attempts to institutionalise psychoanalysis in the country, but failed. It seemed that the project of bringing Freudian theory to the Jewish intelligentsia of Palestine and keeping it from deteriorating into a cultural and ideological curiosity would require a special brand of psychoanalytic emissaries whose self-conception as Zionists would not be incommensurate with their identities as psychoanalysts.

Max Eitingon (1881–1943), who would found the Palestine Psychoanalytic Society in 1933, was just this combination, a committed political Zionist as well as a staunch adherent of psychoanalysis in its clinical, less ideological version. Prior to his emigration from Berlin, the Russian-born son of Leipzig's *Pelzkönig* ("king of furriers") was mostly known to his associates as the first of Freud's students to undergo a training analysis by the old master. As Freud's most loyal representative in the "Secret Committee", the group of Freud's closest disciples who took it upon themselves to protect the movement against schismatics, his personal wealth also made him the movement's most important financial benefactor. By 1933, he had assumed a number of important administrative functions and key positions in the psychoanalytic movement, in addition to what became his historically most significant role as the founder, in 1920, of the Berlin Psychoanalytic Polyclinic, the movement's first out-patient treatment centre and its most esteemed training facility.

While most biographical accounts of Max Eitingon Eurocentrically highlight his Berlin years, the two surviving products of his labours, living evidence of his vision and creative powers, are the psycho-analytic training scheme (known as the Eitingon Training Model) he developed in Berlin during the 1920s, and the psychoanalytic society and training institute he established in Jerusalem during the final decade of his life. The current volume, while not a biography in the strict sense of the term, endeavours to fill in several biographical lacu-nae and to cast some light on Eitingon's enigmatic persona. This is the first study to make use of Eitingon's private papers, which have recently been catalogued and archived at the Israel State Archives in Jerusalem.

Beginning in the 1930s, Hebrew culture gradually facilitated a par-ticular hybridisation between the socialist "Russian" Freud, who was understood to have had constructivist–collectivistic aspirations, and the "German Freud", notorious for his individualistic, critical, and pes-simistic *Weltanschauung*. To be sure, the encounter between psycho-analysis and the Yishuv cannot be considered a precise mirroring of the encounter between psychoanalytic theory and Russian Marxism. It did, however, bear the most prominent markers of the reception psycho-analysis received in Russia. Despite the essential conflict between the constructivist–utopist characteristics of Soviet socialism and the social pessimism in Freud's later writings, his Zionist readers preferred to bridge the gap between these different perceptions of man by a selec-tive reading of psychoanalytic theory. The local debate on the tenets of psychoanalysis took place at the watershed of two conceptions of psychoanalysis—an ideological–political conception and a scientific–therapeutic one. Additionally, the medical–therapeutic discourse in psychoanalysis was strongly influenced and shaped by the ideological leanings of Zionist physicians and pedagogues of the time. Clearly, psychoanalysis's arrival in the Yishuv provides ample evidence that Freud's teachings make it possible to interpret, disentangle, and recon-struct the boundaries of different discourses.

To answer the question of whether psychoanalytic man and Zion-ist man contradicted each other, I cautiously offer a prosopography— a group biography—of the first psychoanalysts to work in the Yishuv and the state of Israel. If a Central European model was indeed simply transferred as it was to Mandatory Palestine, we must examine what enviornmental and mental conditions allowed Eitingon and his colleagues to maintain, in Jerusalem, under British rule, a Freudian institute, one that operated on the same rigorous terms as did the Polyclinic in Berlin during the Weimar Republic. Furthermore, despite the willingness of these German-speaking psychoanalysts to maintain and integrate their psychoanalytic and Zionist identities, a question remains. Is the psychoanalytic point of view, which is, by nature, a critical, interpretative, and individual one, not fundamentally different from the constructivist and collectivist conception that guided Zionist ideology and the self-perception of most Jewish settlers in the Land of Israel? Is there not in psychoanalytic theory and practice something fundamentally, profoundly opposed to the view of humanity and to the intellectual spirit that prevailed in mainstream Zionism? Is Sigmund Freud's "interminable analysis", the universal analytic project, a product of the Diaspora, which Freud's school proposed as a remedy for the angst of the modern age, consistent with the radical historical solution that the Zionist movement proposed for the New Jew? Can psychoanalysis as a psychological–critical theory and Zionism as an ideology and consciousness really live together? Finally, did historical reality and the new Hebrew culture play a role in shaping local psychoanalytic practice and ethics? Beyond the fact that psychoanalysis has clearly flourished in Israel, can we speak today of a specifically Israeli kind of psychoanalysis, or, at the very least, a local "interpretive community" (Fish, 1980) with a distinct analytic identity?

This book thus seeks to be both historical and critical, but by no means "psycho-historical" (Rolnik, 2001). My intention is to reconstruct and place in context the interactions between history and theory. More specifically, I look at the migration, separation, and loss, continuity, and new beginning during psychoanalysis's formative years. And I do this in a place that, while remote from Europe, was shaped mainly by the intellectual legacy, cultural images, and political *débacles* of that continent. Indeed, if the genesis of psychoanalysis in *fin-de-siècle* Vienna epitomises not only the genius of its Jewish founder, but much of modern European self-understanding, then the coming of Freudian psychoanalysis to pre-state Israel, where it rapidly penetrated the discourse of pedagogy, literature, medicine, and politics, becoming a popular therapeutic discipline, could also be regarded as an integral part of a Jewish immigrant society's struggle to establish its identity in the face of its manifold European pasts and its conflict-ridden Middle Eastern present.

Notes

1. Secularisation is a contested concept which describes a movement (grad-
    ual or dramatic) from an other-worldly orientation to an inner-worldly
    orientation and the marginalisation of religion and religious institutions
    (cf. Asad, 2003; Taylor, 2007).
2. The immigration of Jews to the Land or state of Israel is termed, in
    Hebrew, *aliyah*, meaning "ascent". This term, taken from the Bible and
    Talmud, denotes both a literal and metaphysical ascent to the Holy Land
    or the Holy City, Jerusalem. The term is thus infused with the religious
    sense of sacred pilgrimage.

CHAPTER ONE

The Freudians and the "new man" of the Zionist revolution

"We love the nude youth, he who remains a boy in his youth, who exalts the pleasures of the flesh and does not abhor them. . . . I see before me the man who breaks down the walls that generations have erected between spirit and flesh, between rationality and instinct. In this way we create, instinctively, the most primitive and the most cultured man, who cleaves to his woman and his companions, to Lake Kinneret and all of creation"

(Meir Ya'ari, 1921)

Sigmund Freud's conception of himself as a Jew has preoccupied historians of psychoanalysis and the public at large for almost a century. But most practising analysts are very suspicious of the motivations for asking whether his theories are in any way based in his Jewish identity. If the theories of the founder of psychoanalysis are scientific, they maintain, his religious and ethnic identity should be as irrelevant to psychoanalysis as Einstein's is to the theory of relativity. The members of this school—the so-called Ethnic Minimalists—categorically deny any inherently Jewish component in the development of psychoanalysis. Ranged against them are the Ethnic Maximalists,

1

who view Freud's work as a direct outgrowth of his Jewish origins, and even view psychoanalysis as a "Jewish science" (cf. Aron & Henik, 2010; Bakan, 1958; Frosh, 2005; Gay, 1987; Klein, 1985; Krüll, 1979; Oxaal, 1988; Rice, 1990; Richards, 2010; Robert, 1976; Roith, 1987; Slavet, 2009; Yerushalmi, 1991).

The Ethnic Maximalist tradition has a long and diverse history. Its adherents include scholars who are careful to distinguish Freud's personal identity as a Jew from his professional life, and others who claim that everything Freud wrote bears the marks of his Jewish origins. From its inception, psychoanalysis has always been plagued by attempts to limit the validity of Freud's teachings to the scope of the hereditary, peculiar "Jewish spirit". According to this claim, Freud's writings are based on reasoning that grows out of his specific cultural heritage, and were shaped by the social and historical circumstances in which the psychoanalytic movement developed.

The question of a relationship between Jewish culture, or more diffuse notions of a Jewish "spiritual essence", and the origins of psychoanalysis does not arise only from Sigmund Freud's religious or intellectual upbringing. The polemical tradition that has claimed to diagnose an essentially Jewish element in the mental makeup of the Jews has pervaded European culture for several centuries, and reached its climax at about the same time that Freud began to formulate his ideas on the human mind.

The preoccupation with the Jew's body, spirit, and sexuality became, beginning in the second half of the nineteenth century, one of the hottest topics in medicine. Physicians and scientists collated the symptoms and ills unique to the Jews and argued about the causes of the physical and mental distinctiveness of their Jewish patients and experimental subjects. Some offered racist, biologistic explanations, while others claimed that the causes were external: social conditions, and the low levels of sanitation and nourishment suffered by Jewish communities in Eastern Europe. The scientific–medical discourse on the uniqueness of the Jews drew its inspiration from traditional stereotypes and created new ones. A number of these were then adopted by popular anti-Semitic culture. Some found their way into turn-of-the-century chauvinistic and racist philosophies and ideologies; some were adopted by Jewish doctors, who passed them on to their Jewish clients. The participation of Jewish doctors in the discourse about Jewish distinctiveness helped Jewish patients identify with most of these stereotypes and made it easier to integrate them into the Zionist thinking and conceptions of the Jewish nation. Jewish physicians and scholars played an active role in the stigmatisation of the Jewish body, and reinforced the myths on which it was based with the demographic and epidemiological data they collected. Both Jewish and non-Jewish scholars festooned their studies with tables and illustrations: internal, gynaecological, surgical, psychiatric, bacteriological, anthropological, sociological, and statistical. These variously catalogued and quantified Jewish diseases. The dialectic relationship between science on the one hand and myth and ideology and the other played itself out with regard to every one of the Jew's organs and features. His flat feet, hooked nose, scant hair, high forehead, weak eyes, curved spine, nervous stomach, and, of course, his legendary circumcised Jewish penis were all subjects of learned discussion by the best minds. It was argued, for example, that Jews were peculiarly susceptible to haemorrhoids, short-sightedness, and diabetes, but also naturally immune to infectious diseases such as plague, tuberculosis, and cholera—diseases that Jews had been accused of causing from medieval times. The Jew's defective, imperfect body also rendered him unfit for military service, perpetuating the image of the Jew as a *luftmensch*, an air-man, a rootless parasite who could not be an integral part of the body of the European nation (cf. Berg, 2005; Efron, 1994; Gilman, 1991, 1993a; Hart, 2000; Hödl, 1997; Mosse, 1985).

The Jew's peculiarity and otherness was stamped on his body. Every physiological or pathological datum was interpreted as a sign of illness and degeneration, or, alternatively, as a mark of exceptional intelligence and sublime spirituality. Jewish doctors stressed the Jewish body's capacity for endurance and survival. They attributed this to Jewish religious customs: circumcision, religiously mandated dietary restrictions, and kosher slaughtering techniques, which were hailed as particularly hygienic. In part, the positive stereotypes, those that ascribed to the Jews, as the people of the book, exceptional intellectual capabilities, also encouraged Jews to adopt as part of their identities the negative ones about their physical inferiority. Jewish statisticians proclaimed that Jews had made decisive contributions to human culture and knowledge far beyond their numbers, noting Jewish scholarly traditions and the fact that the number of Jewish university students was seven times larger than their proportion in the population as a whole (Efron, 2001).

As a rule, Jewish and non-Jewish mental health professionals agreed that their Jewish patients formed a distinct group. But psychiatrists were divided with regard to the causes of the Jews' mental afflictions. Those of the biologistic–essentialist school sought racial and biological explanations, whereas the environmentalist school rejected the thesis of hereditary degeneration and attributed the putatively typical Jewish mental illnesses, hysteria and neurasthenia ("nervous weakness") to social and historical circumstances. Jewish doctors who wrote on nervous maladies sought, self-consciously and explicitly from their ethnic and religious points of view, to defend Jewish interests as they understood them. Yet, they remained trapped within the particularist conventions of racial discourse. True, they did their best to attenuate, undermine, and ward off the potential and actual anti-Semitic uses of such medical data. But as a rule they did not, prior to the First World War, reject hereditary explanations (Brunner, 2001).

Rafael Becker, a Swiss psychiatrist, explained "nervousness among the Jews" (1919) as a result of their inferior living conditions, which fostered a sense of inferiority. He concluded from this that Zionism was "the radical therapy" for the eugenic nervous maladies of the Jewish people. Max Sichel, a Berlin psychiatrist, who was sceptical about the statistics claiming to show that Jews were particularly prone to mental illness, nevertheless highlighted another epidemiological finding, the high rate of depression and suicides among Western Jews. This seemed to contradict the thesis that the proud and developed Jews of Western Europe differed from the oppressed and backward Jews of Eastern Europe.

Shifting the explanatory burden from biology to sociology, Sichel explained what he acknowledged was a Jewish disposition to mental illness by reference to the conditions of ghetto life, pogroms, and persecutions, all of which put the Jews' nervous systems under constant strain. Yet, Sichel also argued that the proportionally higher ratio of Jews in mental hospitals did not prove that the Jewish population suffered from proportionally more mental disturbances. The hospitalisation figures, he maintained, should be attributed to sociological factors, among them Jewish concentration in urban areas, as well as their greater wealth and better education, which made them more aware of mental illness. Sichel concluded that, while race and heredity were indeed aetiological factors in mental illness, the two were evoked, all too often, without any proof. In fact, he wrote, physicians and scientists often cited race and biology when they could not explain phenomena otherwise. Cesare Lombroso, an Italian psychiatrist of Jewish descent, portrayed the Jews' mental ills as the inevitable by-product of the Jewish mind's superior creative powers, which had allowed the race to contribute so much to European culture.

Despite its biologistic rhetoric, the degeneracy paradigm was thus not as deterministic as it might seem. A Jew could, for instance, slow or even halt the degenerative process by living virtuously. If the Jew adopted a morally rigorous, healthy, self-disciplined, and clean lifestyle, pursued physical beauty and cultivated masculine strength, he purportedly need not fall victim to his racial dispositions. These ideals were promoted by hygiene societies, leagues against prostitution, temperance movements, eugenic associations, and physical culture clubs such as Max Nordau's Maccabi Zionist sports association, which aimed to produce "muscular Jews" (Zimmerman, 2003, 2006).

At the Second Zionist Congress, convened in Basel in 1898, Nordau, a neurologist and Theodor Herzl's partner in founding the Zionist Organization, termed Zionism a political medicine for the revival of the body of the young Jew, which had been devastated by 1,800 years of exile. Zionist doctors promulgated the maximalist version of the sociological and environmental thesis. Some distinguished between the filthy, degenerate, pogrom-beset Jews of the backward villages of Eastern Europe and their Western brethren, who owed their vigour to their superior living conditions and assimilation into German culture. Alexander Marmorek, a bacteriologist, had been hailed as early as 1903 as the one doctor who could inject the Zionist "antidote" into the poisoned Jewish soul (Hart, 2000, p. 272).[1]

Zionist doctors did not stop with attributing Jewish ailments to a lack of hygiene in the ghettos. They claimed that emancipation and assimilation could not ameliorate the Jewish people's physical illnesses. Arthur Ruppin, the father of Jewish sociology and later one of the shapers of Zionist colonisation policy in Palestine, looked at the bio-statistical data and concluded that in fact it was Jews of the upper socio-economic classes who suffered the most from modern culture. In support of this claim he noted, for example, that the incidence of stillbirths, birth defects, and feeble-minded children was higher among Jewish women of high socio-economic status. Likewise, he cited data showing that the suicide rate among Orthodox Eastern European Jews was lower, while the world-weariness (*Weltschmerz*) of

Western Jews led more of them to put an end to their lives. Thus, he argued that, paradoxically, Jews who enjoyed equality and prosperity in the West were plagued by creeping degeneration.

The Zionist scientific discourse about the mental and physical state of the Jews generally tried to move the discussion's centre of gravity outward, from the Jewish body to the ills of the non-Jewish environment. While Ruppin at first used the term "Zion" to refer to a metaphysical condition, rather than a geographical location that could provide for the survival of the Jewish nation, within a few years he became a political Zionist and unambiguously advocated settlement in Palestine as a cure for the ills brought on by the conditions under which most of Europe's Jews lived. Others offered an alternative model that viewed East European Jews, who had more pristine cultural and historical identities than did their assimilated Western brethren, as those most fit to take part in the task of building the nation anew (cf. Biale, 1997; Bunzl, 1997; Gilman, 1986; Gluzman, 2007).

It was only natural for psychoanalysis to get drawn into the modernist vortex in which theological concepts were exchanged for psychological ones, the same current that swept in political–Zionist and medical—Darwinist images. "Psychoanalysis offers contentment to no man, and I do my best to keep my distance from it", Franz Kafka wrote in his diary, "but as a commentary of the Modern Jew, it's no less real and alive than the Rashi commentary" (Kafka, 1982, p. 529). Note the intuitive link implied in Kafka's words between psychological theory and theological text. This connection would be made by many of Freud's Zionist readers, whether implicitly or explicitly, and would become an inseparable part of the story of psychoanalysis's acceptance in the Yishuv.

One of Freud's students believed that psychoanalysis could become a "Jewish science". Otto Rank, born Otto Rosenfeld, was considered by Freud to be his most gifted student up until he left the group in 1926. In an essay of 1905, "The essence of Judaism", Rank stressed the vital role played by Jews in the fight against repression.[2] He argued that the Jews had remained, through their religion, in touch with the repressed, primal element of their psyches. In this they differed from the Gentiles, who had immediately jumped on the bandwagon of culture and civilisation. Turning the stereotype of the mental makeup of the Jew on its head, Rank claimed that the Jews possess knowledge of radical treatment of neurosis that sets them apart from all other nations, such that their historical role as psychoanalysts is how to help others recover from their mental illnesses (cf. Klein, 1985, Lieberman, 1985, Rudnytsky, 2002).

This was precisely what Freud feared—that his students would turn psychoanalysis into a particularist commentary on the Jewish condition. Again and again he argued that psychological problems should be formulated in psychological terms, and that the term "degeneration" implied that there once had been a perfect race whose descendants had gradually deteriorated. Such perfect beings, Freud claimed, had never existed, so it was not proper to call the Jews, or anyone else, "degenerate" (Spiegel, 1986). While in Paris, he called on Max Nordau with a letter of introduction, but he found him vain and stupid (Jones, 1953–1957, Vol. 1, p. 204).

Freud's early writings present a striking contrast to both the established paradigm and the Jewish response. With the completion of *Studies on Hysteria* in 1895, explicit rejections of hereditary conception of neuroses become a regular feature in Freud's papers. In a letter to Wilhelm Fliess in 1897, he declared that he had made it his task to dislodge "the factor of hereditary disposition" in order to shed light on the problem of neurotic illnesses (Masson, 1985, p. 265). The unauthorised critical footnotes which he inserted in his translation of Jean-Martin Charcot's *Lecons du Mardi a la Salpetriere,* were meant primarily to dislodge his esteemed mentor's hereditary doctrine (Roith, 2008). In later writings, Freud continued, with increasing fervour, to oppose the degeneracy paradigm. In the opening pages of his *Three Essays on the Theory of Sexuality,* he wrote, "It may well be asked whether an attribution of 'degeneracy' is of any value or adds anything to our knowledge" (Freud, 1905d, p. 138). By refusing to write as a scientist in a Jewish cause and remaining silent on his own and his patients' Jewish affiliations, Freud departed no less radically from categories used by other Jewish physicians than he did from the dominant paradigm of nervous diseases (Brunner, 1991).

Whenever Freud was queried about the connection between his Jewish origins and his teachings, he made sure not to leave any room for misunderstanding. His analytic and professional identity, he maintained, was completely distinct from his personal and ethnic identity. The only thing he ascribed to his Jewish heritage was his familiarity with the fate of being in the opposition and of being put under the ban of the "Compact Majority" (Freud, 1925d). In his view, it was the historical fate of the Jews, not their racial makeup, that made them natural partners in the project of universal psychoanalysis, a project that demanded of its followers free thought, willingness to fight, and an unrelenting quest for the truth. He thought that it was easier for Jews to accept the radically subversive and innovative nature of his universalist theory and to join his movement. They possessed what he called "our ancient Jewish toughness", and were not misled by the racial myths and mystical beliefs that blinded Gentiles to his message. His address to the Vienna branch of B'nai B'rith makes this explicit: "[A]t a time when no one in Europe listened to me and I still had no disciples even in Vienna, you gave me your kindly attention. You were my first audience" (Freud, 1941e[1926], p. 273). He further admitted to a "racial preference [Rassenvorliebe]" for Jews, that he felt close to Karl Abraham because a "racial kinship", and "consanguineous Jewish traits [verwandte jüdische Züge]" bound them to one another (Freud & Abraham, 1965). Yet, psychoanalysis would do well not to get itself identified as "a national Jewish matter", he warned his most senior student in Berlin. He made sure to conceal the Jewish ethnicity of his patients, even at the price of expurgating Jewish experiences and life circumstances that should have been included in their clinical narratives and which could have cast light on the analytic process (Blum, 2010). But when it came to personal friends, choice students, or the ethnic factor's impact on the ability to comprehend and internalise his ideals, Freud's preferences were categorical. On the occasion of David Eder's death in 1936, he wrote to Barbara Low "We were both Jews and knew that each of us bore within that miraculous common thing that, inaccessible to any analysis so far, makes the Jew" (Freud to Barbara Low, 19 April 1936, in Freud, 1961, pp. 427–428).

Max Eitingon—first encounter

Max Eitingon was invited in 1907 to take part in one of the meetings of Freud's students, the Psychological Wednesday Society. There he had an opportunity to observe, close up, Freud's determination to prevent psychoanalytic theory from becoming part of the racial discourse then under way among European psychiatrists regarding the Jews' fundamental mental distinctiveness.

Born in 1881 in Mogilew on the River Dnieper in White Russia, Eitingon was twelve years old when his family moved to Germany and settled in Leipzig. By the 1920s, his father, Chaim Eitingon, was known as the "Rothschild from Leipzig". With branches in New York, London, Paris, Stockholm, and Moscow, the "Chaim Eitingon Aktiengesellleschaft", the leading German fur wholesaler, enjoyed, at its peak, an annual turnover of 26 million Reichsmarks. Chaim's nephew Motty, who took over the American branch of the company, further upscaled the Eitingons. From well to do merchants they became internationally famous finance magnates and philanthropists. Although a stutter prevented him from completing his secondary education, Max Eitingon became proficient in seven languages and developed an interest in philosophy, literature, and art. His cultured upbringing made him a connoisseur of many artistic fields, and his ample private means gave him the opportunity to cultivate his tastes. He studied for a year at the University of Leipzig and was eventually able to enrol in medical school at the universities of Heidelberg, Marburg, and finally in Zürich, where he graduated and remained until 1908 as a junior resident working under the supervision of Eugen Bleuler, Carl Jung, and Karl Abraham in the Burghölzli psychiatric clinic (cf. Brill, 1943; Jones, 1943; Neiser, 1978; Pomer, 1965; Schröter, 2002, 2004; Wilmers, 2009).

Eitingon's colleagues in Burhölzli gave him the somewhat improbable nickname Oblomov, the name of the protagonist of Ivan Goncharov's classic novel. This Oblomov was a typical Russian aristocrat, good-hearted and well-intentioned, but lethargic and incapable of action. Eitingon was hugely enthusiastic about the analytic studies being conducted by Freud and his school, and he decided to write directly to the professor and ask him if he would consent to take on as a patient one of Eitingon's friends, a young Russian woman, a philosophy student, who, in his opinion, suffered from hysteria. He reassured the professor that the young woman's material resources were not such as to offer a "serious counter-indication" to spending an extended time in Vienna, and that he himself intended to accompany her (Eitingon to Freud, 3 January 1907, in Freud & Eitingon, 2004, pp. 49–50).

So, at the age of twenty-six, Eitingon came to Vienna and participated as the first guest from abroad in two of the Wednesday gatherings. The surviving minutes of these meetings preserve a telling exchange between the young doctor and the founder of psychoanalysis, the man who would be his mentor and idol for the rest of his life. Eitingon asked whether Jews were especially prone to neurosis, and whether a "social factor" in the development of neurosis should not be postulated along with its sexual aetiology. Freud commented that "[t]he questions raised by Mr. Eitingon are indicative of the tendency of our Swiss colleagues to deny the theory of the sexual aetiology of the neuroses" (Nunberg & Federn, 1979, Vol. 1, p. 94).

Eitingon's ethnic and social sensibilities might have interfered at that time with his ability to grasp the radical essence of Freud's theory of sexuality. Whether or not that was the case, both his future activities within the psychoanalytic movement and the personal choices he made during his lifetime would bear witness to his preoccupation with Jewish identity and social solidarity.

Freud liked him from the first. The two men together walked the streets of Vienna and the alleys of Florence. Jung enviously watched as a close friendship developed between the two. He promptly wrote to Freud to offer his opinion of the newcomer:

> I consider Eitingon a totally impotent gasbag—scarcely has this uncharitable judgment left my lips than it occurs to me that I envy him his uninhibited abreaction of the polygamous instinct. I therefore retract 'impotent' as too compromising. He will certainly never amount to anything; one day he may become a member of the Duma [the Russian parliament]. (25 September 1907, in Freud & Jung, 1974, pp. 87–88)

With characteristic self-irony, Freud tried to mollify Jung's jealousy: "He [Eitingon] seems to have taken up with some woman again. Such practice is a deterrent to theory. When I have totally overcome my libido (in the common sense), I shall undertake to write a 'Love-Life of Mankind'" (19 September 1907, ibid., pp. 89–90).

Freud sought to manage his relationship with Eitingon in accordance with the latter's clinical and intellectual abilities. He assigned the new acolyte a task: to proffer to the Vienna circle a survey of the case of Anna O (Bertha Pappenheim), the young Jewish woman treated by Josef Breuer in the years 1880–1882. At the time Freud assigned the project, Anna O was already recognised as psychoanalysis's first patient. Eitingon accepted the challenge with enthusiasm and produced a learned, if critical, assessment in which he reviewed, in light of current psychoanalytic knowledge, Breuer's diagnosis and treatment. Freud must certainly have been pleased by the swiftness with which Eitingon had assimilated the analytic approach, which views the universal sexual drive, rather than particularist ethnic factors, as the heart of neurosis. According to the young doctor, had Breuer been, in 1880, in possession of current psychoanalytic knowledge about the symbolic meaning of snakes, he could have helped the young woman rid herself of the distressing black snake hallucination that troubled her during her treatment. According to Eitingon, this was a manifestation of the patient's repressed incestuous fantasy, which she transferred onto her doctor (Hirschmüller, 1998).

It might well be that the very things about Eitingon that had infuriated Jung were what made Freud fond of him. The wealth of this son of Russian immigrants, his affluent lifestyle and his larger-than-life bigheartedness, no less than his potent "polygamous instincts", played on a hidden string in the soul of the master, who was himself the ambitious son of immigrants from Moravia who had suffered, for most of his life, from penury and hypochondria. Eitingon could easily represent for Freud a kind of heterosexual lordly masculinity of the type that the gentile Jung was naturally blessed with, and which Freud himself so longed for—passionate, potent, and free of neurotic inhibitions. In any case, the fact that the skirt-chasing Eitingon was to become Freud's preferred candidate for marriage to his daughter, Anna, and the fact that Eitingon was destined to be the only "true Zionist" among Freud's disciples, were, at the very least, another link in the convoluted chain of evidence that points to the existence of an ethnic–gender Jewish and masculine code common to the two psychotherapeutic projects that *fin-de-siècle* Vienna—a culture addicted to fatigue and convalescence—produced: psychoanalysis and Zionism (cf. Boyarin, 1997; Heller, 1992; Young-Bruehl, 1994).

In 1909, Freud notified his Hungarian student Sándor Ferenczi, that he intended to train Eitingon as an analyst in an "ambulatory" fashion (letter dated 10 November, in Freud & Ferenczi, 1993–2000, pp. 97–99). Twice a week, for a month and a half, Eitingon accompanied the professor for a night-time walk through the streets of Vienna. This was the first "training analysis" in the history of the movement.

From 1919 on, Eitingon assumed a large number of important administrative functions and key positions: among others, as a committee member; as director of the Berlin Polyclinic and of the Berlin Psychoanalytic Institute; as chairman of the International Training Committee; as secretary, and then, for seven years, president, of the International Psychoanalytical Association (IPA); as confidant and adviser to Freud on the funding and organisation of the Internationaler Psychoanalytischer Publishing House; and as editor of the *Internationale Zeitschrift für Psychoanalyse*, the movement's journal.

Over the course of thirty years, Freud and Eitingon would exchange more than 800 letters, some of them on clinical–theoretical subjects, but most addressing the psychoanalytic movement's internal politics. Their personal correspondence is notable also for its ample use of Hebrew and Yiddish words, usages that Freud eschewed in his formal writing and relegated to his private communications. When Freud reported to Eitingon about his plans to get dental treatment from a Jewish doctor, he put it this way: "Having endured so many years of plodding goyische [gentile] clumsiness, I will gladly put my trust in Jewish sechel [intelligence]" (6 August 1927, in Freud & Eitingon, 2004, p. 539).

The rationalist from Odessa and the wizard of Vienna

Given Theodor Herzl's huge popularity during his final years, it is reasonable to presume that a sympathetic review of Freud's *The Interpretation of Dreams* by the head of the Zionist movement would have given the book a boost. Had he read Freud's book, he would have discovered that one of the dreams that Freud analysed there involved seeing Herzl's play, *The New Ghetto*. He might then have responded differently to Freud's request that he, or his associate editor Max Nordau, who was himself a neurologist, publish a review in the *Neue freie Presse*, an important Viennese daily newspaper. The correspondence between the father of psychoanalysis and the prophet of the Jewish state, who lived a few doors from each other on the same street, consists only of a few arid lines that firmly resist any attempt at historical or analytical fleshing out (cf. Falk, 1978; Goldhammer, 1958; Loewenberg, 1970, 1971):

Many thanks for your generous letter and your book, which I shall read with great interest. I do not know yet whether I shall be able to

write about it. That is to say, whether I will feel that I have the necessary skills for the purpose. (Herzl to Freud, 1 October 1902: AFM)

Freud repeatedly complained that his dreams book, first published
in 1899, was not accorded the recognition that it deserved in medical
circles. He could take solace from the fact that, despite the psychiatric
profession's chilly response to his dream theory, *The Interpretation of
Dreams* quickly broadened the interest in psychoanalysis beyond
academic circles. Artists, literary scholars, folklorists, historians, and
even jurists all came knocking on Freud's door, seeking to participate
in the frenzy of dream interpretation that had taken hold of the first
generation of psychoanalysts (cf. Marinelli & Mayer, 2003). Bible and
Kabbalah scholars were among the first to respond to Freud's conclusions, and also to see in his theory a manifestation of his Jewish
identity.

From the moment of the book's publication, the question of the
Jewish origins of psychoanalysis would plague Freud and his successors. Alter Druyanov, folklorist, historian, Zionist, and author of the
Hebrew book *Sefer ha-Bediha ve-ha-Hidud* (Book of Jokes and Wit),
wrote to Freud from Odessa to draw his attention to the affinity
between his innovative theory of dreams and the interpretations of
dreams in Talmudic and kabbalistic literature. Freud was of a different opinion, "The remarks in the Talmud on the dream-problem have
frequently been brought to my attention. It seems to me, however,
that the similarities with the ancient Greek understanding of dreams
are far more striking" (Freud to Druyanov, 3 October 1910: AFM),
thereby signalling clearly his preference for universality over ethnic,
Jewish particularity.

Like his contemporary, Shaul Tchernichovsky, who, in his poem
"Before a Statue of Apollo" (published the same year as *The Interpretation of Dreams*), expressed a wish to participate in the Greek
cultural experience and not only in the Jewish one, Freud looked
towards classical Greece in his quest for the ancient layers of human
culture in general and of infantile sexuality in particular. The Hebraic
tradition, with its interpretative emphasis on words and text, and the
Greek philosophical tradition of *logos* informed his writings. His
hermeneutics were both Jewish and Greek, exegetical and rationally
scientific (Salberg, 2010). But Athens and Rome, not Jerusalem,
inspired Freud's phantasmagoric world. It was to them he would

make pilgrimages. His study and desk overflowed with hundreds of clay vessels, figurines, and statues from ancient Greece, Rome, and especially Egypt, on which he spent the better part of his money. He called them "my ancient and filthy gods" (Armstrong, 2005; Marinelli, 2001).

Druyanov was not the only member of the literary circle in Odessa that was re-establishing Hebrew as a literary language to delve into psychoanalytic theory. Ahad Ha'am (Asher Ginsberg), the rationalist founder of the spiritual and elitist stream of Zionism, lauded Freud. Even though he once sarcastically referred to Freud as "the wizard of Vienna", that did not prevent him from bringing his ailing daughter, Leah, to Freud for consultation, as mentioned in a letter to his sister, Ester, dated 2 June 1912 (Ahad Ha'am, 1912; 1956–1960). Her unstable mental condition had required her hospitalisation in a sanatorium near Berlin in 1909 (Zipperstein, 1993). When Leah agreed to psycho-analytic treatment, Eitingon, who knew Ahad Ha'am, referred the writer's daughter and her husband to Freud.[3] At the time, the couple lived in Haifa, in the home of Ahad Ha'am's sister, who was a physician. She approved of Leah's decision to seek treatment with Freud, writing to Ahad Ha'am on 19 May 1912,

> I think that his [Freud's] influence on her will be very good because her illness is one of those that he cures. He attributes all hysterical phenomena to sexuality, and this is indeed the case with Leah. For some reason, she does not have a normal sex life, and from what I have been able to divine from her, the cause is entirely moral.

Freud recommended Eitingon. But, as Eitingon complained, "Like Russian patients, who are not prepared to accept authority", Leah did not accept the recommendation and decided in the end to choose another therapist, from Berlin. The correspondence concerning Leah (letters from Eitingon to Freud, 18 June and 10 July 1912, and one from Freud to Eitingon on 23 June 1912, Freud & Eitingon, 2004), who sought Freud's help when he had no more than fifty students throughout Europe, testifies to the rapidity with which psycho-analysis was becoming accepted at the time. And Russian Jewish intellectuals played a key role in this process. Ahad Ha'am himself, who suffered from bouts of depression, was sent at the end of 1920 to a sanatorium in Berlin. He was visited there by Anna (Anyota) Smil[i]ansky, the house doctor at the Berlin Psychoanalytic Institute, who was the sister of his good friend Eliezer Smilansky, a writer and farmer who had settled in Palestine during the First Aliyah (Ahad Ha'am to Rivka Ginsberg, 9 August 1920, AHA).

While the Ginsberg family was still debating whether to send the hysterical Leah from Haifa back to Europe for analytical treatment, psychoanalysis' most pronounced hysterical ex-patient, Bertha Pappenheim (Anna O), started making a name for herself in the Yishuv. The Hebrew press offered extensive coverage of Pappenheim's visit to Palestine. She arrived in her capacity as a social worker, as part of her campaign against trafficking in women and prostitution. Pappenheim was becoming known as a pioneer of feminism in Germany and as founder of the League of Jewish Women. She was not, in her adulthood, a devotee of psychoanalysis. "No, never. Not as long as I live!" she responded when someone proposed sending one of the girls under her care for psychoanalytic treatment (Brentzel, 2002).

Anna O's transformation into the feminist Bertha Pappenheim has provided fertile ground for psychoanalytic and feminist interpretation. It could be argued that her feminist activism served as a public outlet for those unconscious strivings that had caused her hysteria. Some have presented the story of her mental affliction as a symptom of a collective illness that European masculine society imposed on middle-class women, especially Jewish women (cf. Decker, 1991). It seems doubtful whether her illness could be subsumed under just a few such sweeping psychological and sociological formulations. After all, in Jewish society at the turn of the nineteenth century, powerlessness (whether expressed as hysteria or as neurasthenia) was a malady that afflicted men and women equally. In fact, as the masculinity of the Jewish male eroded, the Jewish woman underwent an opposite process of masculinisation and enjoyed the reputation of being a resourceful *balbusta* (homemaker) who ruled, at least in the domestic realm (Boyarin, 1997). The encounter between Josef Breuer and Anna O, like that between Freud and Dora (Ida Bauer), psychoanalysis's second most famous patient, exhibited most of the signs of traditional patriarchal repression and silencing. But, in a historical perspective, they can be seen as a turning point that contained the seeds of something new, loquacious, and subversive, that would eventually spread beyond the gender rules of Jewish society and contribute its part to the change that took place in the position of women in Western society. During her visit to Palestine, Bertha Pappenheim lectured before a full house at the auditorium in Jaffa. Her listeners were hugely impressed and her talk impelled labour circles in the Yishuv to accept her claim that there was a direct connection between prostitution and the social repression of women (Alroey, 2004, pp. 161–162).

Revolutionary Russian psychoanalysis

Even before the incorporation of psychoanalytic ideas into the ideological repertoire of the leaders of the Zionist youth movements, Freud's followers were often given the opportunity to observe close up the manipulation and use of psychoanalysis by revolutionaries and idealistic reformers. Eitingon's referral of his Russian friend to Freud, like the case of the Russian aristocrat Sergei Pankejeff, the "Wolf Man", or Ahad Ha'am's appearance at Berggasse 19 with his daughter, were not coincidences. Psychoanalysis had special cachet among the German-speaking Russians who attended German and Swiss universities at the time. Russian intellectuals, like American doctors, began taking an interest in Freud's ideas well before the German academy started taking him seriously. Just as the Germans Kant, Hegel, and Nietzsche had been hugely influential among the Russian intelligentsia, Freud's theories were eagerly taken up by Russian psychiatrists, in part precisely because they came from the German-speaking world.

The Russians' reception of psychoanalysis is important to understanding its acceptance in the Yishuv because of the large proportion of Russian Jews who immigrated to Palestine in the early years of the twentieth century. Furthermore, the Russian reception of psychoanalysis offers a wider context for understanding the ideological and cultural debate over psychoanalytic ideas in Jewish Palestine.

Two waves of Jewish immigration to Palestine, first between 1905 and 1914 (the Second Aliyah), then between 1918 and 1923 (the Third Aliyah), contributed in a decisive way to the ideological foundations of the Jewish immigrant community of Palestine under the British Mandate (1918–1948). One of the chief accomplishments of these immigrants, whose views in many respects represented those of the Russian intelligentsia, was the transformation of utopian–egalitarian ideas and socialist myths from Eastern Europe into concrete Zionist programmes. Of course, the initial encounter between psychoanalysis and the Yishuv did not precisely mirror the encounter between psychoanalytic theory and Russian Marxism. But it did resemble the Russian case in major ways. The first attempts to transpose Freudian concepts into the notion of the Socialist New Man were made in Russia after the abortive revolution of 1905. The revolutionary impulses released by the advent of psychoanalytic theory, along with the possibilities it opened up in the study of culture and for the treatment of the mentally ill, made it attractive to many young Communists, whose conceptual world offered space for a notion of "soul" not bound to class or nationality. Many of them believed that psychoanalysis could liberate the victims of bourgeois society's repressive mechanisms from their past-centred angst. Even after the October revolution, for as long as it was possible to uphold the analogy between individual mechanisms of repression and those of bourgeois society, revolutionaries such as Trotsky and Joffe fashioned psychoanalysis into a scientific–ideological party instrument aimed at reconciling the "new science of the soul" with Pavlovian physiology.

The Russian Psychoanalytic Institute, with about thirty members in 1922–1923, then made up about an eighth of the entire membership of the International Psychoanalytical Association. And the Soviet state officially supported the work of analysts. An experimental boarding school for small children, run along psychoanalytic lines, was funded by the government, and one of Stalin's children was a pupil there (cf. Etkind, 1994, 1997; Kloocke, 2002; Knei-Paz, 1978; Miller, 1990, 1998; Rice, 1993).

Freud kept an interested but, as was his wont, suspicious eye on psychoanalysis's progress in Russia. In his polemic, "On the history of the psychoanalytic movement", he wrote, "The contributions written by Russian physicians and psychiatrists are not at present noteworthy. Only Odessa possesses a trained psychoanalyst in the person of M. Wulff" (Freud, 1914d).

Moshe Wulff (1878–1971), accepted in 1911 as a member of the Vienna Psychoanalytic Society (the successor of the Wednesday Group), was not the first or the most famous of the Russian psychiatrists who sought association with Freud during the years preceding the First World War, but he was the most talented and serious of them. He assumed the task of translating some of Freud's work into Russian, and before long an article of his appeared in the central psychoanalytic journal. When Freud commenced treatment of the Wolf Man, Wulff, who had previously treated Pankejeff's father, offered his assistance (interview with Kurt Eissler, 27 July 1962, FCLC). Wulff's clinical papers were exceptional in the Russian analytic discourse, which was devoted largely to social and pedagogical issues. He quickly gained the confidence of Freud and the Secret Committee as the only Russian with interest in the clinical applications of psychoanalysis.

The great popularity of Soviet Freudianism placed Russian analysts at the centre of a political debate over Marxist psychology and, in particular, sexology. For the Bolshevik press of the early 1920s, psychoanalysis was a weapon that could be used to fight against Russia's bourgeois past. Yet, the Bolsheviks were also uncomfortable with the concept of the unconscious. A philosophical dispute raged between Marxist "mechanists" and "dialectists". The former argued that social institutions were the chance and unpredictable outcome of clashing forces, whereas the latter believed that social structures were deliberate human creations. In the realm of the life and natural sciences, the mechanists were unequivocal determinists, viewing humans as no more than the sum total of the biological and hereditary forces acting on them. The corollary of this position was that individuals could not be held fully responsible for their actions and urges. Ivan Pavlov's physiological studies and his concept of the conditioned reflex were taken up by the mechanists. The dialectists spoke of revolutionary breaking points at which sudden and far-reaching changes occur in history and in the social structure. The debate between these two camps was not just a theoretical one—each position implied specific revolutionary views and practices that should be inculcated in human beings. The debate had implications for both the social and life sciences. A fundamental assumption that shaped the concept of the Soviet man was that the human organism was malleable and could be changed. One of the central questions that occupied Marxist psychologists and sexologists was the relative role played by biological and social forces in implementing such changes. The dialectists held the upper hand until the end of the 1920s. This approach, which maintained that both biology and environment shaped human behaviour, gradually gained strength. But this theory of the "two factors" was officially condemned in 1936 in a Bolshevik Party declaration. The individual, liberated just years previously from environmental and biological determinism, was now subjected, once and for all, to the ruling ideology. An individual's free will, Soviet ideologues now declared, was achieved by attaining harmony between the individual's needs and society's interests. Desire, personality, and consciousness were given precedence over their subversive unconscious counterparts, and Bolshevik thinkers discussed the question of how to manage the proletariat's sexual resources and harness them to the collective needs of the working class as a whole. Oscillating between advocacy of sexual abstention, condemning the sex drive as an impediment to the individual's ability to dedicate himself to the mission of building society, and calls for total liberation from any bourgeois inhibitions to sexual freedom, Soviet sexologists, psychologists, and Freudians stripped the soul of its determinist and unconscious elements (cf. Bauer, 1952; Halfin, 2003; Naiman, 1997). Moshe Wulff, one of the founders of the Russian Psychoanalytic Association, even offered some observations on the sexual functioning of bus drivers and tram conductors in Moscow (Wulff, 1928). This research, carried out prior to Wulff's emigration to Berlin, demonstrated some of the characteristics of Marxist dialecticism. In another article, "The Resistance of the Ideal-Ego and Adjustment to Reality," Wulff maintained that the appearance of psychoanalysis on the stage of human history was an expression of the cultural crisis humanity confronted in the face of the growing power of the Oedipus complex: "We should not be surprised that psychoanalysis appeared on the stage of history at precisely this stage in human development.... Our social and cultural development depends on psychoanalysis's ability to expose the Oedipal complex in all its forms, to deprive it of its excess influence, and in doing so to bring about the spiritual liberation of humanity." (Wulff, 1926).

A similar view, one that saw the Oedipal complex as a consequence of society's repression of the individual's instinctual strivings, was held by the designers of communal education, in its Zionist version. And Moshe Wulff was part of this context as well; even before his move from Berlin to Palestine, he made a name for himself among educators in the Yishuv's labour movement and agricultural settlements. Thirty years later, this time in Tel Aviv in the 1950s, Wulff again addressed the mutuality dependence of the individual psyche and society. In his essay, "Revolution and drive", he proposed a less utopian and more sober analytical model of the link between internal mental processes and social upheaval. This time he placed the death wish at the centre, the clinical conceptual importance of which was recognised by few of Freud's heirs at that time. Marx's reductionist approach, Wulff argued in this work, viewed the revolution as an expression of the repressed working class's frustration and material subordination. It did not, however, take into account the existence of opposing instincts in the human mind—the sexual urge and the destructive and aggressive urge. Sexual anarchy and the direct assault on the bourgeois family gave vent to destructive forces that threatened to subvert human social existence (Wulff, 1957).

According to post-revolutionary Bolshevism, the past, in the form of the society that had been overthrown, consisted of a system of economic and moral values that needed to be expunged entirely. But Freud had placed the meaningfulness of the past at the centre of his theory: the past was to be confronted and grappled with, not destroyed. Furthermore, Freud's concept of a repression mechanism focused on universal conflicts within the psyche that had their source in infantile sexuality, whereas the Bolshevik view was that human conflicts were fundamentally external, directly caused by class conflict. In the political context, Lenin himself attacked the bourgeois nature of psychoanalysis. In psychological circles, it was Alexander Luria, one of the greatest neuropsychologists of his generation, the scientific secretary of the Russian Psychoanalytic Institute during the early 1920s, who led the anti-Freudian attack during the 1930s.

Once it became clear that "Freudian man" was devoid of any utopian yearnings, revolutionary discourse in its Soviet version turned away from Freud's teachings and psychoanalysis was officially removed from the party's ideological armamentarium.

Ethos vs. Eros

Freud, as noted, did his best to prevent his science of the mind from being reduced or limited to the problem of the Jewish people or from being co-opted by revolutionary ideology. He could not be counted among the cultural pessimists of the late nineteenth century, such as Schopenhauer and Nietzsche, who offered their readers narratives of decline and degeneration. Neither was he an optimistic Whig who celebrated history as an inexorable march of progress toward enlightenment and human happiness. While opposing any deliberate attempt to place his new science of man within the confines of a particular *Weltanschauung*, it was only natural that the discourse on psychoanalytic ideas resonated, explicitly or implicitly, in the self-conceptions of the thinkers who shaped the image of the Zionist revolution's New Man. The New Jew had embodied, often simultaneously, the different philosophical schools current in European Jewish society. He was not an exclusively Zionist product, being shaped also by the thinking and personalities of figures external to the Jewish national discourse. Zionism was never an isolated ideology—it was characterised by an eclecticism of ideas. At the same time, gender and sexuality played a central role in Zionist thinking. Eros, whether in its metaphysical or psychological sense, was seen by the leaders of Zionist youth movements as a "revolutionary engine" with which the young Jew would break down the barriers of tradition and past generations. Whether he chose to identify with Herzl's model of the New Man, or that of the Hebrew author Micha Josef Berdichevsky, or that of Ahad Ha'am, of the socialist revolutionaries, or of Friedrich Nietzsche and Otto Weininger, Freud was never very distant from the centre of his world.

The Jews of Central Europe had a special connection to Ahad Ha'am. Many appreciated his moralistic exactitude, his evolutionary concepts, and his natural aversion to revolutionary shortcuts. The politics of Herzl and his colleagues were revolutionary in character. They rejected the evolutionary mode, stressing the urgent need to remedy the Jews' physical, aesthetic, and mental weakness. Zionism, Herzl argued, was a sort of "new Jewish treatment" for the nation's ills. Palestine was, thus, seen as a healthy place for the nation, where the Jewish body could be healed and develop physical and mental strength through possession of the Land. The model proposed by Herzl in his utopian novel, *Altneuland*, was, in many ways, paradoxical, in that it linked the process of transforming the Jew into a political–sovereign subject with the makeover of traditional Jewish identity markers, while adopting Christian–European norms of behaviour. For Herzl, these were the necessary components of a healthy national life. The Herzlian model thus required identifying, in a way, with the anti-Semitic stereotype of the Jew's ugliness. Max Nordau was similarly criticised when he offered his medical–hygienic explanation, both for the plight of the European bourgeoisie at the turn of the century and for the presumed feebleness of the Jewish mind and body. Herzl and Nordau sought to change the Jewish people from the outside in. These Zionist leaders sought to begin with the visible Jewish phenotype and habitus as expressed in the nation's way of life, mannerisms, and traits, and to proceed from there to the eugenic project of upgrading the fundamental Jewish genotype, which lay at the core of each Jew's self-conception and identity (cf. Geller, 1995; Shapira, 1997a,b).

The socialist model of the New Man in its Zionist version would also play a central role in the acceptance of psychoanalysis by the Jewish intelligentsia. One of the classic trademarks of the socialist movement was its educational–constructivist element. The religion of labour, the return to nature, and collectivist socialism were perceived as remedies for the social anomaly of Jewish social life in Eastern Europe. Revolutionary romanticism gained a firm foothold among the young Russian intelligentsia and this gained a hegemonic ideological and cultural status in the Yishuv (Shapira, 1997b; Sternhell, 1998). As we have seen, the first attempts to harness Freud's teachings to the enterprise of creating a new socialist man were made in Russia following the revolution of 1905. But when it turned out that casting off one's past was neither imperative nor even desirable in Freudian terms, and that Freudian man was not a utopian, Soviet revolutionary discourse spurned Freud's students. This was not, however, the case in Palestine. There, unlike in the Soviet Union, the acolytes of revolutionary Marxism did their best to synthesise Freud and Marx and to find in Freud's theory a place for their ideological and pedagogical repertoire. The encounter between psychoanalysis and Yishuv society was, in part, a replay of the encounter between psychoanalytical theory and Russian Marxism, but in another aspect it was a direct continuation of the complex negotiation conducted by central Zionist thinkers with the vitalism and Gnosticism of German Neo-romanticism.

Young Jews who sought an acquaintance with psychoanalysis outside socialist territory could visit the analytic clinic run by Frieda Reichmann (later Fromm-Reichmann). She opened a clinic in Heidelberg in 1924, a short time after completing her analytic training, where she sought to integrate the Orthodox Jewish education she had received from her parents with her new psychoanalytic identity. The patients in her sanatorium, where the Sabbath was strictly observed, dined together on kosher meals. Before each meal, the patients together read and studied a traditional Jewish text (Simon, 1998, pp. 217–218). Among the clinic's famous patients at that time were Akiva Ernst Simon (later director of the Hebrew University's School of Education), Erich Fromm (who married Reichmann a short time later), and Leo Löwenthal, the Frankfurt School's leading expert on the sociology of literature and mass culture (who later headed the sociology department at the University of California at Berkeley). The "Torahpeutikum", as her clinic is called in the writings of her contemporaries, did not last for long. In his memoirs, Gershom Scholem claimed that, with one exception—Simon—all Fromm-Reichmann's patients turned their backs on Orthodoxy during their treatment (Scholem, 1982, p. 186). So did Fromm-Reichmann herself, even before she left Germany in 1933. After a short stay in Palestine, where she lived with her niece, Esther, wife of the Hebrew writer Shmuel Yosef Agnon, she settled in the USA. There, she turned her back on Freudian orthodoxy as well, preferring the views of Harry Stack Sullivan.[4]

Micha Joseph Berdichevsky, one of the most important Jewish writers of his time, a fervent Zionist sometimes referred to as the Jewish Nietzsche, proposed an explanation for the spiritual predicament of the Jewish people that differed from that of both Herzl and the socialist Zionists. He distinguished between the contemporary theological–Diaspora existence of the Jewish people and their original, natural existence as ancient Hebrews. Berdichevsky was one of the central channels through which the European vitalistic discourse entered the Jewish world. Beyond his fiction, he was noted for his wide-ranging academic studies of Jewish antiquity. Ancient Jewish civilisation held a fascination for many Zionist thinkers who sought to reconstruct their people's mythical past as part of its modern national revival.

While Ahad Ha'am argued that the individualism that had taken hold of young assimilating Jews was a pathology of the national sensibility, Berdichevsky claimed that this same individualism was an expression of natural awakening, a healthy response to a religious deformation that could no longer be borne (Schweid, 2008). Freud and Breuer wrote, in their studies of hysteria of 1895, about the "hysterical patient suffering from his memories"; Berdichevsky declared in his essay, "Age and youth", that "We are the slaves of our memories". The writer's great popularity was, thus, attributable to his ability to put into words the ambivalent attitude that many young Jews had toward the traditional Jewish world with its "excessive spirituality", on the one hand, and to secular European culture, on the other. Similar repugnance for the traditional Jewish world, if less learned and more misogynic and nihilistic, was voiced by Otto Weininger, whose book *Sex and Character* became a cult work for the young people of Vienna (Sengoopta, 2000). Abba Ahimeir, then of the labour movement and later a leading advocate of armed rebellion against the British regime in Palestine, in 1925 devoted an article to Freud's and Weininger's theories of sexuality, and to the view of humanity that each of these theories implied. There was no limit to Professor Freud's faith in science, Ahimeir complained, but "the light that he casts into the darkest corners of the soul of the glory of creation [humankind] blinds more than it illuminates". What Ahimeir found lacking in Freud was the dualism he found aplenty in Weininger and Marx. Freud was a "undeniably monotheist". His theory was not concerned with who was good and who evil, and, while it claimed to explain everything, to remove the veil of secrecy from all parts of life, it could turn out to be "particularly dangerous if it were to leave the room of the learned" (Ahimeir, 1925). An even more pointed critique of psychoanalysis was offered by the Zionist philosopher and journalist Jakob Klatzkin, who offered the most characteristic identification of Freud as a negative icon by the proponents of the Philosophy of Life (*Lebensphilosophie*), while, at the same time, stressing his centrality to his opponents who rejected both Kantian abstract philosophy and scientific positivism. This Philosophy of Life, which grew out of the thinking of Henri Bergson and Wilhelm Dilthey, took a holistic view of life and maintained that it could only be understood from within.

Klatzkin's alternative theory of the mind stressed the tragic rift between life itself and the spirit, between the living, original, unmediated soul (*seele*) and the spirit (*geist*), expressed by reason and its principal product—culture. This rift, he maintained, caused human beings to live in constant alienation from the world instead of being within it. In his book, *The Urge to Know and the Principle of Life and Death* (1935), which he termed an "ontological study of the soul", Klatzkin proposed erotic love, or, more precisely, the erotic–narcissistic immersion of man within himself, as a way of connecting with the original, true, and natural, of experiencing one's true self and obviating the rational law to which one is subject. The metaphysical process

proposed by Klatzkin was meant to have historical and cultural implications for relations between the sexes, marriage, and the Jewish experience. In particular, it bore on the national solution he advocated for
the Jewish problem. Both his metaphysics and his cultural critique fed
into his radical Zionism (Hotam, 2007a).

A student of Hermann Cohen, the neo-Kantian Jewish philosopher, and a founding co-editor of the *Encyclopedia Judaica*, Klatzkin
promoted a Gnostic Zionism. His philosophical work maintains that,
in creation, the intrusion of the spirit divorced the world from the
original life force. From that point on, the history of the world has
been a saga of ongoing detachment, alienation, and decline of life, a
process in which "life eradicated itself". For Klatzkin, as a life philosopher, this dualistic split between life and spirit particularly charac-
terises human existence. Divided between rival spheres, one original
and emotional and the other derivative and rational, human existence
is a paradigm for the cosmic process of the decline of life and the
triumph of the spirit. Thus, Klatzkin argued, as mankind progresses
and his knowledge advances, reason moves ever closer to its origin,
"the divine spirit of nothingness". This process finally controls the
human soul, to the extent of destroying the human and biological
world, cooling human life and killing it with a "kiss of nothingness".
For Klatzkin, the "true Jew" is only conceivable as a national, that is,
political, being. This being was lost during exile, because exile or diasporic existence means a Jewish reality alienated and detached from
the original (national) "life on the land". This absent political being is
the essence to which Jewish existence should return. Zionism, therefore, meant, for Klatzkin, a mere return to what was forgotten during
exile: a return to a genuine national Jewish existence. The Zionist path
showed the way to the establishment of the "political" on the ruins of
the "theological", liberating the buried vital forces of Judaism as it
originally existed. In contrast, he said, psychoanalysis, despite its
success in freeing humankind of certain neuroses, could also be dangerous. A state of over-consciousness could weaken the forces concealed in the "juices of the unconscious", which provide energy for
vital life functions (Hotam, 2008). Klatzkin also voiced his opinions on
questions of psychoanalytic technique, and seems to have been
acquainted with some of the issues that divided analysts of his time.
For example, he referred to Ferenczi's position, put forth in 1911,
about the use of "rude" words in analysis. Klatzkin wrote,

Freud indeed advised analysts to prefer euphemism to explicit speech when referring to intimate parts of the body and sexual functions, but it was Ferenczi who told analysts to be aware that avoiding explicit use of "rude" words referring to the sexual organs would, in many cases, cause associations to cease and depression to ensue. (Klatzkin, n.d.)

Klatzkin sent a copy of his bio-philosophical essay, "The Urge to Know and the Principle of Life and Death" (1935) to Freud and requested a consultation with him. "You cannot imagine how hard it is for me to delve into speculative philosophical work," Freud replied, hinting that he was not impressed by Klatzin's attempt to trace the development of consciousness to vital powers (cf. Farber, 1937; Klatzkin, 1935). With his chilling candour, he rejected the Zionist philosopher's critique of psychoanalysis and his request for a meeting:

The impression I have received is that you lack the necessary experience (in hypnotic phenomena, interpretation of dreams, and the analysis of patients) that has led us to be persuaded both that there are mental processes that can only correctly be called "unconscious," and that there is a way to make them conscious. As a result, there is no path connecting your starting point and ours. The meeting that you wish for would not be able to change this fact and the exchange between us would be equivalent to that between a polar bear and a whale. (Freud to Klatzkin, 14 February 1935, Klatzkin Collection, CZA)

Freud took exception to attempts like Klatzkin's to synthesise his ideas and the vitalistic spirit of the times. Yet, this did not prevent members of the Zionist youth movements from continuing to assimilate eclectic ideas from the fields of philosophical, social, historical, and psychological theory into their political activism. Martin Buber, a charismatic philosopher, took up the challenge of combining philosophy, pedagogy, and psychology.

Between Freud and Buber

Ever since Sándor Ferenczi's lecture on "Psychoanalysis and education" at the First International Psychoanalytic Congress in Salzburg in 1908, Freud's followers had debated the field's applicability to pedagogy (Ferenczi, 1949[1908]). In contrast with the German psychiatric establishment, European educators, for the most part, displayed a keen interest in psychoanalysis. Freud's ideas did not undermine the German ideals of proper education (*Bildung*) and proper behaviour (*Sittlichkeit*) that had prevailed in bourgeois society since the mid-eighteenth century. On the contrary, with his emphasis on the means by which one could fight and sublimate the forces that prevent individuals and society from exploiting their full humanistic and cultural potential, Freud avoided any suspicion that his theory was subversive. The advocates of proper education could, thus, adopt large parts of his theory (Körner, 1980).

That reason and individuality were separated by a chasm was an essential element of the intellectual drama of the end of the nineteenth century. It can be seen in the art, literature, philosophy, and science of that era. The core essence of each individual was seen to be external to the laws of reason, so the inner self struggled endlessly against cultural and social constraints. The "true" or "authentic" inner self did not conform to cultural laws or norms, but, rather, lay beyond and had to be shielded from them (cf. McGrath, 1974; Rose, 1998; Schorske, 1981).

These trends found expression in Zionist thinking as well, especially in the images and messages of the Zionist youth movements. Many of the prophets of the New Man and the vitalistic youth culture that flourished in Europe in the 1890s were active in the German cultural sphere. The Jewish youth groups sought to create a new kind of Jew by adopting the German neo-romantic values of physical culture, the return to nature, and anti-intellectualism (cf. Berkowitz, 1993; Hotam, 2007b; Peled, 2002). *Wandervogel*, the German youth movement founded at the turn of the century, served as a model. Most of the changes that the *Wandervogel* groups advocated were metaphysical and structural rather than ideological and political. They promoted camaraderie, condemned social hypocrisy and falsehood, proclaimed inner truth, and preferred what they called "indirect" education, involving emotionally charged images and myths, to "direct" education, which merely conveyed information. To the search for a unique individual identity and rebellion against all that the generation of their parents represented, members of the *Wandervogel* tended to identify utterly with exemplary figures at the same time that the movement demanded that they give up their individuality and become one with the group. Charismatic orators knew how to give their young listeners a feeling that the individualism of Nietzsche, Schopenhauer, and even Freud could be consistent with the collectivist socialism of Marx and his Soviet commentators. On the other hand, the veneration accorded to the movements' leaders and the ideological collectivism advocated by their members contradicted the principles of free choice and the primacy of the individual conscience. This duality also characterised the attitude of the youth movements' leaders to sexuality. The "New Man" of the youth movements was a manifestly masculine concept. Hans Blüher, in 1912 published his book, *The German Wandervogel as an Erotic Phenomenon*. In this work he preached the ejection of women from the movement and from politics, and extolled the friendship of men united by the (non-sexual!) homo-erotic forces that pulsed within them. The book described the role of eroticism in male companionship as a process of sublimation that goes beyond the erotic urge, thanks to the capacities of the charismatic leader. Indeed, according to the youth movements, a counsellor's job was to channel male eroticism into social and cultural activity.[5] The positive attitude toward the nude body did not imply sexual liberation. On the contrary, celibacy, asceticism, and puritanism were intended to neutralise threatening sexual urges (cf. Borinski & Werner, 1982; Laqueur, 1962; Mosse, 1980, 1985, 1996b; Williams, 2001).

On 1 March 1914, one *Wandervogel* group, the Berlin Ramblers' Association, invited another such movement, *Blau-Weiss* (Blue-White), to a meeting where they united to form *Blau-Weiss*—The Association for Jewish Youth Hikes in Germany. Freud was one of the famous intellectuals and public figures who signed a statement calling for the establishment of a Vienna chapter of this organisation. *Blau-Weiss* was not an ideological movement—its agenda did not include Jewish problems or anti-Semitism. The movement's members came from middle-class, mostly well-off families for which Zionism held little appeal. These were assimilated teenagers who sought Jewish companionship as a solution to their adolescent angst and their crisis of Jewish identity. Like its non-Jewish counterparts in Germany, *Blau-Weiss* took a manifestly critical line against society and civilisation and acclaimed anti-rationalism and anti-intellectualism (Schatzker, 1992, 1998).

It was Gustav Wyneken (1875–1964) who infused the German youth movements with an individualistic ethos. He sought to expand the youth culture—a term he coined—and to bring it into the schools and educational system. His individualistic views differed from those of previous youth movement leaders, downplaying *völkisch*-popular ideas and stressing individual freedom. He published his ideas in a periodical, *Der Anfang*, which began to appear in 1913 under the editorship of Martin Buber and Siegfried Bernfeld (Massen, 1995). Bernfeld, born in the city of Lemberg (Lvov) in Galicia, embodied what an integration of the teachings of Freud, Marx, and Buber could offer to Jewish youth. He completed his philosophical studies at the University of Vienna, where his doctoral thesis was entitled "On the concept of youth". He believed that youth were a revolutionary force and declared that they possessed moral and spiritual sensitivity and were endowed with a natural capacity to rise up against injustice. In light of this, he founded, in 1918, a revolutionary organisation, the Jerubaal Youth Order.[6] National Jewish ideas gradually made their way into the Order's activities. Alongside his pedagogical work, Bernfeld began publishing a periodical, also called *Jerubaal*, meant "to enable youth to make their voice heard and to be aware of the powers beating within it". Bernfeld had joined the Vienna Psychoanalytic Society, and from this point on used the Freudian concept of "repression" to explain the problem of split identity experienced by Jewish youth in Germany. His view was supported by Leo Baeck, Akiva Ernst Simon, and Hugo Bergmann. The members of this generation had received a European cultural education and were pushed by parents into German careers. Yet, they lived with a constant sense of inferiority, because the non-Jewish society in which they lived constantly confronted them with the charge that they were different— no matter how they looked, what language they spoke, and what level of achievement they reached. The constant need to hide their origins and the language of their parents fed their conflict between identification with the Jewish community or with their German environment. The factor that united young Jews was, thus, their disappointment with the idea that assimilation alone could guarantee their acceptance into the non-Jewish society in which they lived (cf. Bunzl, 1992; Ekstein, 1996; Hoffer, 1981; Rechter, 2001; Utley, 1979; Volkov, 2006).

Even before he completed his own analysis with Hanns Sachs, Bernfeld had made a name for himself as the most popular lecturer at the Psychoanalytic Institutes in Berlin and Vienna. In 1925, he published a book, *Sisyphus or the Limits of Education*, in which he examined psychoanalysis's attitude toward Marxist theory and critiqued the foundations of education. A somewhat ironic expression of Bernfeld's deterministic tendencies at the end of the 1920s can be seen in his attempts to develop a "libidometer" to measure the quantity of a patient's libidinal energy (Bernfeld & Feitelberg, 1931). Following his move to France in 1934, he devoted himself to finding a common ground between psychoanalysis and biology and, in collaboration with his wife, wrote a scientific biography of Freud. In 1937, he emigrated again, this time settling in San Francisco, where he joined the local Psychoanalytic Institute.

Bernfeld had a talent for finding his way into the hearts of young people, the Zionist movement's major target population. Along with his ties to the members of the HaShomer HaTza'ir ("The Young Guard") youth movement in Vienna, the first Zionist Jewish youth movement to be established in Europe, he served as a consultant to the founders of the Activity School in Tel Aviv. The founders wished to adopt the principles of progressive education promulgated by Maria Montessori and John Dewey and to integrate them with the values of physical labour as the foundation for Jewish national and cultural revival in a society based on social justice and equality (Reshef & Dror, 1999). Enthused at being the first in the Yishuv to implement modern psychological principles in education and teaching, they planned for the school to include a research institute like the Institute for the Study of Jewish Youth that Bernfeld had established in Vienna. They hoped that researchers would conduct "psychophysiological observations" at the school. Bernfeld donated to the school a stock of books and articles from German educational journals, and served as a member of the editorial board of the first pedagogical journal to be published in Hebrew, Hachinuch (Idelson to Bernfeld, 9 September 1921; June 1921: Bernfeld Collection, YIVO).

When the school in Tel Aviv closed in 1925, Bernfeld recommended to one of its founders, David Idelson, that he hone his pedagogical skills by seeking psychoanalytic training at the Institute that had just opened its doors in Berlin. Idelson traveled to the German capital and became the first Yishuv educator to experience psychoanalysis. His Berlin diary shows a daily meeting denoted by a single word: Wulff (Diary: Idelson Collection, AJE).

The Zionist movement made good use of the revolutionary potential of Jewish youth. One way it did so was by creating a parallel between the young Jew's doubts about his identity and the fuzzy identity of the collective he belonged to. These young people had a natural tendency to express their identity problems in collectivist ways and to follow leaders who could speak convincingly about sexual identity, relations between the sexes, generational independence, honesty, and loyalty. Thus, these young people became the standard-bearers for the new Jewish ideal. In the same year that Freud published *Totem and Taboo*, 1913, the HaShomer HaTza'ir movement was founded in Galicia. Beyond the important historical role this movement played in the framework of the Zionist movement and settlement of the Land, it had a key part, in its early years, in establishing the model of organisation and activity adopted by other Zionist youth movements founded in the 1920s and 1930s, as well as in the acceptance of psychoanalytic ideas in the Yishuv during the four decades preceding the founding of the state. *HaShomer HaTza'ir* began as a non-ideological movement shaped by the modernist neoromantic discourse that permeated the German cultural sphere at the turn of the century. Beginning in 1920, when the first of its members settled in the Land of Israel, it became ideological, adopting Marxism and a clear political and settlement programme. The modernist culture of Vienna at the turn of the century made a deep impression on how members of the movement viewed themselves during *HaShomer HaTza'ir*'s early years. Siegfried Bernfeld was instrumental in mediating between elite German culture and the "young guards". His political ideology, which placed youth at the vanguard of the nationalist enterprise, was a huge influence on the movement's thinking. Thanks to Bernfeld, Freud was also a key influence on their social worldview (cf. Margalit, 1971; Mintz, 1995; Peled, 2002).

Meir Ya'ari, the charismatic leader of the movement's first group to settle in the Land, quickly proved himself to be one of the most articulate spokesmen for integrating Freud into the movement's programme:

> I want you to develop a precise acquaintance with Freud and his school, I don't know whether many of us can accurately grasp his theory, yet I hope that it will at least cleanse the charged atmosphere. I want to sanctify the primal urges through this experience. Please be aware of the power in you, when masculine eroticism unites you despite your inner resistance. (Ya'ari, 1921, cited in Mintz, 1995, p. 353)

The belief in a primal, hidden, true self that expressed itself outside law, culture, and other constraints, was part of the idealisation of youth. In the communal context of the youth group, the young person's journey into himself was rendered in psychological terms through confessions like those familiar in religious contexts. Ya'ari, although using Freud's terminology, conceived this metaphysically in the form of what had been known in the second half of the nineteenth century as "Philosophy of life", of which psychoanalysis was, in fact, the direct opposite. Even if both grew out of a common philosophical tradition that viewed introspection and self-knowledge ("know thyself") as a necessary condition for knowing the world, Freud's scientific psychology, which demonstrated the centrality of primal, unconscious mental processes, never came out against rationalism and never saw the subject's experience of sinking into himself, and certainly not extreme subjectivism, as a means for liberating mankind. Meir Ya'ari spoke of the pure and open-hearted generation that had come to Palestine, a generation which had broken free of the hysterical neuroticism of its parents and from sanctimonious, bourgeois repression of natural instincts. "We wish," he proclaimed, "to extol the unfettered young person who as an adult remains a child, who prizes and acts on his instincts, rather than treating them with contempt"(Yaari, 1921, in Mintz, 1995, p. 374). The symbols that the movement's members adopted for themselves when they settled in the Land demonstrated that they retained their links to the *völkisch* repertoire of images of the *Wandervogel*. The Young Guards was a brotherhood of labouring men who, with their perspiring bodies, fertilised the soil—the true spouse of the Zionist pioneer. In the primordial HaShomer HaTza'ir tribe, woman's role was to underline that men could and would live without her. Women were not the object of desire for the members of the movement—they desired, rather, mother earth. But women were needed to prevent the men of being suspected of homosexuality (cf. Nur, 2004; Ufaz, 1991). The eroticisation of manual and agricultural labour was closely tied to the historical image of the Land of Israel as a lover of the Jew. Ya'ari, the first to marry a woman at a HaShomer HaTza'ir kibbutz, expressed in his letters of this period unambiguous and extreme anti-feminist and anti-family sentiments, attitudes that would be current in the kibbutz movement for many years to follow. He vividly expressed the tension that Freud's romantic readers experienced between rationalism and the concept of the unconscious:

I must operate on and slice into thought like a cold razor. And indeed I conclude that psychoanalysis is delving deterministically into the depths and illuminating them precisely to amplify the mystery all the more, in order to be overpowered in the end at the final barrier. Without a flash of creativity, without completely self-sufficient caprice, without an act of sovereign will, you will not get through the shell, not experience nor create . . . I seek, with all the powers of my mind, to penetrate into my unconscious universe and reveal myself. I feel that this is the only way to independence, that only thus will life burgeon and grow. Your eyes see it, I am speaking in the language of Freud. (Ya'ari, 1921, in Mintz, 1995, p. 376)

It is hard to imagine Freud endorsing Ya'ari's faith in the ability of the will and the intellect to "get through the shell". Creativity and "self-sufficient caprice" were, for Freud, objects of scientific study, not means of liberation from the repression and conflict built into the individual psyche. Ya'ari's psychoanalytical critique, thus, remained loyal to German Philosophy of Life and neo-romanticism, which viewed self-searching itself as the key to salvation. The goal of this sort of self-enquiry was to allow a person to uncover his real nature and the essence of things as they are.[7] Note that exposing a person to his true nature was not an expression of a desire for spirituality, for unification with nature and liberation from physicality. On the contrary, the aspiration for the immanent, the natural, the corporeal, the physical, with the goal of being liberated from reason and rationality, was meant to free man of his cultural inhibitions and connect him with his source. Like the revolutionary Russian version of this doctrine already cited, the HaShomer HaTza'ir account of the Freudian sexual revolution was overly optimistic. Freud never promoted either sexual liberation or abstinence. He did, however, point out that human beings must reconcile themselves to living with some measure of psychic conflict, mental pain, and want. True, some of Freud's early writings, such as his essay, "'Civilized' sexual morality and modern nervous illness" (1908d), could be cited by advocates for reforming the institution of the family or marriage in its Roman–Christian form. But putting all the onus on society for being the central cause of the development of neurosis was never a position that spoke to Freud. The different understanding of the place of infantile sexuality in shaping the path followed by the adult is evident not only in the HaShomer HaTza'ir interpretation of Freud, or in the pedagogical practices that the movement fostered in the framework of communal education, but also in the desire to integrate the teachings of Freud with those of Martin Buber, who, at that time, had already come out explicitly against psychoanalysis.

Buber was hugely influential among Zionist youth in his time. His links to the vitalist spirit were evident as early as his first lectures, in which he stressed the concept of experience (*Erlebnis*), which was a central concept in German Philosophy of Life. Buber's interest in Jewish mysticism and Hasidism is often seen as an expression of his search for a new model for Judaism as a living community that does not suffer from the internal rupture that sustained the sense of crisis at this time. For him, Jewish nationalism and political revival through Zionism were tantamount to heresy against the life prescribed by Jewish law and the transcendent God. Zionism was a way for the Jew to return to the primal state, in the metaphysical sense, to connect with immanent nature (cf. Cohen, 1983; Hotam, 2007a; Wehr, 1991). Buber had met with Freud in 1908 and tried to interest him in contributing to the series of writings on society that he was editing, but Freud declined. Buber disagreed with Freud's dream theory and argued that Freud did not display "sufficient awe" toward the process that created dreams. He also expressed reservations about *Totem and Taboo* (1912–1913), which he maintained was based on assumptions that had long since been disproved (Martin Buber to Kurt Eissler, 22 April 1960, FCLC). Buber's critic of Freud focused on the ability to feel "existential guilt", which, according to Buber, was something that Freud, who emphasised unconscious feeling of guilt, had failed to appreciate. Whereas existential guilt presupposes mans' accountability for the consequences of actual interpersonal relations, Freud's idea of unconscious guilt, so Buber, reduces guilt to a single cause: a moral transgression which is akin to the fulfillment of an oedipal murderous striving (Agassi, 2008). In his opening lecture at the Third International Pedagogical Convention in Heidelberg in 1925, and published a year later, Buber came out against the idea that the sexual drive explained all. He did this, as was his custom, without mentioning Freud's name and without using the term "psychoanalysis":

> It is important that we recognize the 'originator instinct' in its independence and primordiality. The contemporary theory of the soul tends to attribute the multifaceted nature of the human soul on a single primal foundation—libido, the will to power, and so on. In fact,

this does nothing but generalize certain states of degeneration in which one instinct not only overwhelms the other instincts but also permeates and expands them. (Buber, 1926[2005], p. 136)

According to Buber, the human being is fundamentally a dialogic entity who cannot realise him or herself except in a state of encounter with the world. Self-realisation takes form only through the creation of dialogue. Humans have two fundamental drives that are dialogic in essence: the instinct of communion and the originator instinct.

Children, according to Buber, are dominated by these two instincts, and they, not the libido or the will to power, are the keys to education. The Buberian originator instinct is the child's intrinsic drive to form and shape the world. It is not aimed at "having", but at "doing". The originator instinct is not sufficient, however, since it does not lead to mutuality and sharing. The originator is solitary until somebody takes his hand—not just as a creator, but as a creature lost in the world. The task of the genuine educator is to channel the creative forces of the child in the right direction—toward communion.

The communion instinct is the "longing for the world to become present to us" (ibid.).

Buber illustrates this desire by describing a child lying with half-closed eyes in the darkness, faced with a frightening night, waiting restively to experience her mother's communion. According to Buber, a harmonious person can only be formed through trust in communion. Hence, the task of the educator is to channel the child's presence into his own life, into communion (Yaron, 2000). The educator's prime concern should not be to influence the child's primal urges, whether to liberate, suppress, or sublimate and convert them into socially desirable activity. Instead, Buber stressed the encounter between the child and the adult:

Not for the liberation of any one of the instincts, but rather for the forces that confront him with the redundancy of his bonds: the forces of the educators. It depends on them, their merits and truthfulness, their power to love and their humility, what coupling the released element will find, and what fruit will grow. (Ibid., p. 242)

The originator instinct, Buber argued, was not enough to ensure "true human life". Education based only on the drive "to create something" "will impose on human beings a new loneliness, one full of agony".

Rather, the child should be taught "to find a partnership in working with another". This is the drive to commune.

If the soul could be analysed, Buber argued, it would be shown to contain mechanisms that allow a person to grasp the world and the figures within it: "The soul gives birth in the individual to the man, and he 'educates' the person". The point of education is to enable the world to act on the pupil. The educator should perform his craft "not from within the pupil's reality", that is, without a systematic set of values and ideals to be poured into the child's soul, but, rather, with an openness to the child's needs at any given moment. The Buberian educator, thus, needed to empty himself of all desire or positivist knowledge.

Buber clearly issued a challenge to the German ideal of *Bildung* (proper education), which maintained that children should be educated in values and exposed to exemplary figures and works of art. In a world in which "all likenesses have been shattered", Buber argued, the educator found himself in distress. But, when all forms of education "grope in the darkness of the abyss", the only true human path emerges, the path that leads to the spirit of the Creator, "to the spirit of God moving over the face of the waters",

Although he never published a systematic critic of psychoanalysis, Buber's correspondence with his friends Hans Trüb and Herman Menachem Gerson, reveal his ambivalence to Freud. In 1957, in a seminar on the Unconscious Buber said:

> Freud remained until the end a radical physiologist . . . never speaking explicitly about the soul, but only about the psyche, which he never paused to define. Freud was a simplificateur, just like Marx in the social field. That is, someone who places a general idea instead of repeated research of reality. Fifty years of psychotherapeutic thinking have been based on this dangerous way of thinking. These days are over now. (Buber, 1957[2008], p. 221)

Notes

1.   Marmorek was Herzl's model for the character of "Professor Steineck", the bacteriologist, in his utopian novel, *Altneuland*.
2.   Ironically, Leo Baeck wrote an essay with the same title. It was published in the same year as well, in response to an essay of 1900 by the German

theologian Adolf von Harnack, called "The essence of Christianity". Rank's thesis shares some features with Theodore Lessing's claim that the Jews had the task of mediating between mythos and ethos, and with Jakob Klatzkin's Radical Vitalism, which sought to cure both Jewish existence and Western civilisation by evoking authentic Jewish life in ancient times.

3. Few years later, it was Eitingon's turn to seek Ahad Ha'am's advice. In a letter to the Zionist leader, who was living in England, Eitingon inquired if the British law would allow him to remarry before the divorce procedures from his first wife have been completed (Eitingon to Ahad Ha'am, 6 December 1912: AHA).

4. Later well known for her pioneering work with psychotics at Chestnut Lodge in Rockville, Maryland, she was the model for Dr Fried in Hannah Green's autobiographical novel, *I Never Promised You a Rose Garden*.

5. Blüher avoided using the term "homosexual" because of what he called its "suspect" connotations, using instead the Freudian term "invert".

6. Jerubaal being another name for the Israelite Judge Gideon, who smashed the altars on which his fellow Israelites were burning offers to the Canaanite god Baal.

7. It is undoubtedly not coincidental that, in Hebrew, Ya'ari used a word charged with kabbalistic meaning—*klipa*, or shell—to refer to the false outer countenance of the human being. In Jewish mysticism, the word also denotes a foreign or false covering that keeps the spirit from expressing itself and from being known.

CHAPTER TWO

Psychoanalytic pioneers and their discontents

"At Edward Bernays's we once met the leader of the Zionist movement, Dr. Weizmann. A clever man, agreeable, hasn't a clue about psychoanalysis, and reveals himself in his stories as one who identifies (unconsciously) with Joshua (the prophet). He comes to America every winter in order to collect the budget for the next year in Palestine. If only we were so popular!"

(Sándor Ferenczi, 1927)

Before the outbreak of the First World War, the German cultural sphere was represented in Palestine by the settlements of the Templars, a sect founded in southern Germany in the mid-nineteenth century, whose members settled in the Holy Land for messianic religious reasons. This community of about 2,000 individuals influenced the economic, agricultural, and educational models adopted by the members of the Jewish Yishuv. But, following the war, the two major groups of agents of German culture in the newly constituted British Mandate in Palestine were Eastern European Jews educated in Germany or in the German cultural tradition, and Jews born and bred in German-speaking countries. This latter group was small, but they held key positions in the Yishuv's economy and culture. The Zionist youth groups were also channels through which Central and Western European culture penetrated post-war Hebrew culture (cf. Elboim-Dror, 1996; Gelber, 1990; Stone, 1997).

Between Vienna and Mecca

Two psychoanalysts living in Palestine during the first half of the 1920s each sought, in his own sphere, to interest the local intellectual community in Freud's ideas. The name of David Eder (1865–1936), son of a London diamond dealer, was a unique embodiment of liberal, socialist, psychoanalytic, and Zionist ideas—not to mention pure adventurism. In his youth, Eder had shared an apartment with his cousin, the writer Israel Zangwill. He was close to D. H. Lawrence and George Bernard Shaw, and took part in the psychoanalytic frenzy that swept through London's literary elite. With Ernest Jones, Eder founded the London Psychoanalytic Society, but the organisation's life was short, curtailed by the shock-wave released by Jung's schism (Hinshelwood, 1995, 1998). Before falling under the allure of the Land of Israel and the Zionist movement, Eder travelled to Brazil as Zangwill's emissary, to examine the possibility of settling Jews there; hatched with Jones a plan to establish a psychoanalytically orientated colony in Mexico; trekked through the Andes; was accused of espionage; and, sailing ever closer to the wind, fell prisoner to a cannibal tribe (Eder, 1927; Feigenbaum, 1936; Glover, 1945). So, when he joined, at the establishment of the British Mandate, the Zionist Commission that arrived in Palestine in 1918 under the leadership of Chaim Weizmann, this looked like just one more trip to an exotic clime. But from the moment of his arrival he took on a number of public positions. For all intents and purposes, he ran the commission, which served as the Yishuv's autonomous governing institution in the years between the Balfour Declaration and the establishment of the Jewish National Council (the *Va'ad Le'umi*) two years later (Segev, 2001). His busy public life did not, of course, enable him to pursue his clinical work. But when he established the Yishuv's Orphans' Committee, the approach taken by the educators involved began to change. Under his direction, the Committee adopted an approach that was not popular

among the Yishuv's teachers. The natural inclination of these pedagogues was to remove children from indigent families and place them
in the practised hands of educators in orphanages. Eder, in contrast,
instructed the Committee's staff to ensure continuity in children's
relations with their families, even if the family situation was far from
optimum from a pedagogical and social welfare point of view
(Weiner, 1984). In surveying the status, in 1918, of Jerusalem's 300
Jewish orphans (out of a total Jewish population of 27,000), Eder noted
that Zionist policy-makers preferred collectivist approaches to education. They undervalued the importance of the family and took every
opportunity to remove responsibility for the education of children
from parents and place it with the community. He said,

> The younger the child at the death of his parents, the happier a teacher
> is to grab him; a child lacking both parents is, quite naturally, a more
> important object for education than a child deprived only of a mother
> or father. (Cited in Weiner 1984, p. 62)

Eder assigned the Orphans' Committee the task of finding place-
ments for First World War orphans and supervising their care. No
long-term national or ideological goals were considered. He preferred
to place orphans with foster families rather than handing them over
to institutions, and this programme was pursued with great success
during his time in Palestine and then until 1928, when the Orphans'
Committee was dismantled. But, beginning in the 1930s, collective
approaches again became ascendant, and even educators familiar
with psychoanalytic theory tended to view the group, not the family,
as the proper educational milieu. In this view, the counsellor or
teacher would become acquainted with the psychology of each individual child and establish a personal relationship with him in the
framework of the group of children or educational institution; the
family took second place.

Eder lectured and wrote extensively about the need to instil
"cultural and political instincts" in the Jewish people. He claimed that
the Jews of the Yishuv and their leaders had a tendency "to be ruled
by their emotions and lacking in discipline" (Stein, 1945). This Zionist
psychiatrist and analyst sparked the imagination of those who maintained that the Yishuv's political plight was a kind of disease. And
there was no lack of such people in the Zionist leadership. The Zionist

jurist Norman Bentwich, who served as the Mandate administration's attorney general, maintained that

> the principal characteristic that governed Eder's professional and public life was his firm wish to cure the defects of the soul, whether of the individual or of the nation in difficulty. . . . A psychiatrist in the simple sense of the word, a doctor of the soul, he devoted himself utterly and without prejudice to his patient, the Jewish people. (Bentwich, 1937)

As noted in the previous chapter, the medicalisation and pathologisation of the public political sphere was not new to Zionist discourse. But this was a time when most of Freud's students were not part of the Zionist interpretative community that sought to link the individual Jew's physical and mental ailments to the infirmities of the Jewish nation. In contrast, David Eder, in his person and in his actions, was the archetype of the interdisciplinary analyst who seeks to expand his analytic field of action beyond the treatment room and to integrate analytic insights with public life. He believed that psychoanalysis could illuminate not only the masses' relationship to their leaders, but also the leaders' relationship with the public they were supposed to represent. In support of this, Eder cited the "veil of secrecy" that he and his fellow Zionist leaders used to cover up facts that were known to all:

> During the time that I filled a political role in Palestine I noticed in myself (and in my colleagues) the satisfaction it gave me to have secret information, knowledge, which must on no account be imparted to others. Of course good reasons were always to be found: the people would misuse the information or it would depress them unduly and so on—pretty exactly the parents' attitude about imparting information, especially of a sexual nature, to the children. Indeed when our secret information was common knowledge we still tried to keep it to ourselves, just as we do with our children though we have ourselves been through the same schooling. (Eder, 1924, p. 141)

Eder also supplied his colleagues with psychological profiles of Arab leaders. And not just Arabs: when the British sentenced Ze'ev Jabotinsky to fifteen years in prison and he began to serve his time in Acre, Eder wrote to Weizmann that firm action should be taken to obtain his release: "He is in a pathological condition and I truly fear for his mental state" (Segev, 2001, p. 120).

Eder was a Jewish psychoanalyst serving in the Zionist leadership, but he was not the only Zionist politician to comb Freud's writings for a theoretical foundation for the establishment of a governable collective political culture. Arthur Ruppin, the father of Zionist settlement in the Land of Israel, was deeply impressed by Freud's *Introductory Lectures in Psychoanalysis* (1916–1917), which he read in 1923. He also regretted that he had come too late across Freud's *Group Psychology and the Analysis of the Ego* (1921c): "Freud opened up for me new perspectives on my mental life, on the lives of others, and on unconscious religious and emotional life in general. . . . It's too bad that I didn't have the opportunity to study him earlier" (Arthur Ruppin letter to Hanna Ruppin, 22 December 1923, in Ruppin, 1985, pp. 356–357). Ruppin was, however, critical of Eder's inclination to view the Orient from a psychological perspective. He doubted whether a British Jew could truly understand the Arabs, who constituted an issue that the Zionist leadership had tended to neglect. "One can't expect of Eder that he turn into an Oriental, and my feeling is that the task doesn't appeal to him, either" (ibid., diary, 22. February 1922, p. 335), Ruppin wrote. He was reading much Freud in those years. After coming across Freud's work on religion, *The Future of an Illusion* (1927c), Ruppin himself considered writing about the role played by illusions in world history. Examples of such illusions were abundant, he wrote, and it was certainly possible that they played a greater role in history than that which Marx assigned to production.

A psychoanalyst like Eder, for whom the doors of Zionist and Mandate officials were always open, could have done much to assist other psychoanalysts, had they shown an interest in moving to Palestine. But none did. A letter that Ernest Jones circulated to the members of the Secret Committee included a report on a conversation he had held with Chaim Weizmann, whom Freud held in the highest esteem, in which the Zionist leader wrote of impoverished immigrants from Galicia who were arriving in Palestine with nothing except "Marx's *Capital* in one hand and Freud's *Interpretation of Dreams* in the other!" Jones and Eder, two friends who had worked together ten years previously to disseminate psychoanalysis in Britain, might have believed that Eder's energetic presence and Weizmann's optimistic reports were sufficient to put Palestine on the psychoanalytic map. Jones reported to Vienna that he was working vigorously to use Eder "for propaganda in Palestine" (letter, Jones to Rank, 19 October

1920, in Wittenberger & Toegel, 1999, p. 96). At the same opportunity, he gave an account of his efforts to enlist Weizmann in obtaining financial support for the anthropological work of Géza Róheim, an analyst whose work was based on hypotheses about primal social structures that, Freud proposed in *Totem and Taboo* (1912–1913), were preserved in primitive societies. Ferenczi, who met Weizmann in New York, was also impressed with his public relations skills.[1] The Zionist leader, he wrote to Freud, reveals himself as one who unconsciously identifies with the biblical Joshua (dated 26 February 1927, in Freud & Ferenczi, 1993–2000, pp. 298–303).

The heterogeneous ethnic makeup of Palestine in the 1920s gradually captured the imaginations of analysts, even those for whom the Zionist idea had little appeal. In fact, another student of Freud was on his way to the country.

When Dorian-Isador Feigenbaum (1887–1937), a member of the Swiss Psychoanalytic Society, announced he was moving to Palestine, his decision was noted cursorily in the copious correspondence exchanged by the seven members of the Secret Committee in 1920. Following four flagging years, the psychoanalytic movement had returned to full activity, reaching its acme with the inauguration of the first psychoanalytic outpatient clinic of its kind in Berlin. Feigenbaum must have surprised his colleagues when he informed them of his candidacy for the position of medical superintendent of the only psychiatric hospital in distant Palestine, founded in 1895 by Ezrat Nashim, the country's first Jewish women's organisation. Feigenbaum's application was accepted, and he was also made psychiatric consultant to the Mandate administration. Inspiring his moving to Palestine was his Zionist brother, Aryeh Leopold Feigenbaum, who, at that time, served as director of the ophthalmology department at Rothschild Hospital in Jerusalem.

Ezrat Nashim served an extremely heterogeneous population. Its patients included Syrians, Iranians, Egyptians, and Sudanese, as well as Jews from both Eastern and Western Europe and the Islamic world (cf. Halpern, 1938; Witztum & Margolin, 2004; Zalashik, 2008). Feigenbaum depicted the psychiatric institution in stark colours. Otto Rank disseminated his reports to the other members of the Secret Committee. The babel of languages and cultures was an exceptional psychoanalytic challenge. Feigenbaum's assumption of the director's post heralded the beginning of a new era in the Yishuv's substandard mental health system. A systematic employment of Rorschach tests with these diverse patients made it possible for Feigenbaum to make a contribution to the study of psychoses, a field in which most analysts had no clinical experience.[2] Feigenbaum also authored the first psychiatric study that attempted to offer explanations for mental illnesses among the Zionist pioneers, and in particular for the high rate of suicide characteristic of this population. In the years 1910–1923, suicide reached epidemic proportions, making up some ten per cent of all deaths among the pioneers (Alroey, 1999).

Feigenbaum criticised the local Jewish authorities for ignoring the mental problems of the "Third Aliyah" newcomers, and rejected the formal explanation given by the Zionist leadership, that the suicide cases were merely the result of the dire economic situation and living conditions the newcomers were facing. In an article titled "Palestine must have sound nerves" in *The Jewish Ledger*, he described cases of Jewish youngsters he treated in Palestine who suffered from a traumatic past that made them more susceptible to mental illness:

> Mental shocks, the severing of family ties and starvation as well as persecution and constantly renewed military conscription in the lands of emigration during 1919–1920, had created receptive ground for psychic disorders of all kinds among the immigrants of 1921 and the first half of 1922. All the terrible experiences of their recent past, which are to be considered not as primary, but simply as the provocatory causes of disease, were reflected not only in the usual forms of hysteria, but also in many typical forms of fear, neurosis and states of psycho-neurotic confusion. (Feigenbaum, 1924, cited in Zalashik, 2005, p. 412)

Unconsciously torn between his commitment to realising Zionist ideals and his yearning for his parents, who had not always consented to their sons' leaving them, the young pioneer had to fight a "terrible battle" with himself. "The psychoanalyst", Feigenbaum concluded, "was the only witness of the silent battle the Chalutz [Hebrew pioneer] has to fight, not only with malaria and the stony soil, but with an easily comprehensible longing that has been sacrificed to his ideal" (ibid.).

Notwithstanding these observations, Feigenbaum invited his nephew, Leopold Weiss, to come and stay with him in Palestine:

> I will pay your travel expenses round trip, and during your stay here
> you can live with me in my charming old Arab stone house. . . . I have
> a huge quantity of books, and when you have had enough of the
> Oriental landscapes you can stay home and read. (Feigenbaum, 1922,
> cited in Windhager, 2002, p. 106)

Leopold, a journalist in the making who was sick of Vienna's cafés
and who, by his own testimony, was "drunk on psychoanalysis",
quickly accepted his psychoanalyst uncle's offer. In short order, he
began publishing his impressions of Palestine in the German language
press in Europe.

> It seems to me that one must search for reasons more profound than
> economics and tactics for the Zionist program's lack of success (it is
> still too early to call it a failure). . . . The malady must be sought in the
> foundation of Zionist thinking itself. It is a sick idea to think that the
> only solution for the bitter fate of the Jewish people and its longings
> is the homeland. Those who advocate this idea act blindly regarding
> the reasons for the people's misery and longings; they seek to circum-
> vent them and cover them up—and this is precisely the reason for
> Judaism's sickness! (Weiss, 1923, cited in Windhager, 2002, p. 125)

Was this a sober assessment of the Zionist project or the stereo-
typical self-flagellation of a young Jewish man who had just emerged
from anti-Semitic Vienna? Opinions in the Feigenbaum family were
divided. Some proffered a psychoanalytic explanation for Leopold's
anti-Zionist positions, seeking to attribute his hostility to the Jewish
national movement to his hatred of his father, one that through
displacement became contempt for the faith of his forefathers
(Windhager, 2002, p. 230). But no direct line connects Leopold Weiss's
rejection of Zionism with the profound process of conversion that
climaxed when he decided, in 1926, to abandon his Jewish identity
and convert to Islam. He changed his name, and, thereafter, gained
fame as the Orientalist Muhammad Asad, adviser to the Saudi royal
court and later Pakistan's first ambassador to the United Nations (cf.
Kramer, 1999).

In his memoir, *The Road to Mecca*, Asad recalled Dorian Feigenbaum as a man who did not care much for Zionism, but was equally
indifferent to the Arabs, and as a person whose bourgeois way of life
required him to run from Jerusalem to Haifa for a single pound (of
income) (Asad, 1954).

Eder and Feigenbaum put together a psychoanalytic study group. Among its members were the philosopher Hugo Bergmann, director of the National Library; the ophthalmologist Aryeh Feigenbaum; Siegfried van Friesland, an attorney who served as Holland's consul in Jerusalem and later as treasurer of the Jewish Agency; and Greta Obernik, a teacher and the only member of the group who would later belong to the Palestine Psychoanalytic Society when it was founded a decade later. The group held regular meetings in Friesland's home, where they read and discussed psychoanalytic literature (cf. Gumbel, 1965; Hertz, 1983; Liban, 1999; Moses, 1992, 1998; Rolnik, 1998, 2002, 2007, 2008c; Winnik, 1977). Bergmann, who was then being treated by Dorian Feigenbaum, developed a critical attitude toward Meir Ya'ari's project of harnessing psychoanalytic theory to the communal confession ceremonies conducted by HaShomer HaTza'ir immigrants. In an animated letter to his friend Robert Weltsch in Berlin, he reported a discovery he had made in Palestine:

> I am well acquainted with the states you describe, and I suffer from them to the point that I asked an analyst friend to analyse me. For two weeks I have been in analysis with him and I have great hopes for it. Thanks to my acquaintance with him and my study of a number of books on the subject, I have been persuaded of the huge importance that psychoanalysis can have for the individual, but also for the psyche of the masses and for the understanding of politics, but first and foremost for pedagogy. I am very sorry that I did not become acquainted with and study psychoanalysis when I was still in Europe, that is from the source, because, after all, the soul is ostensibly my profession. In any case, I expect that it will help me know myself and gain a better understanding of my confused life. (dated 7 June 1922, in Bergmann, 1985, pp. 171–172)

But Bergmann's enthusiasm was short-lived. From time to time, he published articles on psychoanalysis in the Hebrew press, in which he criticised Freud for his lack of profound metaphysical thinking, and for his excessive biological positivism. Some years later, he seemed to find a way to battle psychoanalysis's "deductive tendencies". It was Jung's, not Freud's, theories that ought to be taught in Palestine, he maintained (diary entry, 3 March 1935, in Bergmann, 1985, p. 385).

Unlike David Eder, who, during these years, put most of his energies into Zionist work, Dorian Feigenbaum sought to win the local medical community and the Ezrat Nashim staff over to psychoanalysis. He gave a number of lectures on the interpretation of dreams and psychopathology in everyday life. In April 1923, he was invited to give a series of lectures on psychoanalysis in Jerusalem, before an audience that included physicians, educators, and German officials in Palestine. The title of the series was "The mind in health and illness". It consisted of three talks: "The unconscious", "Dreams", and "The modern theory of the neuroses". But the audience reacted so angrily to the first lecture that the hospital management forbade him to continue with the series (Anonymous, 1924, p. 101).

At about this same time, Feigenbaum was invited to give another three lectures, entitled "An introduction to modern psychology", to the graduates of the Hadassah nursing school. Hadassah, under the Mandate, was the most important organisation promoting preventative medicine and hygiene. He gave the first lecture, "Experimental psychology and Freud's depth psychology", in January 1924. The following day he lectured on "The unconscious", and on the day after on "Hypnosis, sleep, and dreams". The audience's keen interest in psychoanalysis led to an additional lecture on "Childhood masturbation".

Shortly thereafter, Feigenbaum was dismissed from his position, and the first attempt to incorporate psychoanalytic theory into the Yishuv's public clinical framework came to an abrupt end, as described in a letter from Bergmann to Weltsch of 27 March 1923 (Bergmann, 1985, p. 180). Feigenbaum moved to the USA, and, together with Bertram Lewin, Gregory Zilboorg, and Frankwood Williams, established the *Psychoanalytic Quarterly*.

Coinciding with the untimely departure of Eder and Feigenbaum from the psychoanalytic scene in Palestine, an anonymous report in *The International Journal of Psychoanalysis* offered a harsh assessment of the state of psychoanalysis in Jerusalem:

[In] Palestine there are many positive difficulties for the psychoanalyst to contend against. On the other hand, in certain quarters (especially amongst the young immigrants) there is a tendency to introduce so-called "psycho-analysis" far too carelessly, and in a "fashionable" and vulgarized form. This, quite obviously, is doing harm, and it is most necessary that psycho-analysts should interfere in the direction of correct exposition and, above all, in checking this injurious growth. Although psycho-analysis has made its first humble beginnings in Jerusalem as described above, its outlook there for the future is still not very hopeful. (Anonymous, 1924, p. 101)

While already in New York, Feigenbaum made one last attempt to familiarise Zionist educators with the psychoanalytic perspective on the child within the adult personality. "I always considered myself an educator", he wrote in the *Journal for Hebrew Educators*, "however, a pedagogue is interested only in children aged 5 to 15 and the psychoanalysts' children are aged 5 to 70" (Feigenbaum, 1929). When he applied for membership in the New York Psychoanalytic Society in 1925, he omitted his years in Palestine from his curriculum vitae, for reasons that can only be guessed at (Feigenbaum to Albert Polon, 26 January 1925: ANYP). Perhaps he feared that the brief Zionist episode in his life would be detrimental to his reputation? Or was he concerned that the Hadassah women might catch up with him in his new home?

But Freud's theories continued to make their way into the Yishuv even in the absence of clinical psychoanalysts trained by the movement

Mohammed Asad: "Drunk on psychoanalysis".

in Europe. Paradoxically, it was during the second half of the 1920s, a nadir in the Yishuv's cultural and intellectual life, that some of Freud's works were first published in Hebrew.

Freud in Hebrew

One day in October 1926, "something so wonderful" happened to Hugo Bergmann that he was impelled to write that same day to his friend Robert Weltsch in Berlin. Some faculty members from the Arab teachers' college showed up in the National Library and asked to borrow books by Freud and Jung (Bergmann, 1985, p. 281). The translation of Freud's writings into other languages played an important role in the acceptance of psychoanalysis outside the German cultural sphere (cf. Bettelheim, 1982; Ornston, 1992). Freud took a keen interest in the translation of his works, and wrote an introduction for the Hebrew edition of two of his works. The translation of psychoanalytic literature from German to Hebrew should be understood not only in the context of how Freud's ideas came to be accepted in the Yishuv, but also in a broader cultural context of how German was translated into Hebrew during the first half of the twentieth century. The revival of the Hebrew language was an integral part of the creation of a modern Jewish nation. Zionists were expected to write in that language and important scholarly and popular works were translated into it (cf. Efrati, 2004; Even-Zohar, 1990; Ornan, 1985; Shavit, 1998). Eastern European Jews were the major players in the Yishuv's translation and publishing projects. Even after the arrival of the first major influx of German Jews, during the Fifth Aliyah of the 1930s, nearly all the translations from German into Hebrew were done by Jews of Eastern European origin. The works chosen for translation were mostly classics, works by Jews, and books that were seen as educational for the younger generation. The relative number of books translated in each of these categories depended on ideological and national circumstances. The two decades before the establishment of the state saw the publication of Hebrew editions of many German scholarly works. Theodor Herzl was the most popular German writer in this group—twenty of his books appeared in Hebrew during this period. Max Nordau came in second, while Freud took third place—eight books by him appeared in Hebrew during this period (Sheffi, 1999,

2011). As a standard for comparison, consider that during this same period, some fifty articles published in Hebrew in Palestine directly or indirectly addressed Nietzsche, who was among the most popular and most widely read thinkers in the Yishuv, but more than 100 were devoted to Freud and his theory (Golomb, 2004; Rolnik, 2004).[3]

The year 1925 was a difficult one for the Yishuv. It began a slide into a severe economic crisis that affected intellectual life as well. But this was also the year in which Freud's book of 1921, *Group Psychology and the Analysis of the Ego* (1921c), appeared in Hebrew translation, the first of his books to do so. The choice of this work was not obvious. It is not easy to read. It is not a clinical work, but neither is it metapsychological. Unlike most of Freud's other works, in which one can easily identify his motivation for writing and the difficulties he had while doing so, this book's origins are a mystery. In 1919, Freud announced that, inspired by "a simple-minded idea [*Einfall*]", he had tried his hand at producing a psychoanalytic foundation for mass psychology (Freud to Ferenczi, 12 May 1919, in Freud & Ferenczi, 1993–2000, p. 354). *Group Psychology and the Analysis of the Ego* had its genesis while Freud was comprehensively revising his theory and arriving at his dual conceptualisation of human drives. But the relationship between this work and its successors is implicit; it seems to be merely chronological. In terms of content, it belongs with earlier works such as *Totem and Taboo* (1912–1913), "On narcissism" (1914c), and "Mourning and melancholia" (1917e). It also contains references to Freud's pre-analytic writings, material he produced while he was interning with Charcot and coming to appreciate the power of suggestion and hypnosis, which had been so central to French psychiatry of the nineteenth century.

Group Psychology and the Analysis of the Ego is devoted to an examination of the connection between groups and their leaders. Freud suggests that mass psychology be understood through the changes that occur in the mental state of the individual. This work is a key text for understanding Freud's political thinking. While it is partly grounded in other parts of clinical psychoanalytic theory, as it was shaped during the years prior to the First World War, it stands on its own as a political–social manifesto (cf. Brunner, 2001; Roazen, 1968).

In *Totem and Taboo*, Freud agues that the members of a tribe must inevitably reach a "contractual" understanding as a result of their rebellion against the primal father who had denied them sexual outlet.

The rebellion against the father elicits feelings of guilt among the members of the primitive tribe and their need to establish a symbolic paternal law. When Freud began his work on group psychology, however, he had at his disposal his psychology of the ego, which offered a foundation for understanding the social cohesion that human beings prefer in other than rational and utilitarian terms. In *Totem and Taboo*, he examines defence mechanisms that operate counter to primal urges, contributing to the creation of neurotic distortions. In *Group Psychology and the Analysis of the Ego*, he conceives of these defence mechanisms as vital and unconscious factors acting within the ego and assisting in the individual's healthy development and ability to adapt. From Freud's point of view, the group, by definition, functions only on the irrational level. The individual, when he is in a group, is capable of displaying deviant moral behaviour inferior to his behaviour as a lone individual, but he also has the capacity to rise up to a higher moral level because of the group's influence. The group is characterised by devotion to the sublime, but also to cruel and unrestrained ideals. The change undergone by an individual when he is part of a group derives, then, from the group's regulation of the mechanisms of restraint and repression that act on his drives.

What are the contending forces when the individual confronts the group? Here, Freud replaces the emphasis that his predecessors put on suggestion, which they said the group and leader used to influence the individual, with the libido, a force that comes out of the drive model. He links the Oedipal complex, as it is embodied in the individual's development, with the process through which the individual comes to identify with the group. Identification, as a psychological mechanism, assumes a central place in Freud's discussion. The individual's identification with the goals of the group is a direct continuation of his internalisation of the father figure, the climax of the Oedipal conflict. While Freud refused, throughout his corpus, to yield on the centrality of drives and the Oedipal dynamic as the sources of human motivations, in this work his formulations of the place of internal objects in the individual's mental and love life are somewhat more complex. Here, Freud offers his own explanation of the development of concepts such as justice and equality. Justice is seen as an outlet for envy. Through justice, he wrote, we deny ourselves and others what we originally sought to deny only to others.

Freud placed particular emphasis on the libidinal forces that tie the members of the group together and to the leader. In contrast, he did not attribute much importance to the leader's personality. Since the primal leader's presence was built into the psychology of each member of the group, the members could unify around a symbolic, super-temporal leader who devolved his power on earthly leaders, who come and go in accordance with historical circumstances. Moses was one such ahistorical leader. And, in fact, the Hebrew/Egyptian Moses, leader of the ancient Hebrews, makes a brief appearance in this work as well. In *Group Psychology and the Analysis of the Ego*, Freud, fifteen years before publishing his thoughts about the Egyptian origin of Moses, cites Moses as the archetype of the leader who mediates between the group and the divine primal father.

In his book, Freud shows that no one, not ourselves and not others, can be "blamed" for the suffering that social life brings us. The forces of phylogenesis and evolution are stronger than that of the brief duration of our rational age, and they cannot be defeated merely via rules and reforms. From Freud's point of view, it makes no difference how humans decide to organise their lives together. No attempt at reorganising the relationships between human beings, and between them and their leaders, can paper over the inherently irrational components of social existence and loosen the Gordian knot that ties the psychology of the individual to that of the group.

The Hebrew translation of *Group Psychology and the Analysis of the Ego* was published by the Organisation of Hebrew Teachers. But why did it choose this work to bring the message of psychoanalysis to the Hebrew-reading public? Perhaps because it is devoted to the origins of social justice and to the formation of the tribe, two subjects that concerned the Yishuv's educators. In contrast with the socialist brand of nationalism subscribed to by most of the political elite that had emerged from the labour and agricultural settlements, the Yishuv's teachers held more liberal views. From its establishment in 1903 into the 1930s, the teachers' organisation enjoyed relative autonomy and conferred on its members an exceptional status. The Hebrew teacher—here the adjective refers not to the subject they taught but to the national cultural agenda which the "Hebrew" designation implies —was perceived as the standard-bearer of the nation's cultural–linguistic renaissance and as a moral guide (Sand, 2000, p. 153). The text chosen by the teachers to acquaint the educated Hebrew reading public with psychoanalytic theory—a text that would soon become required reading for the Yishuv's educators—was a work in which Freud linked the private to the public, "the body politic", and the individual's subjective "politics of the mind". It is also the book of his that juxtaposes the two axes around which ideologies, such as Zionist nationalist ideology, revolve. The first is the self-love that metamorphoses into a sense of partnership and group solidarity, while the second is hostile arrogance toward those who do not belong to the tribe.

Much has been written about the place of the collectivist ethos in the life of the Yishuv's young people and the early waves of immigration. The sense of duty that the individual felt to the group's declared goals was constantly tested, and the tribe had little tolerance for those of its members who deviated from the common ideals. The individual was valued only to the extent that he sought the unity and cohesion of the group. A cruel all-pervading measure, public judgment dominated every walk of private life: mode of speech and dress, male–female relationship, ties between group members, manners— realms where no political party would ever dare venture (cf. Almog, 2000; Reinharz & Shapira, 1996). Freud's book was especially recommended to those "who took part in nationalist propaganda and in the dissemination of new ideas", as one of the reviews written in honour of its publication proclaimed (Strikovsky, 1928).

When Aviezer Yellin, chairman of the Organisation of Hebrew Teachers, notified Freud that the book had been published, Freud responded warmly, but also with a note of caution:

> The translation of my *Group Psychology* into our holy tongue has given me especially great satisfaction. I, an ignorant son of the pre-Zionist era, cannot, to my chagrin, read it. . . . I receive even greater joy from your assurance that this small translation that you have chosen from among my works will not remain solitary, and I can only hope that the sense of alienation that an initial encounter with a psychoanalytic book tends to elicit will quickly give way to more friendly attitudes. (Freud to Hebrew Teachers' Association, 14 September 1928: AFM)

Two central motifs run through this passage, written by Freud in Berlin, where he was undergoing another operation to remove a cancerous growth in his mouth. The first is his complicated relationship with Judaism and Zionism. He terms Hebrew "our holy tongue", but he then quickly segues into the first person singular and describes himself as a "son of the pre-Zionist era", as if he wished to tell his Zionist correspondent that he was, in fact, but a distant relative, a compatriot but also a foreigner. The name of the Father, Freud's father, will always come up in association with his Jewish identity.

It looks as if Freud prophesied the reaction that the publication of the book prompted. And in fact, *Group Psychology and the Analysis of the Ego* had a mixed reception. One critic wrote,

> The days have passed when people awaiting with beating hearts the appearance of each new book by the 'wise man of Vienna'. But since the intellectual upheavals caused by Freud's discoveries have gone over our heads and not reached us, we should certainly welcome the translator's choice of text, which, even if it does not reflect the latest fashion, it is commendable principally to those who speak and write about democracy. (Srikovsky, 1928, p. 475)

And the same writer continued, "The transfer of Freud from German to Hebrew is a field full of obstacles, which we will long ponder before we get to the point of having a scientific, precise Hebrew language, comprehensible and familiar to all and accepted by most professionals" (ibid., p. 479). Hugo Bergmann published an article in which he listed all the errors in the translation and the places in which the translator did not understand German idioms (Bergmann, 1928–1929). At about the same time, Bergmann published two surveys of psychoanalytic theory in the daily press. He sent one of the articles to Freud, and Freud replied, with a promise that he would have the article translated into German (dated 19 May 1926: AFM). Apparently, Bergmann did not send his second, more critical, article to Vienna. In that latter piece, Bergmann criticised the reductionist aspects of Freudian psychoanalysis. He claimed that psychoanalysis trumpeted the individual without taking into account the social fabric that was internalised by him. The neurosis of the Freudian individual could be cured by helping him "establish the wholeness of consciousness"; in other words, by removing the repression that prevented the conscious self from achieving integrity. But Freud, Bergmann wrote, had disregarded the fact that the individual is no more than "a part of a comprehensive consciousness, a cell in a kingdom of cells". The goal of Freudian analysis was thus to repress something of the reality of the individual's life-the fact that "he is not the ultimate unit" (Bergmann, 1928).

Bergmann's desire to integrate non-materialist and non-causal elements into his psychology and epistemology led him gradually to reservations about Freud's biological positivism. The considerable influence that Buber (and Fichte) had on him is evident in his argument that "the action of the I on the you is not accomplished through the material world, but rather directly, as it were, on the non-material conduits that link us all" (ibid.). From the point of view of psychoanalytic theory of that time, the idea of individuals merging with each other in a "unity of the spirit" was a mystical concept of the type that Freud sought to exclude from his theory. But Bergmann, like Hermann Cohen, saw no contradiction between belief in God and belief in rationalism. Thus, he objected to Freud's insistence that religious belief of every kind simply expresses infantile wishes. In an article he published to mark the month after Freud's death, he praised Freud's scepticism, but also indicated that his critique of religion was not on the same level as his scientific work and metaphysical thinking (Bergmann, 1939).

In the same year that *Group Psychology* was published, the translator, Yehuda Dvir-Dwosis, wrote to Freud and asked permission to continue translating his works. He had begun this project when he served as secretary of the Organisation of Hebrew Teachers' cultural committee. Born in the Ukraine, he had worked most of his life as a teacher of Hebrew language and Bible. In the early 1930s, he hosted in his home a reading circle to discuss psychoanalytic ideas. His correspondence with Freud was later supplemented by telephone consultations on translation issues. Since Dvir-Dwosis did not have a telephone in his home, Freud would, at a pre-established time, call a café in Jerusalem's Ein Kerem neighbourhood (Ora Rafael, personal communication). The picture offered by Freud's letter to Yellin, quoted above, is supplemented by one he wrote to Dvir-Dwosis:

> I am delighted and extremely happy that some of my books are being published in Hebrew. My father's command of the Holy Tongue was not less than his command of German, or perhaps even better. Yet he allowed me to grow up without any knowledge at all of Judaism. Only after I reached adulthood did I begin to hold it against him. But thanks to the influence of German antisemitism, which surfaced during my university studies, I felt myself a Jew even before. (Freud to Yehuda Dvir-Dwosis, 15 December 1930: AFM)

The translation was important not only to make psychoanalytic ideas available to Hebrew readers, especially to the younger generation of native speakers who were not fluent in European languages. It also served as a way of officially sanctioning Freud in the Yishuv and placing him on the cultural and ideological agenda of the Zionist elite. As a result, interest in psychoanalysis as a method of treatment began to grow. A number of psychiatrists who had not received psychoanalytic training and who were not members of the International Psychoanalytic Association did all they could to offer their patients treatment based on psychoanalytic principles. These physicians did not hesitate to write to Freud directly or to publish articles in the psychoanalytic movement's central journals.

The first clinical paper by an author from the Yishuv to be published in an official journal of the psychoanalytic movement was published in the same issue in which Freud's paper on *Fetishism* was printed. The contribution, by Curt Jacoby from Tel Aviv, bore the title "An analysis of a coitus interruptus dream" (Jacoby, 1927). It was a most appropriate subject, one that could serve as a metaphor for the mixture of passion and frustration with which the Yishuv grappled as it became acquainted with Freud's ideas.

The publication of an article in a journal in which Freud himself published his works was not inconsequential in an era in which these journals had become an arena of contention among Freud's students. Evidence of Freud's editorial policy can be seen, for example, in a letter he sent to Dr Havkin of Beit HaKerem, a neighbourhood in Jerusalem. Havkin had submitted an article entitled "A case study of falling in love". Freud's response was unambiguous:

> My impression is that you think that your love stories are more interesting than those of others simply because men, rather than women, play the role of the beloved. We do not share this opinion, and if you nevertheless wish to bring to the attention of my students a case of a recovery from schizophrenia, please present it in a proper way, not as pages from a diary, but as a case study from which something can be understood. (Freud to Dr Chavkin, 24 March 1934: AFM)

On mice, Arabs, and telepathy

Immanuel Velikovsky, who moved from Berlin to Palestine in 1924 and lived there until 1939, offered the readers of *Imago* and *The Journal of Applied Psychoanalysis* an opportunity to see how he applied Freud's theories in his clinical work during his Yishuv years. Like many of Freud's Jewish readers, and in direct opposition to the master's explicit wishes, Velikovsky took special interest in Freud's dream theory and its connection to Judaism (Velikovsky, 1933).

He published his conclusions about the connection between his patients' unconscious and the revival of the Hebrew language in the journal *Imago*, which was edited by Freud. In his article, entitled "Can a newly acquired language become the speech of the unconscious?" Velikovsky (1934) claimed that for a person with a limited command of Hebrew, the symbolic meanings of the language are dictated by the sound of words and not by their literal meaning. Thus, Hebrew puns appearing in the dreams of Russian, Arabic, or Yiddish-speaking patients actually play on sounds associated with both Hebrew and the dreamers' mother tongue.

One example Velikovsky offered was of a Yiddish-speaking patient who dreamed of mice on the evening before a lottery drawing. The Yiddish word for mice is *maislech*, similar to the Hebrew word *mazlekh*, meaning "your luck", a word evoking the patient's wish to win the lottery. Another patient dreamed that mice were rummaging through his body; in other words, that his conscience was bothering him. Mice, Velikovsky pointed out, are rodents, a group of animals referred to in Hebrew as *mekarsemim*, literally "the gnawers". When Russian speakers refer to pangs of conscience, they say that their conscience is "gnawing" at them. So, in the unconscious language of symbols, this feeling represented itself as mice gnawing at the dreamer's body.

Another dream Velikovsky claimed to have interpreted through such lexicographical methods involved a married man who was suffering from impotence. He had come to live in Tel Aviv for a few weeks on his own to undergo psychotherapy. In his dream, a man approached him with a request to buy lime. "What do you need lime for?" the dreamer asked the man. "After all, at your place, your home, there is a pit full of lime." When Velikovsky heard this dream, he immediately asked the patient whether he had recently given a gift to a woman in order to secure her favours. The patient appeared embarrassed. He had, he related, always been faithful to his wife, who remained at the family farm up north. But now, during his sojourn in the city, he had met a lady whom he tried to win over by means of a gift. He assuaged his conscience by telling himself that the assignation was necessary to see whether his therapy had been successful and his sexual potency restored. But the woman rejected him. Velikovsky explained to the patient how the dream had encoded the entire story: *sit* means "lady" in Arabic, and in the dream he wants to buy *sid* (the Hebrew word for "lime"), in other words, a woman. His conscience answered him by telling him that he had lime at home.

Another of Velikovsky's patients was waging legal battles with his Arab neighbours over the question of ownership of a plot of land. One night, he dreamt about mice falling into a pail. They tried to get out by jumping up through a hole in the lid. He was worried that they might escape, so he covered the hole with a paving stone. Velikovsky found this dream to be a masterpiece of Hebrew–Arabic wordplay: the *akhbar* ("mouse" in Hebrew) is a cognate of the Arabic *khbar* (meaning both "litigant" and "mouse", according to Velikovsky). Unsurprisingly, then, mice were a standard motif in the dreams of Arabic speakers engaged in legal disputes. The Arab neighbours had tried to "jump" on his lands in a place called Hor al-Wasa (*hor* means "hole" in Hebrew) and seize them, so it was appropriate to *lehapil otam bapah* (a Hebrew expression meaning "set them up", or "make them fall into a trap", but which can also be understood as "make them fall into a pail"). And, just recently, the patient had thought of a way he might be able to convince the authorities that the disputed land in fact belonged to him. His plan was to pave the path to Hor al-Wasa, thereby strengthening his ownership claim. Velikovsky summed up his contribution to dream interpretation in Palestine thus: it "is probably connected with the manner of thinking of the Jewish race; the tendency toward similitudes and jokes is also derived from the same source" (Velikovsky, 1934, p. 239). In Jewish Palestine, the unconscious was not structured just like any language, as Lacan would have guessed; rather, it was structured after the language of the Prophets.

A more systematic attempt to apply psychoanalytic thinking to the study of immigrants' adaptation to their new language was taken by Erwin Stengel, a former member of the Vienna Psychoanalytic Society, who immigrated to Britain. As befitted his earlier interest in aphasia, Stengel's first paper (1939) as a new member of the British Psychoanalytic Society concerned the psychological mechanisms that are involved in the acquisition of a new language. There somehow exists in many people a hope that their language is spoken everywhere, wrote Stengel. In many people, there is a degree of contempt for the new language. They earnestly believe that their native language is the best, the only one capable of expressing adequately the variety of life. The new language is often regarded as poor and somewhat primitive. There is often a feeling that only the words of the native language can reflect the truth, while the foreign words are somehow felt as false. Stengel's discussion clearly lacked the ethnic–national undertone which prevailed in Velikowsky's analysis of his subject matter:

> The adult who comes across a foreign idiom is forced in the direction of regression, i.e. in the direction of the primary process which once created the idiom. His resistance against many idioms is analogous to the resistance of the patients against the analysis of their dreams. We forget idioms just as we forget dreams; we feel the strange effect of foreign idioms because they force on us the pictorial thinking which we experience as a temptation as well as a danger. (Stengel, 1939, p. 476)

In his correspondence with lay readers in Palestine, Freud generally came across as curious, modest, and generous. He did not limit himself to pleasantries; he treated even their unfounded statements seriously, and used them to clarify his ideas for the general public.

Dr Yochanan Lewinson, a dentist who emigrated from Berlin to Palestine in 1933, where he joined kibbutz Givat Brenner, wrote to Freud mostly to express gratitude. Thanks to psychoanalysis, he told Freud, he had been able to make a number of momentous life decisions and give up an academic career in Germany in favour of life in a co-operative community in the Land of Israel. But Lewinson also addressed some issues that appear in the *New Introductory Lectures on Psychoanalysis*, which Freud had published three years earlier.

The first issue pertained to the status, in basic psychoanalytic dream theory, of night terror, a sleep disorder in which a person suddenly awakens in panic. These dreams, which disturb the slumber of people with traumatic neurosis (or, in current psychiatric jargon, post traumatic stress disorder), ostensibly contradict Freud's fundamental rule of dream interpretation, according to which dreams fulfil unconscious wishes.

Night terrors clearly present a problem for the theory, as they seem to be the opposite of wish fulfilment. Lewinson, like Freud, sought a way to square the phenomenon within Freud's conceptual framework.

He pointed out that, in people suffering from traumatic neurosis, frightening dreams could serve to reconstruct the traumatic experience so as to allow the mind to discharge the emotional excess built up by the traumatising situation.

The other issue Lewinson raised in his letter to Freud was telepathy, a phenomenon Freud's book addresses under the heading "Dreams and occultism". During the bloody Arab Revolt of 1936–1939, Lewinson became convinced that a handful of Arab villagers in Palestine possessed telepathic powers:

> I have no doubt that the only method of transmitting information that was available to these Arabs was by means of thought transference. There is evidence that certain people among them broadcast the messages while others receive them. . . . I can imagine that these phenomena might constitute an especially fruitful field of research for the psychoanalyst, but he must be familiar with the language and culture of the Arab population in question. (Lewinson to Freud, 5 August 1936: FCLC)

Freud replied as follows:

> I am happy to reply to your letter, since it is a pleasure for me to discuss [these issues] with such a perceptive reader.

> As to your first comment: I agree with you completely. These anxiety dreams are attempts to cope by means of abreaction. I am aware of this, and I have certainly expressed my opinion on this matter elsewhere. I no longer know why I avoided mentioning this fact in the chapter "Revision of the Theory of Dreams." However, we must not forget that the basic definition of "dreaming," in its Aristotelian interpretation, is any mental activity that occurs during sleep, and therefore we ought to agree to include in dreaming also goals that do not serve wish fulfillment. It can therefore be said of this coping mechanism that it is "beyond the pleasure principle," and that it also influences the choice of dream materials. In the nature of things the dream will repeat the disturbing traumatic content for the purpose of turning it into wish fulfillment, although in the absence of analytic help this attempt will usually fail.

> As for the second matter: I am grateful for your enlightenment! You have surely noticed that when it comes to matters of telepathy, my intention has been to minimize any admission that it exists. Here is how things stand: I believe in telepathy but I do not do so willingly. I

have not yet managed to overcome completely my distaste for what is termed the occult, and therefore I continue to demand further evidence of its existence, and indeed you indicate possible ways of obtaining such evidence. Ever since I learned to observe my dear chow chow dog's behavior in certain situations, my disbelief in telepathy has softened somewhat. (Freud to Lewinson, 18 August 1936: FCLC)

Freud, in fact, did not hide his curiosity about superstitions and phenomena that seemed to be supernatural. It was a fascination he shared with Jung and Ferenczi: the latter once informed Freud that he intended to show up in Vienna and introduce himself as the "psychoanalysts' court astrologer". On another occasion, Ferenczi accompanied Freud on a visit to a mind-reader in Berlin. Both were profoundly impressed by her telepathic abilities. Freud had no doubt that so-called supernatural phenomena could be explained by physical–energetic processes that science was still unable to gauge. As early as 1910, in the third edition of *The Interpretation of Dreams*, he decided to add to this already thick book a discussion of "prophetic dreams" and "telepathic dreams". Wilhelm Stekel went even further, devoting an entire monograph to telepathic dreams. Whereas Jung and Ferenczi wanted to make the study of supernatural phenomena psychoanalytic territory, Ernest Jones and Max Eitingon did all they could to restrain Freud on this point. At times they seemed to be succeeding. But experiments in telepathy and mind reading that Freud undertook with his daughter Anna and Ferenczi led him to conclude that "considerations of diplomacy should be set aside" and that telepathy ought to be addressed in the context of dream theory. "The thought of that sour apple [occultism] makes me shudder, but there is no way of avoiding biting into it", he wrote to Eitingon (letter, 4 February 1921, in Freud & Eitingon, 2004, pp. 239–240). He informed Jones as well, this time unequivocally, that he did not intend to allow public opinion, or scolding by his students, to dictate to him the directions that psychoanalytic research ought to take: "When anyone adduces my fall into sin, just answer him calmly that conversion to telepathy is my private affair, just like my Jewishness, my passion for smoking, and many other things" (Freud, 1926, cited in Jones, 1957, p. 422).

So Freud returned to this old interest and published two articles, "Dreams and telepathy" (1922a) and "Psychoanalysis and telepathy" (1941d[1921]). They left no room for doubt: he was prepared, as befit

Freud: "Ever since I learned to observe my dear chow chow dog's behavior in certain situations, my disbelief in telepathy has softened somewhat."

a psychoanalyst, to balance scepticism and evidence, doubt and conviction, in addressing scientifically phenomena that others would rather relegate to the field of the occult and the supernatural.

Zionism as a mental state

In the early 1920s, Freud joined the list of great Jews whose support for the Jewish people's national aspirations could have advanced the Zionist cause among Diaspora communities and in world opinion. Despite his explicit rejection of the restrictive approach taken by some of his students, who sought to tie the psychoanalytic project specifically to the challenges of politics and gender affiliation faced by the Jews, it can hardly be denied that the "Jewish question" gradually came to occupy a fairly high place on Freud's intellectual agenda. And, from time to time, he was asked his opinion on the national aspirations of the Jews in Mandatory Palestine. His public pronouncements on both these issues had some impact on how the Yishuv's intellectuals related to his theories and to those students of his who became part of their community. Clearly, Freud was not a political Zionist prior to Hitler's rise to power, nor did he become one thereafter. If one were to endeavour to match Freud's enigmatic remarks on the Jewish question to one of the established streams of Zionist thought, the obvious choice would be Ahad Ha'am's cultural–spiritual Zionism. And, indeed, among the Zionist thinkers who were his contemporaries, Ahad Ha'am was the one who attempted to embrace and even foster the paradox of Jewish existence, without condemning the problem of Jewish identity as an illness for which a historical remedy was immediately available. At least the rationalist from Odessa recognised that the complete and "normal" identity that his fellow Jews so desperately sought could not be acquired by suppressing Jewish history and tradition, or by turning Jewish mythology of the past into an eternal, transcendental present. Spiritual Zionism of the type preached by Ahad Ha'am, even if it offered little succour for the Jewish people's immediate distress, was the most "analytic" brand of thought that Zionism produced in its search for a (psychological) solution to the peculiar circumstances of the Jewish people (cf. Rose, 2005; Schweid, 2008).

In fact, Freud's Zionism was even more psychological and structuralist than Ahad Ha'am's. It is best understood as a mental state rather than as a political stance. "The only thing that gives me any pleasure is the capture of Jerusalem and the British experiment with the chosen people", he wrote to Karl Abraham on 10 December 1917 in response to the Balfour Declaration of 2 November 1917, in which His Majesty's Government declared that it viewed with favour the establishment in Palestine of a national home for the Jewish people (Freud & Abraham, 2002, pp. 363–364). In 1925, in a missive in honour of the dedication of the Hebrew University, he wrote dryly, "I find it painful that my ill-health prevents me from being present at the opening festivities of the Jewish University in Jerusalem" (Freud, 1925c). But, at the end of 1933, he did not conceal the emotional factor that prevented him from making such a visit. He wrote to Yehudah Magnes, the university's president: "For me, a trip to Jerusalem is perhaps possible from a physical point of view . . . but not from a psychological one" (Freud to Magnes, 5 October 1933: AFM). Freud also turned down the university's request that he deed his papers to the university after his death, and rejected categorically the idea of including an article of his in a Hebrew journal to be published by the university:

I have never concealed my sympathy for Judaism and for the Hebrew University in Jerusalem, but the publication of scientific papers from different fields seems to me to be a presumptuous move that does not serve the interests of science, since the research in question must be accessible to all. I bring out my work in journals that I publish myself. . . . No one will look for them elsewhere, and if I publish them in another venue my readers will miss them and the readers of a Hebrew publication will most likely have difficulty understanding them. For this reason I am unable to lend my name to the list of your regular authors. (Freud to Immanuel Velikovsky, 15 January 1922: FCLC)

One of the interesting radical attempts to decipher Freud's hardly numerous pronouncements in favour of Zionism has been made by Daniel Boyarin, who places them in the context of the discourse of the gender identity of the Jewish male. Boyarin argues that it was not the wish to return the Jewish people to Palestine that nourished Freud's inner world, but rather "the return to Phallostine", to active masculinity unburdened by powerlessness and femininity. It was not only Freud and his students who viewed Zionism as a marker of masculinity. When Ernest Jones learned that a baby boy had been born to Freud's son, he sent the professor an ironic congratulation: "another gain for Zionism" (Boyarin, 1997, p. 222).

Support for the claim that Freud was a "psychological–emotional Zionist" can also be found in the special introductions that he wrote to the Hebrew editions of two of his works. In 1930, he wrote a brief preface to the Hebrew translation of his *New Introductory Lectures on Psychoanalysis*. Here, he briefly touched on the question of historical continuity between the Hebrew reader of his time and Moses and the prophets, placing in the centre his own life, that of a person not conversant in Hebrew.

The Hebrew reading public, and especially young people seeking knowledge, will find in this book psychoanalysis rendered in an ancient language that is awakening to a new life by the will of the Jewish people. The author is aware and knows well the work of the translator of this volume. He cannot conceal his doubts as to whether Moses and the prophets would understand these lessons in Hebrew. But of their descendants—among whom he himself numbers—who will read this book, the author asks that they not be hasty in rejecting him at the first stirrings of criticism and dissatisfaction. (Freud, 1916–1917, p. 11)

Quite clearly, the thought that his works were appearing in Hebrew touched Freud. But this did not prevent him from expressing a rather subversive idea. Could Moses and the prophets really have understood his introductory lectures in their Hebrew translation? Freud was not at all convinced that these biblical figures were actually Hebrews, the ancestors of the Jews. Yet, Freud viewed himself and his contemporary Hebrew language readers as their spiritual descendants. He wrote to Arnold Zweig on 8 May 1932,

> Palestine has never produced anything but religions, sacred frenzies, presumptuous attempts to overcome the outer world of appearance by means of the inner world of wishful thinking, and we hail from there (though one of us considers himself a German as well; the other does not); our forebears lived there for perhaps half or perhaps a whole millennium (but this too is just a perhaps) and it is impossible to say what heritage from this land we have taken over into our blood and nerves (as is mistakenly said). (Freud & Zweig, 1970, pp. 39–40)

While Freud termed the introduction to the *Introductory Lectures* "cool and to the point", at the translator's request he wrote the one for the Hebrew edition of *Totem and Taboo* in "a warmer tone" (Freud to Dvir-Dwosis, 15 December 1930: AFM). In this preface, written in a year when he was putting most of his energies into his book about Moses, and about five years before that work was published, Freud posed a question identical to that addressed in *Moses and Monotheism* (1939a). The introduction opens with the declaration that he does not speak the Holy Tongue, that the faith of his fathers is as foreign to him as any other religion, and he cannot subscribe to any national ideal:

> No reader of [the Hebrew version of] this book will find it easy to put himself in the emotional position of an author who is ignorant of the language of holy writ, who is completely estranged from the religion of his fathers—as well as from every other religion—and who cannot take a share in nationalist ideals, but who has yet never repudiated his people, who feels that he is in his essential nature a Jew and who has no desire to alter that nature. If the question were put to him: "Since you have abandoned all these common characteristics of your countrymen, what is there left to you that is Jewish?" he would reply: "A very great deal, and probably its very essence." He could not now express that essence clearly in words; but some day, no doubt, it will become accessible to the scientific mind. (Freud, 1912–1913[1934])

In a single sweep of his pen, Freud cites the Hebrew language, the Jewish religion, and Jewish nationalism. Having forfeited all three of these elements of his identity, he could not make a clear statement of what stood behind his sense of affiliation with the Jewish people. Yet, Freud's coquettish ambivalence did not prevent him from offering his reader one of the most surprising definitions of that identity that one could expect from a modern secular Jew: that lacking these elements makes him not less, but, rather, more Jewish. Freud was not prepared to give up in despair and leave the matter in the realm of mystery and enigma. The last two sentences, in which he places his hopes in scientific advancement, will hardly seem out of place to readers of his psychological texts. In large swathes of his theory, he searched for the biological laws governing psychological phenomenon. Thus, he accepted the conventions of the late nineteenth century's racial discourse, which viewed science as the principle arena for the discussion of Jewish race and identity. Yet, in his book about Moses, he offered his own analytic solution to the enigma of Jewish identity. True, one could read the final sentence of the introduction as an example of "avoidance rhetoric", used by Freud in addressing his Hebrew readers. But, in fact, he offered a radical conceptualisation of Jewish identity, one which views language and ethnic affiliation as redundancies that conceal the real essence of Judaism. In this Freudian take on identity, we can see "Freud the man" identifying with "Moses the man". Both of them are situated on the seam between affiliation and foreignness; both stand on the boundary between the political and the psychological. Just as Moses did not need to be a Jew in order to constitute Judaism, so Freud's individual and subjective Judaism was not dependent on conventional markers of tribal identity. Ironically, in 1930, following the previous year's wave of bloody Arab attacks on Jews, Freud refused to enlist in a public relations campaign planned by a Zionist organisation, Keren HaYesod. But it gave him an opportunity to make explicit his reservations about the Jewish people's national aspirations in Palestine:

Dear Doctor,

I cannot do what you ask. My unwillingness to involve the public with my name is insurmountable and not even this present critical occasion seems to warrant it. Whoever wishes to influence the crowd must express something that resonates and creates enthusiasm but my sober estimation of Zionism does not allow me to do so.

I certainly have a great deal of sympathy for their endeavors; I am proud of our university in Jerusalem and am pleased that our settlements are flourishing.

But, on the other hand, I do not believe that Palestine can ever become a Jewish State or that both the Christian and Islamic world will ever be prepared to entrust their holy places to Jewish care. To me it would have seemed more sensible to establish a Jewish homeland on a historically unencumbered soil; I do know that with such a rational plan one could never have won the enthusiasm of the masses or the financial backing of the rich. Also, I regretfully admit that the unworldly fanaticism of our fellow Jews must bear some responsibility for awakening the mistrust of the Arabs. Nor can I summon up any trace of sympathy for the misguided piety that has made a piece of Herod's wall into a national relic, thereby provoking the natives' feelings.

Now judge for yourself whether I, with such a critical attitude, am the right person to act as the comforter of a people whose unfounded hopes have been shattered.

Yours respectfully,

Freud (Freud to Haim Koffler, 26 February 1930: INL)

Admittedly, the founder of psychoanalysis could not have anticipated the Holocaust in Europe and certainly its consequences for the actualisation of the myth of the return to the Promised Land. But his words, as sharp as they might be, do not exhibit any ideological opposition to the Jewish national movement. Nor does he blame the Jewish settlers as a group for being the sole source of political incitement. Freud did not take a stance that in principle rejects, utterly, territorial Jewish nationalism. On the contrary, he cites pragmatic considerations regarding the Jewish settlement project in Palestine. He objected not to Jewish nationalism *per se*, but to the revived Jewish nationalism in Palestine. The point he made is, at base, both practical and psychological: it relates to the "historical burden" that Palestine bears on its shoulders, and the expected refusal of the Christian and Muslim communities to place their holy sites in Jewish hands. A reminder of the importance that the Yishuv leadership attached to the impact of Freud's position on public opinion can be found in the response of Haim Koffler, Keren HaYesod's director in Vienna, to a communication from Avraham Schwadron, director of the National Library in

Jerusalem, who asked for the original copy of Freud's disappointing letter so that it could be added to the library's manuscript collection:

> You cannot imagine how happy I would be at this opportunity to acquiesce in your request, but in this case I must reject your proposal. Freud's letter may be heartfelt and warm, but it does not serve our purposes. And since there are no secrets in Palestine, the letter will inevitably find its way out of the library's and university's autograph collections and become public knowledge. Even if this time I was unable to help Keren HaYesod, I still see myself as bound at least not to harm it. Therefore, if you want to see Freud's letter with your own eyes, I am prepared to send it to you with a tourist who plans to travel to Palestine soon . . . but you must return the letter to her immediately so that she may return it to here. (Koffler to Schwadron, 2 April 1930: INL)

Koffler, like many members of the Zionist leadership, very much wanted the support of the secularism and enlightenment that Freud embodied. But, at the same time, the advocates of Zionism had to act like Koffler and develop silencing and repression mechanisms that would provide a response to Freud's complex position toward the dialectic between logos and mythos, as it is reflected in the human psyche, and in Jewish existence.

Notes

1. Ferenczi met Weizmann at Edward Bernays's, the father of public relations and one of the first to attempt to manipulate public opinion by appealing to the unconscious. His father was Ely Bernays, brother of Freud's wife Martha Bernays. His mother was Freud's sister, Anna.
2. One of Feigenbaum's most significant contributions to clinical theory was the conceptualisation of depersonalisation as a defence mechanism against both neurotic and psychotic anxieties (Feigenbaum, 1937).
3. In 1935, a special subcommittee of Va'ad HaLashon, the Hebrew Language Committee, was established to coin Hebrew equivalents for psychoanalytic terms, and the country's young Psychoanalytic Society petitioned to send an expert to be a member of this body (Va'ad HaLashon to Max Eitingon, 8 February 1935: ECI).

CHAPTER THREE

We've lost Berlin

"I am convinced that the Gestapo, the corridors of which I walked until recently with utter confidence, has no category 'psychoanalysis', but they certainly have a rubric called 'psychoanalysts'"

(Felix Boehm, 1935)

As a movement, psychoanalysis almost ceased to function during the First World War. But between the end of the Great War in 1918 and the Nazi accession to power in Germany in 1933, it scored a series of successes. Freud's followers disseminated his teachings in Vienna, Prague, Budapest, Amsterdam, Berlin, London, Bombay, Chicago, and New York. The psychoanalytic movement, once a small group of brilliant but largely unnoticed intellectuals, became transformed into an elite whose voice was heard in broad swathes of society, and who influenced neighbouring disciplines in the social sciences and humanities.

When Hitler came to power and launched his Aryanisation programme, psychoanalytic organisations faced new challenges for which they were unprepared. Some ninety per cent of the approximately 200 psychoanalysts working in Central Europe during the 1930s emigrated

during the years 1933–1939. This migration had far-reaching consequences. The movement's organisational structure was transformed,
as was the character of the psychoanalytic societies in other countries,
the USA and the UK in particular, that took in most of the exiles (cf.
Ash, 1991; Ash & Söllner, 1996; Gast, 1999; Haynal, 1994; Kurzweil,
1996; Makari, 2008; Peters, 1992; Steiner, 1989, 2011; Thompson, 2010).

By the time the Second World War broke out, the International
Psychoanalytic Association had 560 members. Thirty per cent of them
were in the USA, with the rest affiliated with one of the twelve other
Psychoanalytic Societies in Germany, Vienna, Switzerland, Hungary,
Britain, France, Holland, India, Japan, Finland–Sweden, Denmark–
Norway, Italy, and Palestine. During the war the connections between
these local societies and the international organisation were almost
completely cut off, and in 1942 even the precise addresses of some of
the European associations were not known (Limentani, 1989).

Immigration itself could stretch the cords of solidarity to the breaking point. The psychoanalytic societies in the West that took in
refugees from Europe—or, in many cases, refused to take them in or
accepted them only reluctantly—found that the influx of newcomers
with different outlooks and life histories led to profound structural
changes to the movement as a whole. It was crucial for refugee psychoanalysts to be accepted into the psychoanalytic association of the
country to which they immigrated. Without such acceptance, they
could not practise their profession and support themselves. In many
cases, absorbing countries issued an immigration or residence permit
only to newcomers who demonstrated that their professional community wanted to take them in and would guarantee that they could
earn a livelihood. For the men and women fleeing Central Europe,
then, acceptance by their foreign colleagues could be a matter of life or
death. To a reader of the minutes of the various committees set up to
deal with the issue of absorbing the immigrants and the correspondence between Freud's pupils, it seems as if the internal battles fought
within the psychoanalytic movement might have served, in part, as a
psychological shield. The classic example of the intensity of the theoretical disputes during the years of the war comes from the British
Psychoanalytic Society. So heated was the internal warfare between
Freudians and Kleinians during the "Controversial Discussions" that
Donald Winnicott had to draw his colleagues' attention to the fact that
an air raid was in progress (cf. Little, 1985; Stonebridge, 1998).

Max Eitingon redux

If Vienna had been, at the end of the nineteenth century, the garden in which psychoanalysis sprouted, Berlin was the nursery where it grew during the 1920s, as the discipline underwent its decisive stage of development. The Berlin Psychoanalytic Polyclinic transformed the status of Freud's students. From an elite and isolated group of Jewish intellectuals, they became a society whose members volunteered a part of their time and effort to listen to and treat the troubles and sorrows of the downtrodden inhabitants of a big city (cf. Gay, 1970; Laqueur, 1974; Neumann, 2007; Willet, 1984).

The Berlin Psychoanalytic Polyclinic rose and declined over a period of fourteen years, beginning with its establishment in February 1920 and ending with the emigration of most of its staff in 1934. Just as the immediate needs of the Weimar Republic in its early years made it possible for the Polyclinic to flourish, so did the political climate following the accession of the Nazis to power in January 1933 radically change the nature of the institution and, in short order, bring about its end.

Funded predominantly from Max Eitingon's own resources, the Berlin Psychoanalytic Polyclinic offered poor sections of the population psychoanalytic help either free of charge or at reasonable prices. At the same time, the facility served as a training institution for a new generation of psychoanalysts. It formulated the standard structure of psychoanalytic training, known as the "Eitingon model", still in use today. This tripartite programme included theoretical instruction, the trainee's own analysis by a senior psychoanalyst, and the psychoanalysis of patients under the supervision of an experienced staff member (Danto, 1998, 2005; Frank, Hermanns, & Löchel, 2008).

The Seventh Psychoanalytic Congress, held in 1920 in Berlin, decided to condition membership of psychoanalytic societies on certified psychoanalytic training. The older associations—those of Vienna and London—also set up teaching committees like the one in Berlin. The International Training Committee of the International Psychoanalytic Association was established in 1925 with Eitingon as chairman, a position he held until the committee was disbanded in 1938 (Schröter, 2002, 2008). The standardisation of training enhanced the status of the psychoanalytic institutes of Berlin, Vienna, and London, but also led to friction and disputes between the individual psychoanalytic societies.

However, the Berlin group was recognised as the most important authority in psychoanalytic training, given the considerable clinical experience of its members. The teaching staff of the Berlin institute included, in addition to Eitingon and Karl Abraham, Ernst Simmel, Otto Fenichel, Franz Alexander, Paul Federn, Edith Jacobson, Melanie Klein, Siegfried Bernfeld, Alice Balint, Wilhelm Reich, and Theodor Reik. It also pioneered the integration of women into the psycho-analytic movement. Karen Horney, one of the founders, was the first woman certified to teach psychoanalysis (cf. Müller, 2000; Paris, 1994; Thompson, 1987). The establishment of the Berlin institute led to the first systematic discussions of fundamental therapeutic parameters such as the length of analysis, its cost, its indications, and the relation-ship between psychoanalysis and other psychiatric and psychothera-peutic treatments. Rates were set in consultation with the patient, in accordance with his or her income and ability to pay. Eitingon insisted that therapists not have a financial stake in granting treatment, and did not hesitate to go head to head with his senior colleagues on this issue. Anna Smilansky, who would later move to Palestine with Eitingon, served as a full-time assistant to Eitingon and Simmel. Open twelve hours a day without a break, the Polyclinic offered a total of 300 treat-ment hours a week. The age range of the patients was huge, from five years old to sixty, as was the range of diagnoses. More than fifty chil-dren under the age of ten were accepted for treatment, providing Melanie Klein with the opportunity to conduct her pioneering studies on child analysis. The Polyclinic's budget grew steadily during its early years, but only ten per cent of its operating budget was covered by patient fees. Eitingon, who provided the rest of the funding from his own pocket, took pride in the objective statistical data collected by the clinic, which served the psychoanalytic discipline's efforts to gain recognition in medical circles.

The pioneering work done by Eitingon and his colleagues demol-ished most of the claims made by opponents of psychoanalysis during its early years. One such argument was that Freud's theories were suspect because he had based his findings on research conducted on an unrepresentative population, one composed largely of middle-class Jewish women; another was that psychoanalytic treatment could effectively be offered only in private practice and could never work under the conditions of a public clinic. During its peak years, 120 patients were undergoing analysis at the same time. In January 1930,

Eitingon reported that a total of 721 people had undergone analysis there since it opened.[1]

Nearly from the day of its founding, the Berlin Institute was both innovative and conservative. Several study groups operated there, representing a variety of approaches to analytic practice. Weimar Berlin, not imperial Vienna, was the place where psychoanalysis took its first steps as a socio-critical theory. One of the important forums to emerge from the Institute was the Children's Seminar (*Kinderseminar*), which Otto Fenichel led for more than a decade. It was not a seminar about the analysis of children, but rather a seminar for young psycho-analysts—the "children" of its name being novices undergoing clinical training. But the seminar gradually metamorphosed into a group committed to psychoanalytic social critique from a socialist perspective. Fenichel would continue to be the point man for political psycho-analysis after his move to the USA. He liked to mock diehard Freudians who could not conceive that a patient might have lost his job for mere socio-economic reasons and not just because of conflicts lying deep in his unconscious (cf. Gekle & Kimmerle, 2004; Jacoby, 1983; May, 2008; Rolnik, 2008a).

In 1930, the Berlin Psychoanalytic Institute celebrated its tenth anniversary. By that time it was already clear that even though the controversial seven-headed psychoanalytic oligarchy—the Secret Committee that had managed the movement's affairs in its formative years—no longer operated, organisational decisions still lay exclusively in the hands of three key figures: Anna Freud, Ernest Jones, and Max Eitingon (Grosskurth, 1991). On the occasion of the anniversary, Freud delivered an uncharacteristically laudatory speech in honour of Eitingon, then fifty years old (Schröter, 2004). In this emotional address, Freud quoted several lines from a poem by Ludwig Uhland, "King Charles's Sea Journey": "But at the helm King Charles sat by, / And never said a word, / And steered the ship with steadfast eye / Till no more the tempest stirred".[2] Yet, at that moment, no tempest seemed to be on the horizon. Freud could hardly have anticipated that Eitingon, the psychoanalytic movement's silent helmsman, would soon steer his ship to the very same destination to which King Charles and his twelve knights were navigating in Uhland's ballad—the Holy Land.

Freud gave Eitingon as a gift the manuscript of *Civilization and Its Discontents* (1930a).[3] In this work, Freud argued that all cultural advancement comes at the cost of a loss of feelings of happiness on the conscious level, and an intensification of guilt feelings on the unconscious level. The discontent that is part of human existence, he claimed, is the conscious corollary of this unconscious guilt. *Civilization and Its Discontents* was not a subversive political manifesto, but Freud certainly used the concept of the unconscious to challenge the distinction between culture and civilisation, a distinction often viewed by historians as one of the most fundamental and problematic ideas in German thinking of the previous two centuries. The German view that culture and civilisation were distinct had been explained in different ways. The most important suggestion was that the German middle class had, during the eighteenth century, compensated for its lack of political representation, and for its sense of humiliation and lack of freedom, by creating an apolitical and even anti-political cultural sphere. German idealism, which extolled metaphysics and the inner world of the soul, and the German literature produced by the Weimar classicists led by Goethe and Schiller, predated the German nation-state by about a hundred years. They legitimised the Central European individual's turning away from the political and social sphere to the personal and cultural domain. "Civilisation" was understood as the external, surface level of human existence. Culture, in contrast, was seen as an uncompromising striving for the good, the right, and the beautiful. Culture was the antithesis of politics, which was viewed as ambivalent, shallow, and temporal. As German politics deteriorated, and as that deterioration turned precipitous after the First World War, the German state cult of Goethe and Schiller grew stronger, and was taken to express the true cultural pulse of the nation (cf. Elias, 1982; Lepenies, 2006). The Jews living in the German cultural space had a special interest in adopting this concept of culture and identifying with a tradition that promised affiliation and a sense of belonging even to people who had not yet received full civil rights. Under Nazi rule, Germany's cultural assets would undergo a process of racial classification and mapping. Psychoanalysis itself would be condemned as "Jewish science". Today, we are accustomed to thinking of German National Socialism as the diametric opposite of culture. But it is important to keep in mind that the Nazis did not discard this dichotomy between culture and civilisation and between the realm of the spirit and the realm of power. On the contrary, many British and French statesmen and intellectuals were enraptured by German and

Italian fascism precisely because they believed that Hitler was going to war on behalf of culture.

On 28 December 1932, the Leipzig City Council sent a letter of condolence to Max Eitingon, on the death of his father (LBI). In the letter, the mayor of Leipzig, Carl Friedrich Goerdeler, who later became a prominent adversary of the Nazi rule in Germany, cited Chaim Eitingon's most significant contributions to the community, such as the founding of the city's modern hospital.[4] By the end of 1935, the Leipzig University had expelled all its Jewish professors; it would not be long before the hospital refused to accept Jews. The Etz Chaim Synagogue, the city's second largest, built by the Eitingons in 1922, would be demolished during the Kristallnacht pogroms of November 1938.

A few days after being sworn in as Germany's chancellor on 30 January 1933, Hitler gave a speech at the Berlin Sports Palace that launched Nazi Germany's political terror campaign. On 28 February, a day after the Reichstag fire, the German parliament passed a special law granting the chancellor unlimited powers. On 31 March, Germany's Jewish citizens were ordered to hand over their passports to the authorities, and on 1 April a boycott of Jewish-owned businessmen and professionals, including doctors and lawyers, was declared (Friedlander, 1997; Straus, 1978–1988, 1980–1981; Straus & Roeder, 1983). In mid-April 1933, the country's medical organisations were ordered to remove all non-Aryans from administrative positions. An editorial published in the journal of the German Medical Association (after more than half of its members had joined the Nazi Party) welcomed the Führer's "energetic efforts" to cleanse the medical community of foreign racial elements and in so doing make it easier for young German physicians to make a living. Within a year, the average income of non-Jewish German doctors increased by eleven per cent. In 1933, about 5,500 Jewish doctors had been registered in Germany. Five years later, the chancellor signed an order forbidding the 700 Jewish doctors who had received special permits to treat the Jewish population to call themselves "physicians". Henceforth, they could only use the title "carers of the sick". By 1939, the number of Jewish doctors had declined to 285 (Efron, 2001; Klee, 2001). "Each time I feel a bit alone here I look at the newspaper and all my longing for home vanishes completely", Hans Sachs, a jurist and psychoanalyst who had been a member of the Secret Committee,

wrote to Eitingon on 1 February 1933 (ECI). Sachs had emigrated to
the USA in 1932 and was one of the founders of the Boston Psychoanalytic Society.

The possibility that Eitingon might have to leave Germany was
first broached three months after the Nazis came to power. He refused
to transfer management of the institute to two non-Jewish colleagues,
Felix Boehm and Carl Müller-Braunschweig, who had been quick to
suggest themselves for the job. The two men claimed that this was the
only way that the Institute could continue to run its public psychoanalytic clinic without violating the Gleichschaltung, or laws of
"forcible co-ordination", which forbade Jews to hold administrative
positions in public bodies (cf. Brainin & Kaminer, 1982; Brecht, 1988;
Cocks, 1985; Eickhoff, 1995; Gay, 1988; Lockot, 1994; Lohmann, 1984;
Schröter, 2009; Spiegel, 1975).

Eitingon did all he could to remain at the helm. He first agreed that
he would hand his authority over to another only if he was unable to
carry out his duties. But when it became clear that the Aryanisation
laws would be applied to the Institute, he tried to persuade Freud and
Jones that German psychoanalysis could not function without its
Jewish members, and that the proper thing to do would be to shut
down the Berlin Institute and transfer it to another country. Eitingon
had lived in Germany for forty years, but was not a German citizen.
He stressed to Freud, that he identified completely with the Institute
he had founded and was determined not to resign his directorship
unless forced to do so.

Am I behaving unfairly toward my clleagues here when, in the volatile
conditions prevailing here at this time, I dare cast doubt on whether the
Institute can survive, while at the same time voicing my intention to
talk of taking the Institute with me to wherever I go, if I am compelled
to leave my place of work and the country I have lived in for 40 years?
I mean compelled in the literal sense of the word, because I would not
ever consider leaving a moment before that or under less pressure. So
many of my colleagues have gone in recent years, and others will most
likely stop working here, or will be forced to stop before I am. I have
every right to identify with the Institute, or better to identify the
Institute with me. Some of my colleagues here have already intimated
that they do not understand, or reject, this approach. But that is not
enough to dissuade me. I would very much like to know what your
opinion is, Herr Professor. At the present time, at least, and who knows

for how much longer, it is a hypothetical question. I myself am serene and sure of my position on what I must do and how to do it. That is a great help in enduring a period like this one. (Eitingon to Freud, 19 March 1933, in Freud & Eitingon, 2004, pp. 846–847)

It is clear that this statement of his intentions was written by a man in emotional turmoil who felt that his world was inching towards disaster. Eitingon feared that he might lose the thing he valued most—Freud's confidence—if he were to shut down the Institute. No one could doubt the extent to which he identified himself with the institution he had founded. But some wagging tongues claimed that he had resolved to leave Germany even before the Nazis came to power, and that he intended to take advantage of the current situation to relocate the Institute to his new place of residence. Such allegations did not come only from his non-Jewish colleagues, who wanted to maintain the psychoanalytic project under the new political order. The Zionist educator David Idelson, who was at that time undergoing training at the Institute in Berlin, later claimed that in 1925, during a chat with Eitingon in a café, Eitingon told him, in an undertone, that he intended to move soon to Palestine. Furthermore, Idelson maintained, Eitingon had said that Freud himself longed to see Jerusalem become the centre of psychoanalysis (Idelson, cited in Eitingon, 1950, pp. 64–65). Eitingon met David Eder for the first time that same year, discovering that he was not the only Zionist in the psychoanalytic movement (letter from David Eder to Eitingon, 3 February 1925, ECI). He might have attended the lectures given by two Zionist leaders, Kurt Blumenfeld and Haim Weizmann, on "the development of the Hebrew University" and on "the political and economical conditions for Jewish colonization of Palestine".[5] However, one searches in vain through the intensive correspondence conducted by Eitingon and Freud over the twenty years before the Nazis' rise to power for even a suggestion of Zionist sentiment from either of them. On the contrary, Eitingon seems to have been among the students of Freud who best absorbed the latter's warnings to his Jewish students that they not allow their ethnic identities or patriotic inclinations to impinge on their psychoanalytic work. As with Freud's identification with Jewish nationalism, Eitingon's attachment to the Zionist idea went through several incarnations. A postcard he sent to Freud in 1910, when he made a trip to Haifa, Lebanon, and Damascus, indicates that his identification with the place was of an amorphous, orientalist nature. During the 1920s, a number of Zionist interlocutors appear in his letters—Ahad Ha'am, Zalman Schocken, Arthur Ruppin, David Idelson, and Shmuel Golan. During the last decade of his life, from the 1930s until 1943, his desks in both Berlin and Jerusalem were laden with correspondence relating to the Zionist movement and the Yishuv's needs.

From his long acquaintance with Freud, Eitingon knew that whenever the founder of psychoanalysis faced a choice about the future of the discipline *vs.* the future of a friendship, he would choose the former; all the more so if the fate of the flourishing Berlin Psychoanalytic Institute hung in the balance. Eitingon battled like a lion for Freud's trust. He reminded the professor that he had received invitations to join several of the well-established psychoanalytic institutes in the USA, but that, unlike many of Freud's other students, now dispersed over the face of the earth, he, Eitingon, had preferred to stay close to his teacher. He did not err in assuming that Freud's natural inclination was to hope for the best and to not to rule out the possibility that the Berlin Institute could continue to function in Hitler's Germany.

But Eitingon's non-Jewish colleagues did not sit with their hands folded. Felix Boehm invited himself for a visit to Vienna, where he tried to persuade the professor of the purity of his intentions. Eitingon reproached Freud for naïvely agreeing to meet with Boehm even though everyone knew that "Boehm took the trouble to travel to Vienna in order to receive your consent to his taking my place. . . . I reiterate, he went to Vienna to be anointed by you as my successor" (letter from Eitingon to Freud, dated 21 April 1933: Freud & Eitingon, 2004, p. 857). Freud seems to have tried to play both sides, encouraging Eitingon to accept the needs of the hour and to transfer management of the Institute to one of his Aryan colleagues, but also trying to ensure that Eitingon would not withdraw the generous financial support that had been the mainstay of the Institute's budget from the time it was founded. Eitingon's assertion that he and the Institute were one and the same, and that he intended to take the Institute with him to wherever he might go, was not realistic. Even though he funded it, the Institute legally belonged to the German Psychoanalytic Association, and this body continued to function even after it had been expelled from the International Psychoanalytic Association. Eitingon was compelled, again and again in his letters to Freud that year, to refute the charge that he was planning to dismantle the Institute so that he could transfer it elsewhere. He wrote, on 24 March 1933,

All that I do, I do in full knowledge that I have no intention of leaving Berlin of my own free will, before outside circumstances force such a step. The question of whether moving the Institute to another place will make it easier for me, in one way or another, to secure my own future, is a secondary matter. (Freud & Eitingon, 2004, p. 850)

This may have been the last letter Freud received from Eitingon on the stationery of the Berlin Psychoanalytic Institute. In March 1933, prior to leaving for his Easter vacation, Eitingon signed a document granting power of attorney to Drs Mueller-Braunschweig and Boehm to act in his place if, for any reason, Eitingon was unable to return to Berlin, or if the Berlin Institute was required to replace its executive committee and appoint a new one composed of "Christian members of pure German ancestry".

At Jones' request, Eitingon had prepared, earlier that year, a list of the fifty Jewish psychoanalysts who worked in conjunction with the Berlin Institute, with their individual preferences for emigration destinations.[6] The list also included the names of those who had already moved to the USA in 1930–1932 (among them Franz Alexander, Sandor Rado, Erich Fromm, Hans Sachs, and Karen Horney). Eitingon did not add his own name to the list, perhaps signifying his determination not to leave Berlin. He notified Freud that it was his intention to continue to serve as an "immigration office" for Jewish psychoanalysts even if he himself were forced to leave the country.

Colleagues who lived and worked outside Berlin kept Eitingon up to date on the situation in other German cities. Their reports to him showed that Jewish psychoanalysts who worked elsewhere, not under the aegis of the Berlin Institute, were even worse off than those in the capital. In February 1933, Erwin Hirsch, an ophthalmologist and psychoanalyst who would later move to Palestine, gave a lecture to a small group of colleagues in Stuttgart. The subject was "The psychology of conscience" (Bohleber, 1986). This was the last such talk he was able to make in the city. Therese Benedek, the first psychoanalyst in Leipzig (Weidemann, 1988), reported that same year that she was no longer taking on new patients (Benedek to Eitingon, 29 June 1933, ECI). Eitingon categorically rejected her request to join the Berlin Institute: "[T]he prognosis is extremely bleak and with regard to the Jews we should view everything in a very pessimistic light. With regard to the personal fate of each individual, the decisive factor is our capacity for enduring hardship" (Eitingon to Benedek, 30 June 1933: ECI).

The psychoanalysts who left Germany in 1933 and early 1934 were much better off than their Austrian colleagues who emigrated later. During the first years of Nazi rule, a warm letter of recommendation from Eitingon or a personal appeal by him to Abraham Brill, founder of the New York Psychoanalytic Association, "in the name of the old continent and its current troubles" were enough to open the New York Institute's doors to an immigrant colleague. "The fact that Dr. Happel comes from an old and good Berlin Jewish family should certainly not stand in the way of her emigrating from Hamburg to America", Eitingon wrote on one occasion (19 January 1933: ECI) to Brill. In response to this request, Brill and Sachs did their best to facilitate Clara Happel's move, but she in the end decided to settle in Detroit, where she slid into a deep depression (Brecht, Volker, Hermanns, Kammer, & Juelich, 1985). In 1941, she was arrested by the FBI by proclamation of the president on suspicion of espionage and un-American activities. It was later learnt that she was denounced as the leader of a Nazi spy-ring by a former schizophrenic patient. In September 1945, she committed suicide (Goggin, Goggin, & Hill, 2004).

During the initial months of Nazi rule, it already became clear that the new regime would not permit Jewish psychoanalysts to remain in the country. But some of the community's members thought that if psychoanalysis could rid itself of its "Jewish aspects" it could find a place for itself in Hitler's Germany. This attempt to reconcile the increasing Nazification of German life with the clinical and research activities of the psychoanalytic institutes was pursued by non-Jewish German members of the profession, along with colleagues from outside Germany. The foremost of the latter group was Ernest Jones, in Britain. The hope that therapy and research could carry on after the Jews had gone led to huge tensions between non-Jewish and Jewish members of the German Psychoanalytic Association. This came to a climax when the German Association was expelled from its international parent body. On 6 May 1933, Freud's birthday, which in better times the Institute had celebrated with a large party, the German Psychoanalytic Association voted on whether to Aryanise its ranks and those of the Berlin Institute. Eight members of the executive committee voted in favour, while fifteen voted against. Just at this time, the Nazis issued their official reasons for boycotting Freud's works: "in protest against their corrupting influence on the human psyche, their destructive overemphasis on sexuality, and to protect the noble soul of man" (Cocks, 1985; Lück, 1997, p. 165). On 10 May 1933, his writings were thrown into bonfires throughout Berlin. On 8 July 1933, Eitingon reported to his friend Brill: "Things here are as they were before . . . but our group is shrinking by the day" (ECI).

Before resigning from the German Psychoanalytic Association, Eitingon shepherded through the organisation a decision according to which the positions on the executive committee vacated by Jewish members would not be filled. Three days later, he sent Boehm his best wishes for success in his new position as director and asked him to expunge his, Eitingon's, name from the list of the Association's members (Eitingon to Boehm, 21 November 1933, ECI). For the first time since it was founded, the Berlin Institute had to act without the participation of a member of the Secret Committee—that is, without any direct link to Freud. From Vienna, it looked as if the future of German psychoanalysis had been sealed, and this only six months after the Nazis came to power. On 23 August 1933, Freud wrote to Ernest Jones, "Berlin is lost". Informing Jones about Eitingon's decision to go to Palestine he added, "I think one should find a replacement [for Eitingon]" (Freud & Jones, 1993, pp. 726–727).

Eitingon's standing remained strong even after his coerced resignation. His comportment, diligence, economic independence, and uncompromising loyalty to Freud, as well as his lack of any pretence regarding clinical or theoretical innovation made him a welcome guest at all the psychoanalytic associations that operated under the aegis of the International Psychoanalytic Association. Immediately after the Nazis came to power, he received official invitations from several foreign associations to join them—a gesture they made only rarely, and then only to the most senior and respected members of the field in Central Europe. His decision to move to Palestine, of all places, came as a bombshell to Freud and his daughter Anna. In those years, when new disputes rose one after another in the expanding psychoanalytic community, the importance of Eitingon, with his organisational skills and his utter loyalty to Freud, was huge (cf. Steiner, 2011). Some of the psychoanalysts who worked in the Berlin Institute moved to Vienna in 1933, and for a moment it looked to Anna as if the developments in Germany would breathe new life into the Vienna Institute and restore its previous glory. She hoped that Vienna would prove to be the preferred destination for Freud's most important confidant.

"If you really must leave Berlin, where would you go?" she wrote to Eitingon on 16 April 1933. "Not to Vienna? Should we not build a new analytic center here? I believe we will be allowed to work here, where we could get all the assistance we need" (AFC).

Then, unexpectedly, a voice from outside the psychoanalytic community joined the chorus of objections to Eitingon's choice of Jerusalem as his new home. Albert Einstein, who had abandoned Berlin for the USA in 1932, offered a bleak assessment of what awaited Eitingon in Palestine. The refugee physicist thought that the very idea of psychoanalytic practice or academic research in Palestine was ludicrous. "You are probably surprised to be receiving a letter from me at all, let alone one meddling in your most private affairs", Einstein wrote. "Nonetheless, I am certain you will understand". He continued,

> These are the days when each of us must take a good, hard look at the possibilities open to intellectuals seeking suitable employment, be it here or elsewhere. In fact, I have noticed a lack here [in the USA] of serious, knowledgeable professionals in the field of mental therapeutic methods. Yet I have heard that you are looking into establishing your professional base in tiny Palestine, which has naturally been inundated with doctors in every field. That being the case, I feel obliged to urge you to strongly consider settling in America, rather than Palestine. I am convinced that you would have an easier time finding a broader and more satisfying niche here than in Palestine, where intellectuals merely hinder one another. I wouldn't consider making such a claim to a doctor in any other field, since America's urban centers are teeming with such doctors, and there is no real lack of luminaries.

> As for the university in Jerusalem, I am sorry to say that this institution, whose importance for the entire Jewish intellectual world is so great, and whose realization I myself worked so hard for, is not exactly in good hands. I have been fighting to replace the administration for years, but have yet to see results. While I have managed to get a Committee of Inquiry convened, I have little faith in the ability of the current powers that be to bring about real change for the better. So far, the university's best have also been the ones to turn their backs on the place in bitter anger. Why would you want to put yourself through that?

> Even if you decide to limit yourself to a private practice, the above-mentioned points still apply.

If you find it presumptuous of me to be offering you all of this unsolicited advice, just put this letter away. Still, I could not keep myself from telling you what I see. (Einstein to Eitingon, 18 January 1934, ECI: original German version reproduced in Rolnik, 2008b)

Einstein's letter caused Eitingon much consternation, and he immediately consulted Freud. The latter replied that he himself was not involved in any attempt to keep Eitingon away from Palestine, and certainly not in any attempt to convince him to emigrate to the USA—everyone knew, he said, that Frau Eitingon would not like America. And Einstein's letter, Freud claimed, evoked two of Einstein's best known traits: "He's unable to refrain from doing a favor for anyone, and he must meddle in everything that comes his way" (Freud to Eitingon, 1 March 1934, Freud & Eitingon, 2004, p. 874).[7]

In the framework of his feverish attempts to keep Eitingon in Europe, Jones attributed Eitingon's choice of Palestine to the whims of his wife. He hoped and expected, however, that the moment that her delicate foot stepped on to Palestinian soil, "she would realize the relative unattractiveness" of that country and quickly head back to Europe. Jones hoped that the couple would, in the end, settle in France, and that Eitingon would take the opportunity to put the fidgety psychoanalytic scene in Paris in order and get it back on the high road (letter from Jones to Anna Freud, 19 September 1933, ABS).

Mira Yakovlevna Eitingon, Max's second wife, a beautiful and pleasure-loving Russian actress, had already aroused Freud's wrath by telling him proudly about her huge collection of shoes. Eitingon's other colleagues also considered her a high-dressing lady who spent her time either entertaining ostentatiously or suffering from mysterious migraines. She reputedly resented psychoanalysis for keeping her husband too busy to spend time with her. "She has a feline nature . . . and you know I don't like cats", Freud wrote to Arnold Zweig during one of his bouts of bandying invectives. He added a few more speculations about "the neurotic conditions of the love" shared by the two Eitingons (10 February 1937, in Freud & Eitingon, 2004, pp. 976–978). Yet, Mira surprised everyone by not fleeing back to Europe from Palestine too soon. She instead used her talents to recreate in the Palestine of the 1930s the elegant Weimar lifestyle to which she was accustomed. Not only that, but, despite the heatwaves and her migraines, she outlived her husband. And on top of everything, she controverted the innuendo about her selfish nature. Shortly after her husband's death, she deeded over to the Palestine Psychoanalytic Society the beautiful building in which the Jerusalem Psychoanalytic Institute was housed, with all its furnishings. It was an act of generosity without parallel in the history of psychoanalysis, in keeping with her husband's legendary munificence. The gift ensured the continuing operation of the young society during its greatest crisis.

Eitingon left Berlin and reached Palestine in October 1933, bearing a letter of recommendation from Freud intended to facilitate his application for a work permit from the Mandate administration. He was soon joined by the Viennese professor of neurology, Martin Pappenheim, and several other colleagues from Berlin: Kilian Bluhm, Ilja Shalit, Anna Smeliansky, and Moshe Wulff, all of whom were medical doctors. David Eder in London and Anna Freud in Vienna were made honorary members. Although the letter sent to Eitingon's temporary address (King David Hotel in Jerusalem), was generous and supportive, Freud did not fail to mention his hopes that Eitingon's relocation to Palestine is "incidental" and would be temporary (letter of refrence (*Zeugnis*) from Freud, dated 5 October 1933: Freud & Eitingon, 2004, pp. 869–870).[8] Within four weeks of his arrival, Eitingon reported the establishment of the Palestine Psychoanalytic Society (Eitingon to Freud, 2 November 1933: Freud & Eitingon, 2004, pp. 870–873). As befit the prominence of its founder and the political circumastnaces, the incorporation of the group into the International Psychoanalytic Association was immediate. Anna Freud put the news into its proper historical perspective:

> My father had a letter from Eitingon today. You will soon hear from him about the formation of a new group in Palestine. The members are mostly or all old Berlin members. New groups used to be a pleasure. They are not just now. (Anna Freud to Jones, 7 November 1933: ABS)

Ernest Jones was not so quick to give up on Berlin. Several Jewish psychoanalysts remained there following Eitingon's departure, hoping that the reconstituted management would allow the Institute to continue to operate under the new regime. The International Psychoanalytic Congress in Lucerne afforded the first opportunity, following the Nazi takeover and the forced resignation of Eitingon and the other Jews, for the non-Jewish German psychoanalysts to meet face to face with their colleagues from other countries and their former German associates. Jones sought to prepare Felix Boehm and his non-Jewish German associates for their forthcoming meeting with their Jewish former colleagues:

> You will know that I myself regard those emotions and ultra-Jewish attitude very unsympathetically, and it is plain to me that you and your colleagues are being made a dumping ground for such emotion and resentment which belongs elsewhere and has been displaced in your direction. My only concern is for the good of psychoanalysis itself, and I shall defend the view, which I confidently hold, that your actions have been actuated only by the same motive. (Jones to Boehm, 24 July 1934: ABS)

Jones made a point of sending Anna Freud an advance copy of the keynote speech he planned to make. Something in it rubbed her the wrong way. It seemed to her that he had framed the problem as the Nazis' attitude toward psychoanalytic science, when what actually concerned the Nazis was that many psychoanalysts were Jews. "The facts are, curiously enough, that the government never attacked psychoanalysis or restricted its activity in any way", she wrote. "The 25 members who left did so because they were Jews. Not because they were analysts" (Anna Freud to Jones, 18 August 1934: ABS).[9]

Eitingon's dramatic resignation from the directorship of the Berlin Institute did indeed enable the new management to avert, for a short while, the inevitable head-on collision with the new regime. But the fear of losing its ties to the other psychoanalytic societies, in particular that of Vienna, impelled Eitingon's successors to do all they could to present what had happened as a rescue operation rather than a betrayal. In the short time before the German Society was expelled, Felix Boehm made every effort to persuade the societies in Vienna and London that Germany's new regime did not necessarily pose an ominous development for German psychoanalysis. He wrote to Jones, "I am convinced that the Gestapo, the corridors of which I walked until recently with utter confidence, has no category 'psychoanalysis', but they certainly have a rubric called 'psychoanalysts'" (Boehm to Jones, 15 November 1935: ABS). Jones sensed the danger of a split in the movement, with the Berlin Institute taking a course independent of its sister institution in Vienna. And he was particularly concerned about the relations between Freud and his German non-Jewish followers. After visiting Holland and speaking there with several psychoanalysts who had moved there from Berlin, he reported his impressions to Anna Freud. The profession was not yet doomed in Germany, he insisted. He advocated support for the efforts of the German colleagues who were seeking to keep the field going (Jones to Anna Freud, 2 September 1933: ABS). His hope was based on the assumption that if they could "bring in new blood" and disassociate the profession from its Jewish origins, the Nazis would have no ideological or legal cause to suppress it. He viewed as adequate proof of this the fact that the non-Jewish psychoanalysts were willing to continue to operate under the aegis of the Institute founded by Eitingon and Abraham.

One of the incidents that incensed the psychoanalytic community was the arrest, in October 1935, of Edith Jacobson, a young Jewish psychoanalyst who had gained prominence thanks to her exceptional clinical capabilities. She had quickly advanced, having been appointed a member of the Berlin Institute's faculty. Jacobson was not, however, a protégé of Eitingon, and did not resign with him and his loyalists or leave Berlin with them. Several of her patients were arrested, and one of them was murdered during interrogation by the Gestapo. Its agents later fished a suitcase out of Gruenewald Lake in Berlin that contained documents and leaflets printed by a socialist resistance group. The material identified Jacobson as a member of the underground. On her person when she was arrested was a notebook containing the name of a patient who was a known Communist, as well as an invitation she had received to the German Psychoanalytic Association's general meeting. The invitation was seen as incriminating evidence, on the ground that it closed with the phrase "with friendly greetings", rather than "with German greetings", as the law required (cf. Brecht, 1987: Lockot, 1994; Schröter, Mühlleitner, & May, 2004; Steiner, 2011). Jones took vigorous action to obtain Jacobson's release. But, at the same time, he supported Boehm's claim that any intervention by the German association in the matter of a colleague suspected of undesirable political activity was liable to tarnish the name of the German analysts and bring psychoanalytic activity in that country, Germany, to an end.

The Germans sensed that their colleagues elsewhere were condemning them for their conduct in Jacobson's case. In response, Boehm wrote a long letter to Jones, in which he presented a detailed account of the events that had preceded her arrest. Jacobson, Boehm related, had declared to him that she would adjust to the new regime and its demands to the best of her ability, and denied the rumours that she belonged to the Communist Party. She had also insisted that she would never leave Germany. He said that

> the full confidence that there is no one among us whose ties with Communism can put us at risk was the basis on which I conducted with government agencies, police headquarters, the district medical officer, and others those contacts that have enabled me to defend our [psychoanalytic] society.

After learning that Jacobson's statements "were not consistent with the facts", and that in 1933 she had given several lectures at gatherings of Communist workers, Boehm felt that she had betrayed his trust. She, of all people, who was highly cognisant of the complicated relations he had established with representatives of various government agencies, should have known that even a small slip-up was liable to put the continued operation of the German Psychoanalytic Association in doubt. Boehm iterated that he had assured the authorities that none of the Society's members was engaged in forbidden political activity. Colleagues outside Germany, he claimed, did not understand the country's mood, and were censuring the German psychoanalytic community without appreciating the tremendous efforts it had made to keep psychoanalytic practice going "under impossible conditions", in an environment in which psychoanalysis was identified with Judaism.

> If the Edith Jacobson affair comes to the attention of a representative of the ministry of culture—a development that cannot be ruled out—I will not longer be able to defend my position. One possibility is that the same circles in which I have been received with esteem as a result of years of hard labor will consider me a fraud. The other, if I declare that I trusted a colleague who gave me her word, is that I will be considered an idiot, who out of a strange philo-Semitism took a Jewish woman's word of honor. Either of these reasons would be sufficient to have me dismissed. (Boehm to Jones, 15 November 1935: ABS)

Boehm described his plight in the clearest possible way. The words he chose, while not indicating any identification with Nazi racism, certainly show how quickly Nazi idioms became part of the lexicons of even the most sophisticated German intellectuals. He concluded his letter with the hope that his friends in Germany would one day acknowledge their German colleagues' efforts to carry on the work of psychoanalysis under difficult conditions. "Everyone gazes in wonder at this paradise, a palpable El Dorado, that I have managed to safeguard for our Jewish colleagues and at the courage I have displayed in doing so," he protested. "This society in which Jews and non-Jews work together and enjoy equal rights is without a doubt the only one of its kind in Germany."

"The Edith Jacobson affair", as it was referred to in the letters of those involved in it, did not demoralise the non-Jewish German psychoanalysts. Some of them continued to believe that the Jewish ethnicity of Freud and most of his students was the only thing preventing psychoanalysis from making a place for itself in Hitler's Germany. Jacobson extricated herself from the Gestapo's clutches by the skin of her teeth—she absconded from house arrest. She subsequently managed to make her way to the USA, where she became an important theoretician. One of her lesser known post-war contributions to analytic theory was based on her own experience of incarceration. Jacobson's (1949) analysis of the psychological impact of prison on the ego is a unique scientific text/testimony which barely conceals its "autobiographical" nature (Kuriloff, 2010).

Boehm was able to boast of creating a paradise for Jews at the Berlin Psychoanalytic Institute for only a short time longer. In December 1935, most of the Jewish psychoanalysts who were still members resigned. Boehm reported this to Anna Freud and requested her and her father's consent to continue to back the German society, in a spirit of collegiality and in gratitude to him for having done all he could to delay this painful development (Boehm to Anna Freud, 11 December 1935: ECI).

In 1936, the Institute had been annexed to the German Institute for Psychological Research and Psychotherapy. It became better known as the Goering Institute, after its new director, Matthias Heinrich Goering, nephew and protégé of Field Marshall Hermann Goering. Goering, Boehm, Müller-Braunschweig, and Jones met in Basel, and the latter believed he had managed to persuade Goering that the psychoanalytic training programme did not include "foreign elements that contradict his views". And, in fact, the new director, whose close ties to the top levels of the regime enabled him to obtain particularly generous state funding, enabled fourteen non-Jewish German psychoanalysts to operate in what was called "Section A" of the reconstituted

Institute. They accepted many constraints, among them an absolute prohibition against mentioning the name of the founder of psychoanalysis and any use of psychoanalytic terminology to describe mental processes. They also had to give up the theory of sexuality and the Oedipal complex. It was a golden age for Carl Müller-Braunschweig. Undisturbed, he developed his own neo-psychoanalytic theory, quite different from Freud's. A locked cupboard at the Institute, referred to as the "poison cabinet", held the one remaining copy of Freud's works.

Felix Boehm and Carl Müller-Braunschweig, who took Eitingon's place at the head of the Institute, and the work of the Goering Institute have been the subjects of many studies of German psychoanalysis under Nazi rule. This contentious topic, which casts a shadow over German psychoanalysis to this day, will not be examined here (cf. Bohleber, 1995; Goggin & Goggin, 2001). But whatever one thinks about whether psychoanalysis could really survive in Nazi Germany, it should be acknowledged that German psychoanalysts did not display unusual resilience in standing up to the regime's demands. The Berlin Psychoanalytic Institute fell victim to the official Nazi policy of anti-Jewish discrimination at a relatively early stage. In 1938, there were still symbolic pockets of opposition to the anti-Jewish policy throughout Germany. One of these was the German Society of Art Historians, which refused at this same time to give in to the Ministry of Education's demands that it expel its Jewish members (Friedlander, 1997, p. 252).

The third Diaspora

A short time after the Nazis came to power in Germany, a Berlin psychoanalyst asked his colleague, Otto Fenichel, what questions were at the focus of psychoanalytic research. Fenichel offered a concise reply: "Whether and when the Nazis will seize power in Vienna" (Fenichel, 1998, p. 702). Fenichel reported this conversation in 1938, when he was in the middle of a long period of wandering that led him from Berlin to Vienna, and then to Prague, Oslo, and, finally, San Francisco. In 1933, it might have looked as if the storm unleashed on Germany might bypass little Austria. But, in 1934, the Jews of Vienna received a reminder that their fate was tied up with that of the

Jews of Germany. Surging unemployment—more than thirty per cent—and fear of a Nazi takeover of the Austrian political system helped the country's hard-line nationalist and anti-Semitic, but also anti-Nazi, chancellor, Engelbert Dollfuss, break the back of the socialist resistance in the city that had once been known as "Red Vienna". He arrested the leadership of the Social Democratic Party, plunging the country into civil war. But the one-party rule he set up after winning the internal conflict did not last long. On 25 July, Dollfuss was assassinated during an Austrian Nazi attack on the chancery.

Freud and his Jewish disciples faced a fate different from that of other Viennese Jewish intellectuals. Part of the reason was that most of them operated on the margins of Austrian society rather than at its centre. Only a handful of psychoanalysts were employed by the state or had senior academic appointments. Consequently, they were less vulnerable to the official anti-Semitism of the Austrian fascist regime (Stadler, 1987). Those who were active in political organisations were the first to feel the brunt of repression. Joseph Karl Friedjung, a psychoanalyst and paediatrician who represented the Social Democrats in the Vienna city council, was incarcerated at the Wallersdorf prison camp before emigrating to Palestine. Martin Pappenheim, a member of the Vienna Psychoanalytic Association since 1912 and a professor of neurology at the University of Vienna, was also imprisoned for a time, afterward taking the opportunity to defect during a visit in the Yishuv. Siegfried Bernfeld, one of the pillars of the Vienna Institute, moved to France in 1934. A year later, Felix and Helena Deutsch also left Austria. Before departing from Vienna, Bernfeld tried to warn Richard Sterba, his colleague at the Institute. "Sterba," he said, "if I'm leaving Austria now, it should be a sign for you that the time to do so has arrived. I've always known when it's time to flee" (Sterba, 1985, p. 160).

Following the arrest of Edith Jacobson in Berlin, the Vienna Psychoanalytic Association passed a resolution similar to that approved by its sister society in Germany. Members were forbidden to take part in any form of illegal political activity, and prohibited from treating "politically involved" patients (Huber, 1977). Vienna's Freudians certainly displayed political naïvety in this attempt to erect a barrier between their clinical activity and the political gales surrounding them. But, beyond that, this decision, ostensibly aimed at ensuring that psychoanalytic practice could carry on undisturbed, undermined one of their most fundamental professional and ethical norms. Paradoxically, the neutrality that the Vienna Psychoanalytic Association sought, through its attempt to prevent politics from entering the consulting room, led to a decision that marked the victory of the ideological and political over the private psychological sphere (Rolnik, 2006).

In February 1938, Hitler summoned Dollfuss's successor, Austrian Chancellor Kurt Schuschnigg, to Berchtesgaden, the same Alpine resort town where Freud completed his work on *The Interpretation of Dreams*. The German dictator delivered an ultimatum: Schuschnigg must allow the German army to march unimpeded into Vienna on 12 March. That same day, Freud wrote in his appointment book, "Finis Austriae" (Gay, 1988). That same month a unique letter was sent from Jerusalem to Berggasse 19. It was signed by the sixteen members and friends of the newly founded Palestine Psychoanalytic Society, who extended their condolences to the Professor and expressed their resolve to protect and continue his life long creation (Eitingon to Freud, 26 March 1938, in Freud & Eitingon, 2004, p. 900).

While the persecution of Jews in Austria, and in Vienna in particular, had been more systematic and crueller than Germany's anti-Semitic policies, the dismantling of the Vienna Psychoanalytic Institute began only after the Anschluss. A visit by Gestapo agents to Freud's home was the first sign that psychoanalysis in Vienna would suffer the same fate as it had in Germany. Eitingon, one of the most devoted clients of the psychoanalytic publishing house, began receiving baseless bills that looked as if they were being sent at the behest of the Nazis. He asked Jones for advice on whether to respond to them. Jones suggested paying, even though he believed that it was an attempt at blackmail. In the meantime, Eitingon enquired of his friend, the publisher Zalman Schocken, whether the latter might be able to buy up the inventory of the psychoanalytic press and remove it from Austria, so as to save the books from being destroyed. His intensive correspondence with Schocken's agents did not produce any results, in part because the Nazi authorities, despite their appetite for foreign currency, refused to negotiate. Psychoanalytic literature, Jones said, was at that time a white elephant (Jones to Eitingon, 23 March 1938, 4 April 1938, 13 May 1938, 21 May 1938: ECI).

A large number of psychoanalysts from Berlin moved to Vienna and set up practice there after the Aryanisation of the Berlin Institute.

Letter of solidarity with Freud from the members of the Palestine Psychoanalytic Society.

Even though some of them later left Austria, more psychoanalysts were working in Vienna on the eve of the Anschluss than ever before. Freud's fate was the focus of the world's attention, but the emigration of his followers was not discussed by consuls and foreign ministers. Their fate was left in the hands of Jones and Eitingon, who did their best to demonstrate an equal concern for the Freud family and for the future of the seventy other psychoanalysts who sought asylum. "I truly believe that if we leave the people to their fate at this time of crisis, something might happen and we would be responsible. Don't forget: it would be a pity for these people!" Freud's daughter wrote to

Eitingon before she and her family left Vienna on 4 June 1938 (Anna Freud to Eitingon, 22 April 1938, 19 May 1938: ECI). Jones, who in the first half of the 1930s had gained considerable skill in managing the emigration of psychoanalysts from Germany, immediately upped the frequency of his correspondence with Eitingon and Anna Freud, announcing: "We are, of course, arranging for the third Diaspora as soon as it is allowed" (Jones to Eitingon, 23 March 1938: ECI).

In August 1938, four months after Austria was annexed by the Nazis and after most members of the Vienna Psychoanalytic Association had emigrated, the Fifteenth Psychoanalytic Congress was held in Paris. The political situation, the dissolution of the first Psychoanalytic Association, that of Vienna, and the emigration of the movement's founder, exacerbated the tensions between the American Psychoanalytic Association and the International Psychoanalytic Association. Anna Freud represented her father, who was too ill to attend, and read to the attendees a passage from the third part of *Moses and Monotheism*. The passage, entitled "The advance in intellectuality", could be understood as a metaphor for the new psychoanalytic diaspora, and was perhaps the founder's last attempt to call on his followers to display solidarity with their Jewish colleagues who had been exiled from the lands where they had lived:

> Immediately after the destruction of the Temple in Jerusalem by Titus, the Rabbi Jochanan ben Zakkai asked permission to open the first Torah school in Jabneh. From that time on, the Holy Writ and intellectual concern with it were what held the scattered people together. (Freud, 1939a, p. 114)

Edward Glover, the scientific secretary of the British Psychoanalytic Society, was appointed secretary of "a subcommittee for the examination of the relations between the International Psychoanalytic Association and the American Psychoanalytic Association", He pleaded with Lawrence Kubie, secretary of the American Psychoanalytic Association, to recognise the plight of the psychoanalysts of Central Europe. The first victims were those who lacked medical training:

> It is plain, therefore, that this problem of lay analysts exiled from their own country and unable to gain a livelihood is one that cannot be burked [*sic*]. We cannot believe that you would expect us to expel such analysts from our ranks, the only motive for which would be their

political misfortune, and, since it especially concerns the American
Association, we would ask again for your friendly co-operation and
advice in finding the most satisfactory solution for it. (Glover to Kubie,
21 December 1938: ECI)

Pleas were not enough for the Americans—they demanded painful
concessions. Glover and his colleagues in the International Psychoanalytic Association had to consent to a number of provisions that
they undoubtedly would have rejected had they not needed to placate
the Americans so as to help the dozens of psychoanalysts who were
on their way to the USA. Among these concessions was their retroac-
tive acceptance of the Psychoanalytic Society of Topeka into the
American and International Psychoanalytic Associations. They also
had to give in to the American demand that former members of the
dismantled psychoanalytic institutes (those of Vienna, Prague, and
Rome) would have to join one of the other psychoanalytic institutes in
order to remain members of the movement. Another concession the
Americans extracted was that refugee psychoanalysts from Germany
would not be recognised as members of the International Psychoanalytic Association until they became members in good standing of
one of the other psychoanalytic institutes (Kubie to Franz Alexander,
10 January 1939; Kubie to Glover, 12 January 1939: ECI). These concessions, taken together, marked the end of Europe's hegemony in the
international body. The American institutes' tepid attitude toward the
newcomers from Europe did not apply only to those who lacked
medical degrees. Even though, in 1948, one third of the 150 members
of the New York Psychoanalytic Society were émigrés, for many years
after the war, the acceptance committees of the American institutes
continued to evince suspicion of German-speaking immigrants (cf.
Kirsner, 2000; Thompson, 2010). When Max Stern arrived in New
York in 1943 after completing his psychoanalytic training in Palestine,
the New York Institute's admissions board demanded that he produce
documents proving that he had, while enrolled in medical school,
come down with a stomach ulcer that had required hospitalisation
and compelled him to suspend his studies for several months. Stern
reminded the members of the board of the circumstances of his life in
Berlin and in Palestine:

As you see from this survey, there is in my life a disastrous interaction
of political catastrophes (War–Hitler–Emigration), almost hopeless

disease, and financial difficulties (inflation). I have given all the details, in order to prove that I do not use—as is quite often done—these general emergency situation for a cover of personal inadequacies. In the following, I give you the wished for details for my psychoanalytical work, starting with my training analysis with Dr. Wulff. (Stern to Edward Kornwald, 16 March 1954: ANYP)

As a student of Moshe Wulff, Stern was one of the first graduates of the Jerusalem Psychoanalytic Institute. He authored many articles on the connection between trauma and anxiety and his work was well received by the most senior theoreticians of his time—Ernest Jones, Edward Glover, and Margaret Mahler (Galef, 1976; Stern, 1988). He submitted his article on the condition from which he suffered, "The psychic etiology of the peptic ulcer", to the admissions committee (Stern to Karl Menninger, 13 April 1954: ANYP). One may presume that of all the trials and tribulations he endured in his life, one that stood out was the ten years during which his American colleagues weighed whether he was qualified to be a full member of the New York Psychoanalytic Society.

Separation and individuation

For many German-speaking psychoanalysts, this was not the first time that they had had to emigrate. More than 1.25 million Jews left Russia during the decade preceding the First World War (most of them for the USA). Many members of the first generation of Central European psychoanalysts were immigrants or the children of immigrants, having spent their childhoods in the eastern provinces of the Austrian–Hungarian Empire or in Czarist Russia. Uprootedness, in a broader socio-political rather than strictly geographical sense, must have been prevalent among many young Jews who found their home in psychoanalysis. In any case, the emigration of 1933 or 1938, under catastrophic circumstances, was, in effect, a repeat trauma, since it involved early memories of abandonment and loss of identity (cf. Grinberg & Grinberg, 1989; Haynal, 1994). While only a few—including Bruno Bettelheim and Edith Jacobson—were actually imprisoned in concentration camps, the distress experienced by most émigré psychoanalysts in the 1930s and 1940s, because of their personal histories, impinged on their psychoanalytic practice, and their experiences would occasionally reverberate, in one way or another, in their scientific work. In the USA, many of the young members of the Vienna Psychoanalytic Association became leading figures in their profession. Among them were Kurt Eissler, Heinz Hartmann, Heinz Kohut, Margaret Mahler, and Helena Deutsch, who wrote to her husband soon after she arrived to America:

> One thing is clear: *anyone*, whoever he may be – you, I, famous or obscure – must make his way here from the very beginning. The most glorious past is only a visiting card, which is more likely to cause difficulties, because it raises expectations and makes one more critical. One must close the curtains on one's European past and build only on what one *is*, what one is *capable of*. (Deutsch, 1934, cited in Roazen, 1985, p. 284)

Whether they viewed themselves as representatives of classic orthodox psychoanalysis or as post-Freudians who set off in new directions, only a handful of analysts acknowledged, in retrospect, the formative influence, on their personalities and on their work, of the experience of war, emigration, and adjustment to a new language, culture, and homeland.

A short time after arriving in the USA, Margaret Mahler, born in Budapest, began to conduct observations on the mother–child relationship, and to propose hypotheses about the way in which they shape the child's ability to enter into interpersonal relations and to experience himself as distinct from other individuals. During this period, she learnt that her mother, who had remained in Hungary, had been deported by the Germans to Auschwitz, where she was murdered shortly before the war ended. Paul Stepansky, the editor and compiler of Mahlers memoirs, suggested that Mahler's own life ordeals exemplify her theory of development, particularly its focus on separation and individuation (Stepansky, 1988). Both Hartmann and Mahler chose to be buried in Europe.

Mahler, whose research was central to the psychoanalytic discourse during the second half of the twentieth century, did not hesitate to point to her move from Europe to the USA as necessary for her ability to spread her wings and develop new ideas:

> In Vienna, I had toiled for a decade and a half under the shadow of titans. . . . It was only the stressful situation of emigration that mobilized my creativity, prompting me to bring out of hibernation ideas

that had long been slumbering, to communicate them orally, to write them down. For me, then, the stress of emigration, however genuine, however unsettling, was simultaneously the harbinger of a whole "new beginning." . . . Separation from the Vienna Psychoanalytic Institute was painful, to be sure, but it was also liberating and even exhilarating. . . . I no longer felt I was laboring under the shadow of titans. (Mahler, cited in Stepansky, 1988, p. 121)

Mahler, Hartmann, Jacobson, and Eissler were among the best known of these young analysts who emigrated at the prime of their lives. But not everyone managed to adjust to the new environment and to develop their own psychoanalytic voice in the USA. Some of them were convinced to their dying day that an unbridgeable abyss separated American and European psychoanalysis. Some of them accused American psychoanalysis of doing everything in its power to neutralise and even suppress the social–critical tinge of Freud's thought. Russell Jacoby authored a book titled *The Repression of Psychoanalysis*, in which he first revealed the correspondence of several immigrant psychoanalysts he called the "political Freudians". They constituted, he said, a psychoanalytic subculture that formed in Europe but which could not get itself heard in the central psycho-analytic discourse (Jacoby, 1983). Jacoby argued that the conditions imposed on people like Edith Jacobson and Otto Fenichel for accep-tance into the American psychoanalytic establishment required them to put aside their psychoanalytic critique of society and culture precisely when the issues they raised were, for them, most acute. Only following the publication of all of Fenichel's letters to his colleagues was it possible to comprehend the paradox integral to the Marxist–psychoanalytic critique of culture that they proposed. It was a critique that sometimes obscured the psychoanalytic perspective that they wished to broaden. Fenichel, a devout Marxist, is, none the less, revealed in his later letters to be an enthusiastic devotee of the "American way of life", with its emphasis on the external life circum-stances of the individual and its rejection of the determinism of an overpowering unconscious that controls the fate of the individual. Either way, the migration of psychoanalysis out of Central Europe threatened to put an end to the young discipline's special status, in as much as it stood at the midpoint between the objective and the subjec-tive, between scientific positivism and socio-historical constructivism.

From the 1940s, and even more so in the 1950s and 1960s, a psychoanalytic–objectivist discourse developed within American psychoanalysis. Unsurprisingly, each of the rival camps argued that it represented the most accurate interpretation of Freudianism, and also that it was producing the most vital new findings. Conservative classicalists and energetic idol-smashers proved to be more like each other than they imagined. While the dividing line on these issues did not necessarily run between immigrant and local psychoanalysts and between older and newer immigrants, the question of the status of psychoanalysis as a social and critical theory, as opposed to a naturalistic medical–scientific theory, became the central issue in the dialogue between the different approaches to the field.

The prevailing scientific and cultural disposition in the USA of the 1940s privileged the life and natural sciences. The reverberations of this preference could be observed as well in the social sciences and humanities, which almost completely abandoned any engagement with ethical and political issues. The ideal of mental health was constructed accordingly, as were the theoretical models on which psychotherapists were trained (cf. Cushman, 1995). Some went so far as to maintain that the Central European culture imported into the USA by immigrant intellectuals had a destructive effect: America had beaten Germany in the Second World War, they said, but had been overrun by the same German culture that had brought about the Nazi devastation (cf. Bloom, 1987). In literary circles, it was Vladimir Nabokov who missed no opportunity to disparage and mock the "Viennese delegation" and the "Freudian voodoo" its members spread through American culture during the 1940s and 1950s.

Endearing popular stereotypes, like the stock Hollywood character of the all-knowing psychoanalyst who pronounced his insights with a heavy German accent, did not make the lives of the immigrant Freudians any easier. Ernst Federn of Vienna, whose father Paul had been one of Freud's earliest students, had difficulty finding a place for himself in the American psychoanalytic culture. He maintained that the signature tragedy he and others like him had endured was not the loss of their homelands, status, and property, but, rather, their exile from their philosophic milieu. American psychoanalysts, he argued, did not truly understand Freud because they turned his thinking upside-down. They viewed psychoanalysis first and foremost as a therapeutic method, and only secondarily as a theory that explains the

structure of the human psyche. The American version of the unconscious was no more than a hypotheses to be tested via therapy, but the
truth was that, for Freud, the unconscious was a discovery in no need
of repeated confirmation, just as the existence of the American continent did not have to be proved each time a new settler reached its
shores (Federn, 1988).

Another immigrant who rose to prominence in America was
Bruno Bettellheim. As one of the first "analysts" of the Nazi concentration camp, his 1943 text, *Individual and Mass Behavior in Extreme
Situations*, has assumed the status of a "classic" (cf. Wünschmann,
2012). In later life, Bettelheim accused Anglo-Saxon psychoanalysis
and the monumental translation enterprise of James and Alix Strachey
(the *Standard Edition* of Freud's works) of a systematic misrepresenta-
tion of Freudian language and of divesting Freud's thought of its
humanist underpinnings (Bettelheim, 1982).

Momentous historical events would also reverberate in the biologistic ego psychology of Heinz Hartmann. In *Ego Psychology and the
Problem of Adaptation*, which Hartmann published before his move
from Vienna to the USA, he professed to remain loyal to Freud while
at the same time liberating Freudian theory from its logical contradictions (Hartmann, 1939). But the particular emphasis that Hartmann
and his colleagues placed on the defence and adaptation mechanisms
available to the ego fit remarkably well with the philosophic and
scientific optimism that Freud's American disciples had stressed ever
since they became acquainted with the theory of infantile sexuality at
the beginning of the century (cf. Hale, 1977, 1995). Ego psychology,
being another stage in the evolution of the positivist version of the
psychoanalytic idea, enabled its adherents to combine two worthy
goals: to make Freud's teachings amenable to the American scientific
tradition, and to increase the symbolic capital of the psychotherapist
by reinforcing the field's epistemological link to the natural and exact
sciences. Ego psychology, thus, took psychoanalytic theory back to the
days in which the inner psychic reality was not perceived to mirror
external reality, but, rather, as a factor that could be regulated and
adjusted according to the level of the personality's integration (cf.
Govrin, 2004). Theoretically, at least, ego psychology could offer the
psychotherapist a model in which the psyche, and not historical or
biographical circumstances, determined the individual's destiny.
Through treatment of the psyche, one could expect to see a permanent

change in the way in which external reality would be experienced and interpreted in the patient's inner world. The title Heinz Hartmann chose for his book, *Ego Psychology and the Problem of Adaptation*, which became the most quoted piece of psychoanalytic literature after Freud's works, thus refers not only to the problem of biological adaptation, which preoccupied Charles Darwin during the first half of the nineteenth century. It also addressed an existential psychological issue for Hartmann's generation, people who had lived through two world wars that seemed to bring humanity to the extreme limit of its ability to adapt. It is not unlikely that Hartmann's ego psychology seemed all the more compelling precisely because some of its leading spokespersons were immigrant psychoanalysts whose very personalities embodied the flexibility of the psyche and its adaptive capacity—if it could be freed of neurotic inhibitions. Indeed, this theory, developed by immigrant Freudians, carried on the trend toward interiorisation evident in Freud's writing after his abandonment of the seduction theory during his early years of clinical work. Above all, classical psychoanalysis, as it was dubbed in America during the 1940s, made it possible to deflect the gaze from the external reality to the psyche's mechanisms of adaptation and defence. It is possible to understand why, in the historical circumstances of the 1930s and 1940s, the search for such a theory offered immigrant psychoanalysts a certain measure of consolation.

Among the German-speaking psychoanalysts were some who resumed the ethno-cultural elements of their identities that they ostensibly left behind when they entered the tent of psychoanalysis. Some of them began taking an interest in their Jewish backgrounds. A few, as I will show in the next chapter, would decide to tie their futures to the Zionist movement. Others would develop a solid socialist identity. For still others, the tragic historical circumstances they had lived through enabled them to draw a clear boundary between their past and current lives and to reinvent themselves. Those who became accustomed to treat with empathetic charity the outspoken Christian persona adopted by Heinz Kohut when he reached the USA could not imagine that a day would come when Wolff Hirsch (Kohut's original name), who had been circumcised and who celebrated his bar mitzvah at the Stadttempel, the Great Synagogue in Vienna, and who became one of America's most celebrated psychoanalysts due to his theory of narcissism, would ask one of his colleagues to find out for him the meaning of the term *brit milah* (circumcision ceremony) used by the Jews (Strozier, 2001, p. 323). The reports of some of Kohut's Jewish colleagues raise pointed questions about the active and uncompromising "denial policy" with which this highly influential developer of self psychology greeted every attempt to confront him with his Jewish origins.

Kohut may have been an extreme case; however, for many émigré analysts any discourse linking their theoretical ideas to personal war experiences was unacceptable. Such thoughts were seldom reflected upon in published articles. They were usually left for private talks with colleagues or to interviews given by the analysts towards the end of their life. Discussing one's war experience of migration, separation, and loss was like discussing one's Jewishness in the context of science. It was taboo.

Were analysts apprehensive about linking their theories to their personal histories lest they undercut their scientific claims for objectivity? Were they concerned that by giving credence to the impact of the personal war experience on their theoretical outlook they would have displaced their own gaze from their patient's internal reality and unconscious phantasy, or, worse still, succumb to the seductions of "trauma-centric" theories? In a recent book, Kuriloff (2012) points out that any discourse that would emphasise historical reality and self-experience in the making of theory could potentially evoke anxiety in the analytic community. Such discourse would disclose the authors' subjectivity, thereby undermining her truth claims, or be identified as the return of the repressed of psychoanalysis: a return to Freud's "seduction theory".

Fortunately, after the war, the task of juxtaposing history and psychoanalysis was no longer a prerogative of psychoanalysts, who often mistake the historicisation of their theory with its postmodernist relativisation. A case in point was the work of neo-Marxist refugees aligned with the New York New School for Social Research, who jointly authored *The Authoritarian Personality* (Adorno, Frenkel-Brunswik, Levinson, & Sanford, 1950). For these former Frankfurt School intellectuals, the link between psychoanalysis and anti-Semitism became, once and for all, inextricable (cf. Bohleber, 1997; Frosh, 2005; Jay, 1973). It is as imperative as ever, wrote Adorno in 1959, to arm ourselves with an "exact and undiluted knowledge of Freudian theory" to enable us to diagnose the soil that nurtures the hatred of others—the same hatred that is in turn directed at psycho-analysis. And "not just because Freud was a Jew", Adorno continues, "but because psychoanalysis consists precisely of a critical *self-reflection* that puts anti-Semites into a seething rage" (Adorno, 1986).

Notes

1. The Institute's reports cite hysteria as the most common diagnosis among women (129 female patients were treated for hysteria during the Polyclinic's years of operation), while obsessive neurosis was the second most common diagnosis, among both men and women (Eitingon, 1923; Oberndorf, 1926).
2. Translated by Margarete Münsterberg, www.aol.bartleby.com/177/55. html, accessed 21 December 2010.
3. The manuscript was kept at the Psychoanalytic Institute in Jerusalem until it was transferred, in 1970, to the Freud Archive in Washington.
4. In 1928, shortly after the inauguration of the hospital, an adjacent street was named after Haim Eitingon (Kreuter, 1992).
5. Among Eitingon's letters are two invitations by Albert Einstein to attend lectures in his house by the two Zionist leaders (Einstein's letters to Eitingon, 8 February 1924; 4 January 1925, ECI).
6. The complete list is reproduced in Rolnik, 2004.
7. In an an earlier letter to Eitingon (23 November 1930), Freud comments on Einstein's "complete misunderstanding of psychoanalysis" (cf. Grubrich-Simitis, 1995).
8. "Ich bin der sicheren Überzeugung, daß seine [Eitingon's] Loslösung von der Stätte seiner bisherigen Tätigkeit nur einen Zwischenfall und kein Ende seiner für unsere Sache unschätzbaren Leistung bedeutet".
9. For Ernst Jones' troubling perspective on "the psychology of the Jewish question" (and the Jewish nose) see Jones ([1947]1974).

CHAPTER FOUR

Migration and interpretation

"I heard about the opening of the psychoanalysis institute in Jerusalem and I permit myself to request your Excellency to recommend for me a psychoanalytic in Tel Aviv who can take care of me and help me get rid of the difficult situation that reaches the point of destroying my nerves. . . . Awful fears surround me. All the little things that a normal person doesn't pay attention to, with me are great dangers . . . I get mad at every little thing. . . . I don't talk to people because of my inner anger and because I am always busy with my own thinking. . . . I can pay for the first times ten *grush* for each séance and afterward when the situation of my problems gets better and I work each day and earn money, I will pay more and more. . . . I have a fluent command of Russian. Hebrew I don't know so well and this letter I am writing with the help of a dictionary. . . . I hope that Herr Doctor [Eitingon] will not leave my request without listening and will answer in the closest possible time"

(Mr A to Dr Eitingon, 1934)

The wave of Jewish immigration to Palestine between 1929 and 1939, called, in Zionist historiography, the Fifth Aliyah, increased the population of the Yishuv from 175,000 to 475,000.

Although only twenty per cent of the new arrivals were German Jews, the Germans' influence on the Jewish community in Palestine was striking. Many of them were highly educated professionals and businessmen, who formed a middle class of a new type, differing from that established by the Polish Jews, who had arrived between 1924 and 1929 as part of the Fourth Aliyah. The Germans differed from the Yishuv's leaders, most of whom came from Eastern Europe and whose Zionism was heavily coloured by socialism. The newcomers adhered to German Zionism, which, despite its support of a Jewish settlement in Palestine, retained deep connections with German language and culture and had seen Palestine mainly as a sanctuary for persecuted East European Jews. Between 1933 and 1939, 650 Jewish physicians emigrated from Germany to Palestine. Another wave of a few hundred from Austria followed. But the refugee physicians who arrived at this time in Palestine, among them German-speaking mental health professionals, were not a monolithic group. Some of them, while arriving from Germany, originally hailed from Eastern Europe, or had been born in Germany and Austria–Hungary to parents who had emigrated from the Pale of Settlement. These doctors had the potential to bridge the ideological gap between the Yishuv's new German and established Eastern European physicians (cf. Geter, 1979; Levi, 1988; Niederland, 1985, 1988, 1996; Sela-Shefi, 2006; Zalashik & Davidovitch, 2009).

The second, decisive phase in the establishment of psychoanalysis in pre-state Israel thus began with the onset of the Fifth Aliyah. Although, like previous streams of immigration, the newcomers mostly came from Eastern Europe, the migrants also included some 90,000 German-speaking Jews who fled Central Europe following the Nazis' rise to power in 1933 and Germany's annexation of Austria and the Sudetenland. While the political circumstances that drove them to leave Europe hardly require comment, the way they became integrated into the Yishuv was somewhat different, and depended significantly on the ideological background from which they came. The previous arrivals viewed the German newcomers—whom they derisively referred to as "Yekkes"—as bourgeois and lacking in ideological conviction (cf. Dachs, 2005). As such, they were perceived as potentially dangerous to the Zionist cause. The British authorities had established an annual quota for Jewish immigration, and, with the number of available immigration permits (called "certificates") severely limited, German–Jewish doctors were sometimes accused of filling up the quota and preventing "real" Zionists from coming. Some of the German-speaking "New Zionists" adopted the Zionist idea as a direct result of the discrimination and displacement they had endured in their countries of origin. Highly motivated to integrate themselves into the Yishuv, these immigrants adapted to life in Palestine quite well. The move was much more difficult for the so-called "old-time-Zionists", that minority among the German-speaking immigrants who had absorbed, in their youth, an idealised form of Central European Zionism. They found it hard to reconcile that dream with the reality they encountered. This minority group developed an overwhelmingly critical attitude toward the Eastern European domination of the Yishuv, and sought means to assert their unique, Central European brand of Zionism. "Zionism", claimed Arnold Zwieg, "is a disease one can recover from only in Palestine" (Heid, 2005, p. 36). Another group of German-speaking immigrants lacked any allegiance to Zionism whatsoever. They viewed themselves merely as refugees, or even exiles, having come to Palestine because they had no other choice. They fully intended to return to Europe once the danger had passed. Members of this group—among them writers such as Arnold Zweig, Max Brod, Elsa Lasker-Schüller, and the much younger Wolfgang Hildesheimer—also perceived themselves as part of a worldwide "humanist front" against German fascism. In short, they were self-defined Germans in exile rather than Jews returning to their homeland. Nearly all were outspoken anti-Zionists; most were intellectuals; some were devout Communists. All of them recoiled from Jewish nationalism in its Eastern European form, and from the new Hebrew culture promoted by the earlier arrivals. The Germans gave voice to their cultural isolation at sophisticated cultural evenings, and, in criticism, they published in *Orient*, a German-language periodical, and, mostly, by pining for Europe (cf. Gordon, 2004; Grab, 1989; Lavsky, 1996, 1998; Viest, 1977).

A small notice in the *Palestine Post* informed the public of the opening of the Psychoanalytic Institute in Jerusalem. A large quantity of pictures and furniture, all belonging to Eitingon, had been shipped from the Berlin Institute to Jerusalem. The Berlin Institute's library, which consisted largely of Eitingon's huge private collection, reached Jerusalem intact, as did the Institute's files from Berlin. These material objects bolstered the self-esteem of the founders of the Jerusalem

Arnold Zweig: "Zionism is a disease one can recover from only in Palestine."

Institute. As they saw it, the endeavour that ended abruptly and painfully in Berlin would now be carried forward in Jerusalem. The implication was that the Berlin Institute, though still operating, was no longer really a part of the psychoanalytic movement, neither formally nor in practice.

As members of a subculture within the intellectual emigration from central Europe, the psychoanalysts were confronted with circumstances offering them very limited room for manoeuvre. In contrast with fellow intellectuals whose integration was facilitated by the mediation of academic institutions, and unlike colleagues who had emigrated to other countries and were absorbed by well-established psychoanalytic societies, the Yishuv's émigré psychoanalysts were forced to start by constructing the same framework in which they had exerted their European influence (cf. Ash & Söllner, 1996; Fermi, 1968; Hassler & Wertheimer, 1997; Jay, 1986; Peters, 1992). The founders of the Palestine Psychoanalytic Society shared two biographical traits that would do much to shape the profession as it was practised there during its early years: all of them were physicians, and the great majority had resided, at one point or another during their lives, in Russia or the Soviet Union. It should be kept in mind that about twenty per cent of the half million Jews living in Germany when the Nazis came to power were foreign nationals, not German citizens. When the moment came to leave Germany, the ethno-geographical traditions and historical–individual memories that these immigrants had brought with them from their childhood homes had a major influence on their choice of destination (cf. Aschheim, 1982; Zimmerman, 1992). Furthermore, this group's capacity for absorption into the Yishuv and their ability to spread psychoanalysis beyond the small kernel of German speakers who had been acquainted with the field in Europe was largely ascribable to their command of the Yiddish and Russian languages. The fact that the founders of the Palestine Psychoanalytic Society had a natural connection with the *Ostjuden*, the Eastern European Jews who made up the bulk of the Jewish immigrants to Palestine during the first four *aliyot*, and not just with the *Westjuden*, the German Jews of the Fifth Aliyah to whose ranks they formally belonged, made it much easier for them to find their place in the Yishuv. The native language of Anna Smilansky, Moshe Wulff, Ilja Schalit, Max Eitingon, and Fania Lowetzky (sister of the philosopher Lev Shestov, who joined the group somewhat later) was Russian. The years they spent as students in Marburg, Freiburg, or Heidelberg, or as psychoanalysts in Zurich, Vienna, and Berlin, did not weaken their connection to Russian culture and Jewish ethnicity in its East European version. Testimony to such close and friendly relations and to ties to Zionism can be found in the "private holiday" that the members of the Psychoanalytic Society's founding members celebrated every 3 February, a tradition that began in 1904 in Marburg. Then, as students, sitting together in the room of one of their number following the Kishinev pogrom, they swore allegiance to the Zionist idea (Smeliansky & Nacht, 1941). They did so at a time of crisis for the Zionist movement, in the year that followed the divisive Sixth Zionist Congress in Basel at which Herzl's proposal to establish a Jewish colony in East Africa was rejected, largely because of opposition from the delegations from Russia and Eastern Europe. It demonstrates the strong sense of solidarity that shaped the world-view of these immigrant psychoanalysts in the years in which they received their training and developed their professional identities in the German-speaking world.

But most of the German immigrants of the Fifth Aliyah, the psychoanalysts among them, had not been involved in Jewish national activities prior to their arrival in Palestine. In now declaring themselves Zionists, were they simply seeking to present, after the fact, their decision to immigrate in 1933 as an act of free choice or as the realisation of a long-standing youthful dream? From a historical perspective, it seems that, in this case, the issue extends beyond the debate over the extent to which the Land of Israel was central in the minds of the German-speaking Jews who immigrated to Palestine in the wake of the Nazi takeover (cf. Lavsky, 1998). These psychoanalysts' childhood memories and ties to the members of the earlier *aliyot*, along with the Central European identities they acquired during their studies and adult lives, would prove to be functional in important ways. It enabled them to view themselves as having "made *aliyah*"—to have come to the Land of Israel out of Zionist conviction and identification with the Jewish national collective, rather than having merely "immigrated" because they had no other choice. But, beyond that, it also facilitated the success of psychoanalysis in the Yishuv of the 1930s and 1940s. Most members of this small group of psychoanalysts could present, in addition to the symbolic cultural and intellectual assets they brought with them, a Zionist genealogy that was hardly open to doubt. Anna Smiliansky (Smilansky), for example, was a native of Kiev, and in 1912 went to Palestine for a year; she belonged to the circle of Ahad Ha'am, founder of "Cultural Zionism", a group that also included her brother, the iconic writer and farmer of the First Aliyah, Moshe Smilansky. Odessa-born Moshe Wulff, who joined the Vienna Psychoanalytic Society in 1911, did not need to exert himself to convince the pioneers of the Yishuv's agricultural and labour settlements of the large Russian and Zionist heart that beat within him ever since his move from Moscow to Berlin. Wulff's patients in the latter city at the end of the 1920s had included several members of the HaShomer HaTza'ir youth movement, who would later view him, not Max Eitingon, as the Yishuv's leading psychoanalytic authority. Like many immigrants' societies, Jewish society in the Land of Israel hungrily sought out symbolic hierarchies, ethnic stratifications, and ideological dichotomies. It was only natural, then, that Wulff would assume, upon his arrival, the proletarian Russian guise of his youth in Odessa and Moscow, so as to distinguish himself from his "bourgeois Yekke" colleagues. Ilja Schalit, who originally came from Riga and who began his medical studies at the army academy in St. Petersburg, joined the German Psychoanalytic Society in 1929 and worked for only a brief time at the Berlin Institute before heading for Palestine (Wulff, 1953).

In a letter to Freud, written shortly after his immigration, Eitingon displayed a determination not to let historical and societal circumstances interfere excessively with working to entrench psychoanalysis in Palestine. "The intensive development that characterizes this place forces us to follow our own private path and not become absorbed too early in public life," he declared, adding that, "after all, it is the same people, with the same problems we are used to dealing with, as clearly neither Orthodox Jews nor Arabs are suitable in any way for psychoanalysis" (dated 25 April 1935, in Freud & Eitingon, 2004, pp. 887–888). Blinding himself to the two "Others" of Jewish nationalism (the religiously observant and the indigenous Arab population), Eitingon did not hesitate to deploy the same strategy used by the shapers of the new Zionist self.

Under normal circumstances, the processing of the new Palestine Psychoanalytic Society's application for membership in the International Psychoanalytic Association would have taken years. But the new society was rapidly accepted, creating a sense of continuity that was crucial to the émigré analysts in their new environment (Eitingon to Glover, 31 October 1934: ECI). The casting of the Institute in Jerusalem as the avatar of the Berlin Institute had a great impact on both the analysts and their patients, all of whom felt that they had created for themselves, under the tragic circumstances that had led to their arrival in Palestine, a "Little Berlin" that assisted in their acclimatisation to their new home. The psychoanalysts were no longer merely "agents of knowledge"—they had become the embodiment of psychoanalytic knowledge as such. The Jerusalem Institute's bylaws contained an unusually draconian provision aimed at ensuring that none would use the name of Freud's theory in vain. It stipulated that any member who wished to give a public lecture on any topic relating to psychoanalysis was to inform the Institute's governing committee in advance and receive the committee's consent (Statutes of the Palestine Psychoanalytic Society: ECI).

"The Psychoanalytic Institute in Jerusalem is the direct descendant and heir of the Berlin Institute", stated a report issued by Margarete Brandt to mark the seventh anniversary of the former, "which arrived in this country together with the original spirit, the love and admiration for Freud, and an 'orthodox' stance on the main principles of his teachings"(Brandt, 1941). Even people of the Old Yishuv—the traditional religious community that predated the Zionist influx—who came to receive treatment at the institute evinced an understanding of psychoanalysis. The Freudian system of dream symbolism and interpretation spoke directly to them, and the mystical explanations they offered for neurotic conditions, such as possession by a demon, could be used as an analogy for psychoanalytic concepts. These pious Jews soon overcame their initial disappointment at the fact that these new soul healers did not offer them charms and magic potions. But this was not new, Brandt wrote in her report. In Berlin, too, psychoanalysts had had to cope with a similar kind of disappointment over their not providing somatic treatments of the type that the psychiatric profession never tired of offering. In response, the Yishuv psychoanalysts displayed flexibility and often agreed to incorporate hypnotic therapy into "classic" psychoanalytic therapy, thus significantly shortening the length of treatment.

For quite a few German-speaking immigrants, psychoanalysis, whether in its "applied" critical–cultural guise or in its clinical–therapeutic practice, served as a substitute focus of identity. The analysis that Arnold Zweig underwent with Ilja Schalit in Haifa did not weaken his firm ties to Europe, or to enamour him of Zionism. He had a difficult time in Palestine, and was especially pained by the refusal of the local literary community to accept a writer working in German into their ranks (cf. Gordon, 2004; Worman, 1970). In articles in *Orient*, in letters to Freud, and in the two novels he began writing during his Palestinian sojourn, *De Vriendt Goes Home* and *A Costly Dream*, he displayed his dim view of the encounters between socialism and Zionism and between Zionism and psychoanalysis. His inspiration for the first was the murder of Jacob Israel de Haan, a Dutch-Jewish poet who came to Palestine and eventually became a spokesman for the anti-Zionist ultra-Orthodox community, both in Palestine and in Europe. De Haan was accused of having homosexual relations with Arab boys and was assassinated in 1924 by two members of the Haganah, the Yishuv's defence organisation. We have already met the protagonist of *A Costly Dream*, Dr Richard Karthaus (his name means "house of cards"), the German-speaking neurologist and psycho-analyst who is disabused of his Zionist dream and returns to Europe.

Another such German Jew was Wolfgang Hildesheimer. Born in Hamburg, from a young age this writer could not fully identify with his parents' determination to settle in Palestine. The son of Arnold Hildesheimer, a chemist and industrialist and grandson of Rabbi Azriel Hildesheimer, the moderniser of Orthodox Judaism in Germany, he returned to Germany, served as an interpreter at the Nuremberg trials, and became one of the founders of Gruppe 47, a German literary movement. "It may well have been the psycho-analysis that I underwent during my youth in Jerusalem," he wrote, "that enabled me to avoid the psychosis of the refugee and the tendency to accuse all Germans collectively" (Hildesheimer, 1984, p. 219). Hildesheimer also said of his experience that "I couldn't profit from this analysis throughout my life, but neither could I mentally conceive of myself at all without it" (cited in Buchholz, 2008, p. 150). This biographer of Mozart believed that psychoanalysis had provided him crucial insights into the nature of the human mind, especially into creative phenomena and processes of aesthetic transformation.

The Yishuv's changing demographic profile does not seem to fully explain the considerable interest in psychoanalytic treatment at this time. Certainly, the growing number of Jews of Central European origin, people who had been acquainted with psychoanalysis before their arrival in Palestine, explained part of this expansion, but it was hardly the sole cause. Psychoanalysis posited that the harshness and pain of the real world was not dissociated from one's inner, mental, symbolic world. It claimed that a person could better cope with the travails of his times by familiarising himself with his inner world and transforming it into something less intimidating. Paradoxically, as Jewish life was rendered frightening and precarious by an essentialist fascist ideology that rejected the dynamic concept of the mind, psychoanalysis offered immigrants to Palestine a way to re-examine the borders between inside and out, between their inner fantasy worlds and outward reality.

As mandated by both their psychoanalytic and Zionist self-con-ceptions, the psychoanalysts who came to Palestine did not view their relocation as stressful in and of itself. Margarete Brandt claimed that, among her patients, she discerned no connection between the

Wolfgang Hildesheimer: "I couldn't conceive myself without psychoanalysis."

development of neurosis and the fact that they were immigrants. A person who links her mental suffering to immigration would not, in any case, seek out treatment, she maintained (Brandt, 1941). Her colleague, Ilja Schalit, did not even use the word "immigration" in the address he gave to mark the Jerusalem Institute's seventh anniversary. He referred to the circumstances under which he and his colleagues arrived in Palestine as "the geographical vicissitudes of psychoanalysis" (Brandt, 1941). Arnold Zweig offered a slightly more analytic position in a guest lecture on "Immigration and neurosis" (1937) that he gave at the Psychoanalytic Institute. The experience of immigration and expulsion, Zweig argued, had been deeply etched in the Jewish psyche ever since the destruction of the Temple, and it should be presumed to be responsible for the fact that the Jews had an inborn predilection for mental illnesses, and for giving those around them an impression of social and political instability. The Jewish immigrant was much more dangerous to those around him than was a non-Jewish immigrant, Zweig argued, because he had an instinct that propelled him into the grasp of socialist–revolutionary movements. He attributed the special difficulty that immigrants like him had in adjusting to their new circumstances to memories of the expulsion from the paradise of their childhoods—separation from the mother's body or eviction from the parental bedroom. Zweig took the same opportunity to express his scepticism about the likelihood of a "Zionist solution" to the Jewish nation's chronic migration problem. Palestine, he told his fellow psychoanalysts, was a sham solution. It could never take in all the world's Jews, and its immigrants were led astray by the delusion that their wanderings had reached an end (Eitingon to Freud, 24 January 1937: Freud & Eitingon, 2004, p. 894; Eitingon to Zweig, 6 January 1937: AZA). In 1948, Zweig returned to East Berlin with his family.

Fit candidates

Relations between Moshe Wulff and Eitingon were tense, and would impinge on the group's work. The distance from Europe clouded the disparity in the status of these two pupils of Freud. From the moment they arrived in Palestine, Wulff viewed himself as Eitingon's equal and felt that the time had come for him to spread his wings and not labour in the other's shadow. Wulff was a prolific writer and published frequently. By the time of his arrival in Palestine, he already had more than a hundred articles to his credit, a bibliography that testified to the broadness of his horizons, the breadth of his knowledge, and his clinical sensitivity (cf. Kloocke, 2002). His work would later be cited by leading theoreticians in the field. The papers on infantile sexuality that Wulff published in 1912 earned him a footnote in Freud's *Totem and Taboo*. Donald Winnicott, who was not known for attaching detailed bibliographies to his writings, made a point of stating that the concept of the "transitional object" that he introduced in 1953 was a development of the "fetish object" that Wulff had proposed several years before (Winnicott, 1953; Wulff, 1946). At the beginning of the 1940s, Wulff sent to the central psychoanalytic journal, from Palestine, an article that offered one of the first detailed case reports of homosexuality. Interestingly, the homosexual fantasies of his patient, a married man of Russian–Jewish origin living in a kibbutz, had undergone an outward change since his arrival in Palestine; in the place of Russian peasants, Arabs now appeared, or rather the simple fellaheen of the Arab village (Wulff, 1942). Wulff also engaged in interdisciplinary psychoanalytic writing, producing works in which he traced the psychological roots of Jewish customs (Woolf [Wulff], 1945). He also published popular pieces in Hebrew and missed no opportunity, in the city or in his travels around the country, to give lectures on psychoanalysis to school and preschool teachers. Eitingon griped in one of his letters to Anna Freud, that Wulff acted as if he alone could provide the entire Yishuv's psychoanalytic needs (dated 12 March 1935: ECI). Eitingon, for his part, acted as if he had no need to prove anything to anyone but his master Freud. He devoted all of his not inconsiderable talents as a writer to the internal politics of the psychoanalytic movement, generally preferring to consort with the upper crust of the Yishuv and the Fifth Aliyah leadership. At the end of the 1930s, the Palestine Psychoanalytic Society was but a step away from being plunged into the same kind of civil war that had nearly destroyed the London, French, New York, and Vienna societies in their early years. The climax of the tension between the two men came at the end of the 1930s, when Wulff set up an independent organisation, the David Eder Psychoanalytic Institute, in Tel Aviv. Even though the new institute did not claim to offer full psychoanalytic training, and was not affiliated to the International Psychoanalytic Association, it served as a reminder both of its founder's standing and of his destructive potential (Golan to Fenichel, 15 September 1938: Fenichel, 1998, p. 982; curriculum of the David Eder Institute for Psychoanalysis: David Idelson Collection, AJE). Eitingon tirelessly sought to appease Wulff. Thanks to Eitingon's diplomatic skills, the small psychoanalytic community was able to present, outwardly at least, a unified front. At times of crisis, when Wulff's wounded dignity seemed liable to sabotage a scientific meeting, the secretary of the Psychoanalytic Society would call on Eitingon to write a conciliatory letter, preferably in Russian, and remind him that the two Russian-born psychoanalysts had more in common than they had differences:

But now, Moshe Vladimirovitch, I truly hope that you won't think that your presence at our meetings is not important. After all, we all work for the same goal, and your cooperation is especially important to us, and it really is not our fault that things are not going well. You certainly know the dates of the Society's meetings, and you must make sure to notify us when you are unable to make it to the meetings. We are not, after all, just anyone who casually invites you in, we are rather the Institute among whose members you number, just like the rest of us, and we might expect that you display a warm attitude and even take an active part in it. I very much hope that at our next meeting, on April 13 in Tel Aviv, I will have the opportunity to speak with you about this. (Eitingon to Wulff, 24 March 1935: ECI)

The Hebrew-language newspapers reported the fate of Freud's family following the annexation of Austria, and this further increased the visibility of the immigrant analysts working in Mandate Palestine. Eitingon attributed the large rise in the number of persons who sought therapy in the second half of 1938 to this publicity (Eitingon's Report for 1936–1938: ECI). The Kristallnacht pogroms of 8 November 1938 were especially brutal in Leipzig. Eitingon reported to Freud that the Great Synagogue built by his family had been destroyed, and that the Jewish hospital that the family had contributed to the city had been burned down (letter dated 12 December 1938, in Freud & Eitingon, 2004, pp. 912–913). He made every effort to obtain immigration certificates to Palestine for all of the Freud family's acquaintances, and was also involved in attempts to obtain one for Ernst, Freud's youngest son. A Jewish Agency committee examined the younger Freud's expertise in "Jewish and Zionist matters", quizzing him about Jewish history, the geography of the Land of Israel, and Zionist issues. They did not form a very good impression: they reported that "the boy barely knew who Herzl was" (Martin Freud to Eitingon, 16 July 1935: ECI).

The Jewish community in Palestine did not like to think of itself as but a sanctuary for refugees. Martin Pappenheim was a case in point. In 1933, he was under consideration for the post of director of a psychiatric clinic planned to open in the Tel Aviv area. A professor of neurology at the University of Vienna (the first person in this field with an academic appointment who applied for immigration to Palestine), Pappenheim was a long-standing member of the Vienna Psychoanalytic Society and served as the Austrian representative to the

International Mental Hygiene Society (Else Pappenheim: "Martin Pappenheim—a biography", unpublished manuscript). He seemed to be the ideal candidate for the post. He submitted to the Tel Aviv municipality a detailed programme in which he argued for establishing an open psychiatric ward that would counteract the humiliation that had traditionally been attached to psychiatric hospitalisation. Such a ward, he claimed, would make it much easier for many in need to seek out treatment in the early stages of their disease (Martin Pappenheim to Israel Rokach, 9 August 1933: TAC).

But members of the Jewish community of Vienna wrote letters to Tel Aviv officials warning that Pappenheim's motives were "non-Zionist". As a result, Mayor Meir Dizengoff and Deputy Mayor Israel Rokach cut short their contacts with the candidate. Pappenheim, the letters asserted, had disassociated himself from Vienna's Jewish community; some alleged that he had intended to convert to Christianity. Still others suggested that, had the Tel Aviv opportunity not presented itself, his sympathy for Communism would have led him to try his luck in Russia, a sure sign of an absence of genuine Zionist engagement (Kermenzky and Schnirer to Meir Dizengoff, 28 September 1933; 2 October 1933: TAC). Once these rumours began to circulate, not even such leading citizens as the poet Chaim Nachman Bialik, the senior arbiter of the Yishuv's cultural life, and Chief Rabbi Avraham Yitzhak HaKohen Kook—to name just two men who had been Pappenheim's patients and who intervened on his behalf—could convince the city administration that it was about to make a huge mistake (Heilperin to Rokach, "on behalf of Prof. Pappenheim's friends and admirers", 15 April 1934: TAC). The first Hebrew city broke off its negotiations with Pappenheim and declared, in an open letter to *Die Neue Welt*, a Zionist newspaper in Vienna, that it was committed to "maintaining no contact with those considered traitors to our people" (Meir Dizengoff to the editors of *Die Neue Welt*, 4 October 1933: TAC).

Pappenheim's story demonstrates what difficulties Central European intellectuals and physicians faced in their contacts with the Yishuv leadership. The latter tended to see the German-speaking immigrants, notwithstanding their reputation as excellent doctors, legal experts, or hard-working labourers, as second-class Zionists, and accordingly kept them out of public institutions and organisations (Niederland, 1985). The few analysts who sought haven in Palestine had first to present themselves before Eitingon, so that he might evaluate "their level of suitability for the unique conditions of this country" (Eitingon to Jones, 4 May 1938: BPS).

Five years after founding the Palestine Psychoanalytic Society and after establishing his public position, Eitingon felt confident enough to apply to the Mandate administration to ask that it permit the entry of several psychoanalysts who wanted to immigrate. He told the British High Commissioner about the plight of the Vienna Institute's faculty members, who had been stripped of all they had—students, patients, books, journals, and their publishing house. He presented the plan that he and Jones had drafted for the absorption of some seventy Jewish psychoanalysts from Vienna, along with another twenty of their students who were at various stages of their training. The five psychoanalysts he wished to invite to Palestine, he claimed, would not have any deleterious effect on the status of local physicians, and there was no reason for concern that they would become public burdens, since the local psychoanalytic society would take full responsibility for them (Eitingon to Eric Mills, the British Commissioner for Migration and Statistics, 17 May 1938: ECI). Jones, in London, set up a meeting with Chaim Weizmann, the president of the British Zionist Federation, and his deputy, Selig Brodetsky, to find out whether they could help to obtain certificates for the prospective immigrants. The two Zionist leaders said that the only way for the psychoanalysts to qualify for certificates was under the "private initiative" category established by the Mandate authorities; the requirements for applying for such a visa included a deposit in the sum of £1,000 (Jones to Eitingon, 30 March 1939; 29 April 1939: ECI). Eitingon had no doubt that the practitioners would be able to make their own living, and he was prepared to put up personal guarantees to enable them to receive immigration certificates. The question was only how to direct the "right psychoanalysts" to Palestine. Jones reassured Eitingon that, in Britain, "the Home Office has throughout acted on our recommendation about the desirability or not of granting a permit to various emigrants to practice psychoanalysis in this country".[1] By 1939, the British Psychoanalytic Society took up thirty-nine immigrants (Ash, 1991, p. 111).

The question of the suitability of immigrant psychoanalysts in Palestine also came up in the correspondence between Eitingon and Anna Freud. "I again turn to you with an impossible request," the latter wrote to Eitingon, "but one cannot simply get up and leave here in a time of trouble and leave the people behind. . . . In the end something will happen, and then we will all be at fault" (Anna Freud to Eitingon, 19 May 1938: FCLC).[2] Jones' letters were much more practical: "[I]n addition to analytical capacity, the personal suitability for various countries has to be carefully studied. This is especially the case with England and Palestine" (Jones to Eitingon, 4 May 1938: ECI). Jones' experience in dealing with earlier immigrants convinced him that the "quarrelsome Central Europeans" tend to remain their home habits in other countries (Jones to Eitingon, 3 July 1934: ECI). New arrivals in America, he wrote to Brill, develop a peculiarly rebellious psychology: "It simply means that the son–father complex is still unresolved and keeps being imparted into all sorts of unnecessary situations" (Jones to Brill, 20 June 1933: BPS).

Senior members of the profession who had been Freud's students during Vienna's Social Democratic era, people who could have done much to enhance the status of psychoanalysis in the Yishuv's medical and pedagogic circles, did not go to Palestine. Heinrich Zvi Winnik, born in Romania and a member of HaShomer HaTza'ir, preferred to move from Berlin to Vienna to complete his training. He arrived in Palestine in 1942 and served in a number of key posts in which he set up Israel's mental health system. He also founded the first psychiatric journal published in the country (Edelstein, 1982). Even Siegfried Bernfeld and Otto Fenichel, enthusiastic supporters of HaShomer HaTza'ir in the 1920s, whose ideological commitment to socialism and Zionism made them ideal candidates for the Palestine Psychoanalytic Society, preferred the European or American diasporas to the Jewish homeland. The correspondence conducted by Sigmund and Anna Freud with Eitingon and Jones leaves no room for doubt. With the exception of a handful of individuals like Gershon and Gerda Barag, Aharon Isserlin, Friedrich Rothschild, Daniel Dreyfuss, and Erich Gumbel, all novice practitioners who had not yet completed their training, Palestine was a refuge of last resort for experienced Central European psychoanalysts. They considered it, in most cases, only after their efforts to reach other destinations failed. The exceptions were the paediatrician Karl Joseph Friedjung and the neurologist Martin Pappenheim, both senior members of the Vienna Psychoanalytic Society. Theodor Reik came to Palestine for a visit in 1937 and gave a lecture to the Jerusalem group, but his critical attitude toward Jewish religious practices, as expressed in his books, did not speak to Eitingon, whose fondness for Jewish tradition grew after his arrival in Israel. Even more so, Reik was liable to sabotage the neutral and non-subversive image that Eitingon sought to construct for psychoanalysis in the Yishuv (Jones to Eitingon, 28 March 1938: ECI; cf. Rolnik, 2008a). Some of the immigrants who arrived in Palestine went on, after a short time, to other places. This was the case, for example, with Max Stern, Kilian Bluhm, and Ellen Simon. Else Pappenheim, Martin's daughter, spent only a short time in Palestine. Because she left Vienna before completing her medical studies, Anna Freud and Eitingon both agreed that they should help her go elsewhere, so she, too, went on to the USA and became a member of the New York Psychoanalytic Society (Anna Freud to Eitingon, 22 May 1938; Else Pappenheim to Eitingon, 3 February 1939; Martin Pappenheim to Eitingon, 4 July 1938: ECI). Eitingon was also attuned to the needs of young psychoanalysts who had not yet completed their training. Daniel Dreyfuss, who had, just prior to the Nazi takeover, undergone analysis with Frieda Fromm-Reichmann in Heidelberg, received from her a letter of recommendation that included a few words about his psychoanalytic and Zionist background. Dreyfuss suggested to Eitingon that he could be of use, given his ability to act as a bridge between neurology and psychoanalysis: "I hope to be able to point out some fundamental problems of epilepsy as an expression of narcissistic neurosis and in doing so to expand greatly those observations about traumatic neurosis made by Freud in *Beyond the Pleasure Principle*" (Dreyfuss to Eitingon, 15 January, 15 February, 28 May 1934; Fromm-Reichmann to Eitingon, 7 July 1934: ECI; cf. Dreyfuss, 1936). Fromm-Reichmann, who at that time was planning to travel to Palestine for an extended visit to her cousin, Esther Agnon, went so far as to propose to Eitingon that, during her stay in the country, she continue with Dreyfuss's analysis (undated letter from Fromm-Reichman to Eitingon: ECI). The young people who worked under his guidance were a special pleasure for Eitingon. He was proudest of Erich Gumbel, the first graduate of the Jerusalem Institute. In a letter to Freud, Eitingon forecast a great future for the young man, who indeed became one of Israel's most esteemed psychoanalysts (dated 7 May 1939, in Freud & Eitingon, 2004, pp. 925–926).

Eitingon asked to see Anna Freud's list of psychoanalysts who were considering a move to Palestine, "so that I can judge for myself

if any of them can adjust to the peculiar conditions of this country"
(Eitingon to Jones, 4 May 1938: ECI). He requested that she help him
search out "fit candidates". She took on the role of Jones' and
Eitingon's classification officer with mixed feelings and asked that her
deliberations on the subject of immigration would be kept secret
(Anna Freud to Jones, May 1938: BPS). She did not always see eye-to-
eye with the latter about his criteria, but did her best to supply him
with a psychological and sociological profile of the psychoanalysts
who were prepared to move to the country. During the first half of
1938, the only psychoanalyst in Vienna who was prepared to consider
immigration to Palestine was Bertha Gruenspan, and that only "if the
matter of the capital necessary for this purpose is arranged for her and
if her attempts to emigrate to South Africa fail". Anna Freud wrote to
Eitingon that

> Mrs. Gruenspan is a brave and diligent psychoanalyst who worked in
> the past as a nurse and thus has considerable experience in hospitals.
> She was not endowed with a great deal of imagination, and she
> undoubtedly will never be able to teach psychoanalysis. In that sense,
> she cannot here [in Vienna] offer a great deal of help in the Institute,
> but she is nevertheless a useful member. She has also already
> conducted a number of analyses of children. I think that, in terms of
> her general style, she can suit Palestine well. (22 May 1938: FCLC).

Gruenspan would later settle in Haifa, where she gained an excellent
reputation. She was one of the five training psychoanalysts of the
Israeli Psychoanalytic Society during the 1950s.

As the former director of the Berlin Institute, where the best
psychoanalysts in Europe and America had been trained, Eitingon
was disappointed to discover that, in time of crisis, only a handful of
his senior colleagues joined him in Palestine. Jones, who sensed this
disappointment, tried, in his British way, to offer solace: "We are all
waiting here in anticipation of Hitler's speech this evening. I hope we
won't soon be obliged to seek shelter in Palestine" (12 September 1939:
ECI).

Psychology or ideology

Unlike most of the psychoanalytic societies in Europe, the Palestinian
society displayed unusual vitality during the war years, one of the

most difficult periods the Yishuv had known. During the period of the Arab revolt of 1936–1939 and the Second World War, the Psychoanalytic Institute in Jerusalem held about fifty scientific gatherings. At a time when the trip to Jerusalem was extremely risky because of Arab attacks on Jews, these meetings were held in the homes of members in Tel Aviv. Another interesting number is that some forty of the 130 analyses conducted in the Jerusalem Institute during its early years of operation were conducted in Yiddish or in Hebrew (Rolnik, 2004, pp. 305–314). This challenges, in some measure, the common wisdom that it was the *Yekkes*, the German immigrants of the Fifth Aliyah, and they alone who enabled psychoanalysis to exist as a therapeutic practice in Mandate Palestine. The fact that Eitingon and his colleagues arrived from Berlin, and the fact that they continued to conduct the meetings of the Israel Psychoanalytic Society in German through the end of the 1950s, did not prevent them from fostering connections with the Eastern European Jews who made up an important part of the population that sought out treatment. Eitingon instilled in his small band of colleagues a combination of Central European elitism and profound solidarity with Yishuv society's material needs and national–ideological milieu. One could, of course, find in the local psychoanalytic community a manifestly non-Zionist Central European intellectual such as the Social Democratic paediatrician from Vienna, Joseph Karl Friedjung, who desperately wanted to return to Austria after the war ended and who published, in *Orient*, incisive critiques of the state of the Yishuv's educational system (cf. Gröger, 1986; Hitschmann, 1931; Mühlleitner, 1992; Reichmayr & Wiesbauer, 1979; Woolf, 1945). Another such figure was the pro-Soviet alleged convert to Christianity, Martin Pappenheim. But, as a whole, the Palestine Psychoanalytic Society was, from the start, a group that was interested in being part of Yishuv life. To enhance the reputation of psychoanalysis in the Jerusalem Institute's early years, Eitingon founded a Friends of the Psychoanalytic Society Association, which was joined by a number of writers and public figures who had undergone analysis. The bourgeois psychoanalytic salon run by Mira and Max Eitingon almost precisely recreated the German–Russian ambience enjoyed by those who attended their soirées in Weimar Berlin (captured vividly in the correspondence of Alix and James Strachey: Meisel & Kendrick, 1985). They, too, had operated as a historic crossroads where Eastern European Jews came into contact with their brethren from the West. Unlike his friend Arnold Zweig, who turned a cold shoulder to Zionism from the minute he arrived in Palestine and, thus, became a target of the polemicists of the Hebrew press, Max Eitingon never ceased to demonstrate his sympathy for the Zionist cause and to offer financial support for a variety of the Yishuv's projects. No portrayal of his complex personality would be complete if it did not include the fact that, at the end of the 1930s, he joined a small but eminent group of Yishuv intellectuals and artists who expressed their solidarity with the USSR's heroic war against Nazi Germany by offering covert support to the Communist Party in Palestine, the PKP. Only a small number of these supporters, who included Martin Buber, Akiva Ernst Simon, Judah Leib Magnes, Shmuel Hugo Bergmann, and Gershom Scholem, were anti-Zionists or committed Communists. For the most part, they were content to offer learned critiques of the failings of political Zionism, and made small gestures of solidarity with, and generosity to, the young PKP activists among their students. But Eitingon's support was reportedly more expansive than that of these other Jerusalem professors. One reason might have been the considerable financial interests that his family had in Russia. According to one woman active in the PKP at that time, during periods of crisis the members of the party would receive free treatment from Eitingon, and she herself received from him, from time to time, "substantial sums of money" for the party. The author of a history of the PKP maintained that Max Eitingon was one of the largest contributors to the party (Dotan, 1991, pp. 385–387).

The ideological and nationalist issues of the time were reflected in the Institute's academic activities. Eitingon's paper "Sexuality and dreams in the Talmud" exemplifies the ethnic–nationalist cast of the Institute's work. Notably, neither the murderous anti-Semitism raging in Europe nor the proximate Arab–Jewish conflict openly reverberated or was reflected upon analytically during the society's formative years. While events in Palestine and Jewish nationalism were addressed in the Institute's lecture programme, its annual reports to the International Psychoanalytic Association stressed clinical psychoanalysis as the mainstay of the Institute's interests. The gradual dissemination and acceptance of analytic practice in the Yishuv made it necessary to consider several formal questions and legal precedents. The subject of the minimum fees analysts could charge their patients nearly led to a clash between the Institute and the physicians' association, one of the Yishuv's most powerful organisations. In the end, a compromise was reached: the psychoanalysts were permitted to maintain the Berlin Institute's philanthropic tradition and offer, in cases of need, pro bono therapy. But, in their private clinics, the analysts would not undercut the prevailing rate schedule and would charge the minimum fees set by the physicians' association. In a dig at the newcomers in the psychoanalytic profession, the secretary (director) of the physicians' association also requested that the chairman of the Psychoanalytic Society please write all future letters in Hebrew (Eitingon to the Hebrew Medical Association, 5 February 1936; Medical Association to Eitingon, 16 February 1936: ECI).

This partial submission by the psychoanalysts to the medical establishment would have implications for the question of whether Kupat Holim medical insurance would cover psychoanalytic treatment. The health services' organisation demanded that the psychoanalysts commit themselves to specific terms and frequencies of treatment, and to a fixed price for it. The psychoanalysts claimed, for their part, that their profession should not be constricted by strict rules of the type applied to other medical services. Moshe Wulff endeavoured for a number of years, in vain, to explain to Kupat Holim officials that psychoanalytic treatment differed from somatic treatment:

> The psychoanalyst cannot be bound to the number "three times a week" . . . nor can he be bound by a payment of four pounds a month. In each given case the doctor must determine the number of hours, which might be more or less than the given number, depending on the psychic state of the patient, and the determination of the fee must be left to the discretion of the doctor, in accordance with the patient's financial situation. (Wulff to Dr Meir, 18 August 1944: ECI)

Similarly, Ilja Schalit failed to impress health officials with his explanation that the cost of psychoanalysis in a small private framework was cheaper than hospitalisation in institutions and sanatoriums, not to mention the cost of lost workdays as a result of neurotic complaints. But Kupat Holim continued to refuse to recognise psychoanalytic treatment as part of the services it offered to its members.

Ten years after the minimum fee controversy was resolved, the psychoanalysts won another victory in their effort to maintain their profession's unique character and ethic. Israel's income tax commissioner acceded to the psychoanalysts' position and excused them from having to record the full names of their patients on their invoices and annual tax reports—a precedent-setting decision that benefits psycho-analysts in Israel to this day (Schalit to Bikells, 3 March 1953: ECI).

The insistence on upholding the philanthropic character of the Jerusalem Institute's activities and its respect for the privacy of patients was aimed, in part, at maintaining the profession's autonomy. These principles also testified to the Society's interest in managing its affairs outside the sphere of influence of the physicians' association. But, to do so, the psychoanalysts had to spread word of their practice to new audiences. Eitingon did not rest on his laurels and on the will-ingness of the *Yekkes* to adopt psychoanalysis as their own and to cling to it as specifically German property, a "transitional object" to make it easier for them to acclimatise to Palestine. The psychoanalysts failed to get psychoanalysis into the curriculum of the Hebrew University, which proved that a German pedigree was no guarantee that the profession could flourish in Palestine. The university was constructed on a German model, which took a conservative approach to all fields of knowledge (cf. Mosse, 1996a). The attempts to bring psychoanalysis into the young institution should, thus, be understood not just in the context of the controversial status of psychoanalysis among the sciences, or as one more expression of the unconscious resistance it aroused. It has to be placed in the context of Freud's attitude toward Jewish nationalism and of the dispute between the two largest factions on the university's Board of Governors.

A product of the Jewish brain

From early on, the founders of the Hebrew University in Jerusalem were aware of the unique place in Jewish public opinion that was accorded to psychoanalysis and its founding father. Contacts between the university and several of Freud's students began in the early 1920s, and were due, in part, to Freud's willingness to number himself among those prominent Jews who had joined the university's Board of Governors. Even more important in this regard were the efforts of David Eder, who, in 1925, supported Siegfried Bernfeld's offer to teach psychoanalysis at the university. But Bernfeld's discussions with the university's president, Judah Leib Magnes, produced no results (Eder to Bernfeld, 1 July 1925: SBC).

The establishment of the Hebrew University, which opened its doors in 1925, was a key event for the Yishuv. It led to a sea-change in the complex relationship between the Yishuv leadership and the Zionist movement, on the one hand, and non-Zionist Diaspora Jews on the other. While the Yishuv saw the university's establishment as proof that Jews in the Diaspora were willing to support Zionism's nationalist aspirations, the young institution's non-Zionist benefactors felt they could draw a distinction between Jewish nationalism in its controversial, territorial sense, and an intellectual–cultural endeavour aimed at serving as a focal point for Jewish brain-power around the world. This tension between those who saw the university as an integral part of the Zionist project and those who preferred to view it as extraneous to the context of political Zionism informed the institution's decision-making processes during its formative years (cf. Cohen, 2006; Goren, 1982, 1996; Myers, 1995; Reinharz, 1993).

Chaim Weizmann and Magnes set the tone for the university. The former lobbied British officials and enlisted the support of Jewish scientists such as Albert Einstein and Paul Ehrlich, while the latter gained the trust of American Jewish philanthropists and of the university's Board of Governors in Jerusalem. Magnes, Weizmann, and Einstein had, however, very different views on the proper course for the new institution, on matters as diverse as fundraising, academic appointments, and the inclusion of political declarations in the university's public manifesto. Weizmann attached great importance to the establishment of medical and science faculties, while Magnes's imagination was fired by the Jewish archaeological studies that gradually led to the establishment of a humanities faculty "with a Jewish outlook". The resulting tensions shaped academic policies between 1925 and 1935.

When Freud and some of his students directed their gaze to Mount Scopus, the site of the university's campus, they had in mind a similar endeavour initiated by Karl Abraham, Ernst Simmel, and Max Eitingon some years earlier in Berlin. Freud's disciples in the German capital submitted their proposal for teaching psychoanalysis in the framework of medical faculties to the Ministry of Culture and Science. They assumed that the generational change in the government that had followed the revolution of 1918 had created a new situation in the ministry. They hoped that the ministry's relatively young officials could prevail over the conservative members of the university faculties, whose suspicion of psychoanalysis was well known, and force them to include the field in the curriculum of the medical faculty. Their hopes proved, however, to be groundless. Following a brief exchange of letters, the ministry decided not to accept the proposal (Hermanns, 1994; Kaderas, 1998).

In October 1933, Eitingon approached Magnes with a proposal that a chair of psychoanalytic studies be endowed at the Jerusalem university (Eitingon to Mages, 16 October and 5 November 1933: HUA; Eitingon to Freud, 2 November 1933: Freud & Eitingon, 2004, pp. 870–873; cf. Liban, 1999; Rosenbaum, 1954). The uncharacteristically long letter that Eitingon submitted to Magnes was, in fact, a reworking of the proposal sent to the ministry in Berlin twelve years earlier. The meticulous detail and the effort made to persuade Magnes seem to indicate that, at least during his early months in Palestine, and perhaps even beforehand, Eitingon hoped that psychoanalysis might be able to operate within a public academic framework in the Yishuv and not have to rely on private initiative, as was the case in Europe. Eitingon supplied Magnes with an impressively comprehensive and clear historical and thematic survey. Notably, however, on some essential points the text he gave him differed from the Berlin proposal. Eitingon sought to alter the way the academy grasped Freud's doctrines and to convince the university's academic policy makers to accept psychoanalysis as a field of study—even in the absence of a medical school. He rejected the idea of including psychoanalysis as a subfield under neurology or psychiatry. Experience showed that the official representatives of these two fields tended to view psychoanalysis as being of little value and to present it in a negative light. Furthermore, the plethora of innovations and developments in the field and its burgeoning scientific literature meant that only a few people with great proficiency could teach it to students. Psychoanalysis was a scientific discipline in its own right, Eitingon wrote. He proposed to Magnes, therefore, the establishment of a chair in "general and specific psychopathology", with psychoanalysis serving as the knowledge base for the person who would fill the position. Such a chair would enable doctors and educators to study psychoanalysis, and it could develop, in time, into "the Hebrew University's Freud Institute". Eitingon also surveyed psychoanalysis's contribution to the handling of psychiatric disorders, citing, for example, a study showing that psychiatric institutions that included psychoanalytic insights in their programmes of treatment were better able to cope with intractable patients and to reduce the hospitalisation times such patients needed. He did not neglect to mention the large number of Yishuv educators who had been trained in the Berlin Institute and who had implemented what they learnt there in their work in Palestine. Eitingon sought to decouple psychoanalysis once and for all from its dependence on the medical profession, and viewed his new country as a platform for pedagogic psychoanalytic activity where Freud's students could carve out a place for themselves.

There is some indirect evidence that Freud's ambiguous attitude toward the Jewish people's national aspirations in Palestine, and even toward certain Jewish practices, exacerbated the already difficult task that the friends of psychoanalysis faced on Mount Scopus. Martin Bergmann, a New York psychoanalyst and son of the philosopher Hugo Bergmann, claimed that the book *Ritual and Psychoanalysis*, published in 1928 by Theodor Reik, alarmed the university's decision makers about the subversive potential of the psychoanalytic critique of Jewish customs. Reik's Freudian interpretation of Jewish practices, such as the wearing of prayer phylacteries and the blowing of the *shofar* (ram's horn), Bergmann argued, went far beyond the cultural critique familiar to Freud's readers from *Totem and Taboo* and aroused much antagonism among the Yishuv's intellectuals (Bergmann, interviewed in Liban, 1999). Arnold Zweig believed that it was Freud's complex self-conception as a Jew that closed the doors of the Hebrew University to his students. Zweig put words to this effect in the mouth of Richard Karthaus, the protagonist of his novel, *Costly Dream*:

> We were appalled that the university, which had used Freud's name for its international public relations, just as it had used the name of Albert Einstein, retreated in the face of the irresponsible attacks against Freud and his discipline that appeared from time to time in the daily press. Especially following his brilliant work on Moses, which he himself once called a historical novel. (Zweig, 1989, p. 243)

No more solid evidence than this is available to support the claim that Freud's attitude toward Judaism, as expressed in his writings and those of some of his students, dictated the Hebrew University's attitude toward psychoanalysis. However, it is important to note that, during the 1920s and 1930s, Freud was not demonstratively forthcoming when it came to the university; his support seems to have been strictly declarative. As already noted, he refused to endow his manuscripts to the Hebrew University after his death, and even to contribute an article to a journal published by the institution (Freud to Israel Wechsler, 8 May 1929: Freud, 1960, pp. 383–384).

During the same month that Eitingon submitted his lengthy defence of psychoanalysis to Magnes, Siegfried van Friesland, the treasurer of the Jewish Agency, also wrote to Magnes with a range of arguments for why the world's first Hebrew University should be a pioneer of academic psychoanalysis, the first to endow a chair in the field. Van Friesland explained that his profound interest in psycho-analysis was not limited to its medical value. Of greater importance, he maintained, was its contribution to psychology, pedagogy, and sociology. But at the centre of his case, he put political and ethnic factors:

> This new science can well be called a specific product of the Jewish mind, and as such it is suffering from the persecution of all that is Jewish; it might well be said even, that it is banned from Germany where it was highly developed. It would, therefore, only be fitting to give it a place at the Jewish site of learning, the Hebrew University of Jerusalem. . . .This need not wait for the development of a medical faculty, as psychoanalysis is a science more of the mind and the soul than of the physical side of life. (Van Friesland to Magnes, 21 October 1933: corrected draft with Eitingon's signature, ECI)

Van Friesland no doubt chose to frame Freud's theory as a current ethno-political issue in order to position the issue advantageously in the debate over the young university's priorities, a debate in which Magnes was the advocate of Jewish studies while Weizmann sought prominence for the life and natural sciences. Van Friesland also sought to indicate to Magnes that he should not allow financial considerations to impinge on his decision, since Max Eitingon promised to bear a part of the costs of establishing a department of psychoanalysis. The latter, who received a draft of van Friesland's letter, asked him to strike out this promise. As part of the Jewish Agency treasurer's lobbying campaign, he dashed off letters to other members of the Board of Governors, stating that if his proposal were rejected he would write an article with the title "Why I am not a member of the Association of Friends of the Hebrew University". In the piece, he would explain that his reason was the university's refusal to include psychoanalytic theory in its curriculum (van Friesland to David Eder, undated; Eitingon, "Nachruf auf Van Friesland", read on 16 December 1939: ECI).

Eitingon reported to Freud about his contacts with Magnes and his sense that Magnes harboured a great appreciation for psychoanalysis and its founder. "Struck's portrait of you hangs in his office at the university", he wrote to Freud on 2 November 1933 (Freud & Eitingon, 2004, p. 871). But Magnes preferred to admire Freud rather than support his theory. At first he argued that budgetary limitations prevented him from giving psychoanalysis a place in the university. When he was given promises that the chair in psychoanalysis would be funded by outside sources and not be a drain on the university budget, Magnes again began weighing the issue, and wanted to convene a committee to consider the proposal. Eitingon's impression was that his proposal would be considered favourably precisely because he had publicised his intention to open a psychoanalytic institute in Jerusalem. And who knew better than Max Eitingon, son of the famous philanthropist Chaim Eitingon, how to find the right balance between symbolic and material capital? "The rumor about my decision to open a psychoanalytic institute here", he wrote, "has become public knowledge and made an impression on everyone—they are founding an institute among us, here, in this place; something of that great Jew who has won world fame will arrive here! And all that without them asking anything in return" (ibid.).

Freud's Zionist disciple knew how to read the rules of the game and the rhetoric of the Yishuv leadership. He would continue to pluck these strings of pride and act as a munificent patron to a variety of constituencies, from the Hebrew Writers Association through Habima—The National Theatre to the Bezalel Academy of Arts and Design. Eitingon's ears, and pocket, were open to all comers. He also regularly offered both financial and professional support for social projects, such as Youth Aliyah, an organisation that rescued 22,000 Jewish children from the Nazis.

At the margins of these efforts to endear psychoanalysis to the university's patrons, there was also a battle over who would be Freud's ideal candidate to fill the chair, were it to be established. Eitingon discovered, to his astonishment, that his colleague Moshe Wulff believed that *he* was Freud's favourite. Freud confirmed that he had indeed made a promise of this sort to Wulff, but neglected to say that he had met with the philosopher David Baumgardt, a member of the Board of Governors, to discuss the matter (Freud to Eitingon, 1 March 1934, in Freud & Eitingon, 2004, pp. 874–876). For whatever reason, Freud kept from Eitingon the fact that he had, as early as December 1932, written to Baumgardt to say that he believed Wulff to be the most appropriate person to receive the chair in psychoanalysis in Jerusalem (Freud to David Baumgardt, 17 December 1932; Freud to Wulff, 26 June 1932: FCLC). Freud's support of Wulff also came up in Freud's meeting with Baumgardt in London (Freud to Baumgardt, 3 November 1938; 27 April 1939; Kurt Eissler to Baumgardt, 7 July 1952: LBI).

While Eitingon and his Jerusalem colleagues were trying to find the code that would open the Hebrew University's doors to psychoanalysis, Freud managed to make the issue a personal one, perhaps sabotaging their efforts. He told Magnes that Eitingon would establish the Palestine Psychoanalytic Society whether or not the university decided to teach psychoanalysis in Jerusalem, and that the only question was if and in what way the university would want to co-operate with him. Magnes, for his part, was not aware of Freud's great sensitivity when in contact with academic organisations. He wrote to Freud that "The prevailing notion here is that it would be best not to bring psychoanalysis in too early, that is, before the university has a chair in psychological studies" (Magnes to Freud, 27 November 1933; 22 December 1933: AFM). And, as if to rub in the insult, he asked Freud for his opinion of the leading candidate for the psychology position, Professor Kurt Lewin from Berlin. As Freud saw it, Magnes's doubts, even before he mentioned Lewin, the founder of the Gestalt school, bore one of the classic marks of opposition to psychoanalysis, the attempt to subordinate it to academic psychology. He told Magnes that, as far as he was concerned, this was a veiled rejection of Eitingon's initiative, and that all that was left for him to do was to take comfort in the fact that his student in Jerusalem was determined to practise psychoanalysis outside the university (Freud to Magnes, 17 November 1933; 5 December 1933: AFM).

On 14 February 1934, the university Senate held a meeting in which it approved the appointment of Martin Buber as professor in the department of sociology. At the same meeting, it took up Eitingon's proposal, discussing the "scientific character" of psychoanalysis. It was decided that the university would ask for the opinion of a reputable scholar before making its decision (van Friesland to Eitingon, 25 March 1933: ECI; Minutes of the university's Senate from 14 February 1934: HUA). The fact that two candidates to offer the opinion were mentioned at the meeting—Buber and Kurt Lewin-helps to explain the thinking of the decision makers about psychology in general and psychoanalysis in particular. Buber made a point of voicing his esteem for Freud, but said—not for the first time—that when the time was right he would come out openly against psychoanalysis. Lewin was a practitioner of research-orientated Gestalt psychology, which, at that time, was perceived to be the polar opposite of psychoanalysis (cf. Bargal, 1998).

The university decided not to accept the negative evaluation drafted by the committee. It set up a new committee chaired by Andor Fodor, a professor of chemistry who was a member of the Friends of the Psychoanalytic Society. His committee produced a most sympathetic recommendation and Fodor himself asked that this message be conveyed to Freud:

> Not all the teachers at the university are parasitologists and Orthodox scholars of the Bible; there are among them also those who are very well aware of how great a debt the entire world, and the Hebrew University in particular, owes to Freud, and what they must do about it. (Andor Fodor, cited in Eitingon's letter to Freud, 21 July 1934: Freud & Eitingon, 2004, pp. 878–879)

A striking picture of Freud's special standing at the university at this time was supplied by a minor scandal, when Fodor wished to place a stone portrait sculpture of Freud in his chemistry laboratory. Opponents enlisted the biblical commandment "Thou shalt not make any graven image" and demanded that the statue be removed. In the end, a compromise was reached—the sculpture was placed in the staircase of the university library (Schalit, cited in Brandt, 1941).

The lobbying effort was joined by the American neurologist Israel Wechsler, another member of the Board of Governors. He mobilised several of the university's financial supporters in the USA to raise the $100,000 needed to endow a department of neurology and psychiatry at the Hebrew University. He also approached Abraham Brill, chairman of the American Psychoanalytic Association, saying that he wanted to include psychoanalytic studies in the department he wished to set up. Brill pledged $5,000 for a chair in psychoanalytic studies, on condition that Eitingon fill the post. He also enlisted several well-known American psychoanalysts in the campaign. But concern that the university would accept the money but then use it for other purposes was aroused when Brill was told that the inclination of the university administration was not to explicitly use the word "psychoanalysis" in the chair's name, but rather to prefer the terms "psychology", "psychiatry", and "neurology" (Brill to Eitingon, 19 January 1935; 30 March 1935: ECI). The arguments in favour of psychoanalysis did not seem to cut much ice on Mount Scopus. Psychoanalysis had to wait more than forty years longer in the library stairwell before it came into its own at the Hebrew University. In 1977, Jerusalem hosted the first meeting of the International Psychoanalytic Association ever to be held outside Europe. That same year, the Sigmund Freud chair of psychoanalysis was dedicated, its first occupant being the British psychoanalyst Joseph Sandler.

Berlin in Jerusalem

Freud showed little empathy for Eitingon's concerns about the fate of the Jews in Palestine; neither did he conceal his scepticism about Eitingon's Zionist sojourn. But Anna Freud took a keen interest in the fate of the Levantine branch of the psychoanalytic community. Eitingon, by nature practical and often reserved, wrote to her of his travels through the country; of his excursions to the desert and to Petra, the ancient Nabatean capital cut into red cliffs east of the Dead Sea; the intoxicating smells of citrus trees in bloom, and the clear, warm weather (Anna Freud to Eitingon, 11 and 30 January 1934, 4 April 1934, 4 and 30 March 1935; Eitingon to Anna Freud, 12 March 1935, 21 April, 1935, 17 July 1935: Anna Freud Collection, FCLC). He shipped crates of oranges and grapefruits to Vienna; Anna replied that "such grapefruits, unlike any sold in Vienna, even Papa devours with rapture, although he is forbidden to eat fruit" (Anna Freud to Eitingon, 4 March 1935: FCLC).

The analysts soon had plenty of patients. Eitingon was treating nine on a daily basis, allocating one hour a day to his Hebrew lesson. The small Palestine Psychoanalytic Society managed to maintain a façade of solidarity even at times when some members were brought before a disciplinary board on charges that they had strayed from "classic Freudian psychoanalysis". This was an accusation that psychoanalysts everywhere tended to make against each other—a practice that helped to keep alive ancient rituals and memories of Berlin and Vienna. The seminars for teachers and educators held by some of the Institute's fellows became increasingly suspect of straying from the original spirit of psychoanalysis. Moshe Wulff, who succeeded Eitingon as chairman of the Society, was shocked by some of the things Fania Lowetzky (who was analysed by Sabiene Spielrein and by Eitingon) wrote in the popular newsletter for teachers, *Mental Hygiene*. He suspected her of instructing the kindergarten teachers she trained to spoil children. Lowetzky was summoned before a special panel to prove that her theoretical positions had not strayed from those of "classical Freudian analysis". She refused to appear and the panel stripped her of her training position. A few years later she left Palestine and settled in Zurich (Gumbel, 1995; Nagler, 1965) (Lowetzky, "Report on teaching activities 1940–1944; Lowetzky to Schalit, 19 May 1951; Schalit to Lowetzky, 9 June 1951: ECI).

What was the "classical Freudian analysis" that was ostensibly meant to unite the members of the Jerusalem Institute, and which, if not upheld, would be grounds for questioning whether the Institute's fellows indeed practised psychoanalysis? It was a question that had dogged the psychoanalytic movement since Freud's publication, in 1914, of "On the history of the psychoanalytic movement" (1914d). But it took on special importance after the psychoanalytic exodus from Europe and the closure of the institutes in Berlin and Vienna. The term "classical" might have carried with it an additional symbolic and psychological meaning for those who had been severed from their work environment, their language, and their culture. Above and beyond its controversial clinical or theoretical signification, the concept of "classical psychoanalysis" served the émigrés as an alternative identity signifier during their years of adjustment to their new home in Palestine (cf. Will, 2001). Regardless, however, of just how "classical" each individual analyst wished to perceive himself, in Palestine the old battles of psychoanalysis had to be fought anew on a daily basis. The field had articulate and well-established opponents in Palestine, among them Martin Buber and Gershom Scholem, who had to be dealt with gingerly but firmly. Others frequently criticised Freud's ideas in articles in the popular press, in particular in *Ha'aretz*, a Hebrew-language daily popular among the German immigrants.

Eitingon did not take this sitting down. He protested to an editor at the newspaper, who replied, in an undated letter to Eitingon (ECI): "I hereby sincerely assure you that I do not oppose psychoanalysis itself but rather the public's blind faith that it is of aid and assistance in all cases. I hope that this letter will clear up any misunderstanding".

But there were critical voices within the Psychoanalytic Society as well. One psychoanalyst, Shmuel Goldschein (Golan) a member of a kibbutz, complained to Otto Fenichel that analysts in Palestine were undergoing "privatization". He wrote that

> Dr. Eitingon wants to continue the noble Berlin tradition and is lead-ing the Society according to the principle of *nolo me tangere*. The public can wait, he says—all we need to do is let people seek us out. He is avoiding any active struggle, deliberately refraining from any popu-larization of psychoanalysis. (Golan to Fenichel, undated, in Fenichel, 1998, pp. 193–195)

Internal struggles and purges over theoretical issues had been part of the daily fare in psychoanalytic societies from the time they were first established. But how, then, was the Jerusalem Institute different from those in Vienna or Berlin? Even Anna Freud wanted to know whether the future of the Jewish nation in the Land of Israel would affect the state of psychoanalysis, and whether Zionism's emphasis on rooted-ness in the land and soil would cause Berlin analysts ensconced in Palestine to suddenly turn into landowners or even farmers. She found herself caught up in Eitingon's idyllic descriptions of nature. "Last night I had a vivid dream of Jerusalem," she wrote to Eitingon "But it was a mixture of Vienna Forest and Berchtesgaden. It seems that my imagination cannot reach any further than that" (Anna Freud to Eitingon, 11 and 30 January 1934, 4 April 1934, 4 and 30 March 1935: FCLC).

The ideological and national issues confronting the Zionist move-ment and the Yishuv were soon reflected in the Institute's academic activities. For example, Greta Obernik-Reiner gave a lecture entitled "On the contribution of individual observations in groups of children to the construction of collective education"; Eitingon presented a paper on "Sexuality and dreams in the Talmud" (cf. Rolnik, 2004). Modern Jewish nationalism, as radical and revolutionary as it might have been during its early years, was not overly tolerant of those who questioned the basic tenets of Zionism. "More deeds, less words" was the Yishuv's motto; sceptical philosophical contention, non-partisan criticism, and self-reflection were seen as undermining change, group cohesion, and construction. The individual was constantly on trial: would he forgo his convenience, his personal gain, and his desires for what the collective defines as "must be done" or "there's no choice"? The public takes a dim view of individualists who defy its will, and frowns upon non-conformists. According to built-in group expectations, the individual must view submission to public authority as a normative procedure, and readily accept it (Shapira, 1996, p. 807). HaShomer HaTza'ir's educators in fact rapidly distanced psychoanalysis from attending to the psychological needs of the individual and turned it into an instrument to fulfil the ideological needs of the group. Paradoxically, in an ideological environment that tended to appropriate the private sphere of the individual for the benefit of the public interest, Freudian psychoanalysis offered the immigrant an instrument to re-examine the borders between inside and out, between his inner world and the real world outside.

Did the price that psychoanalysis had to pay to establish itself in the Yishuv require that it give up critical aspects of Freudian theory? Did the collectivist and ideologist atmosphere of pre-state Israel lead Eitingon and his successors to steer psychoanalysis on to a pronounced anti-intellectual path, thus narrowing its horizons? The formative years of psychoanalysis in the Yishuv were shaped by perpetual tension. While popular psychoanalytic discourse worked ceaselessly towards defusing the social pessimism that was part of Freud's works, it was left for the analysts to safeguard the therapeutic function of psychoanalysis.

That the Yishuv's psychoanalysts could withdraw into their private clinics was of great importance. "The minute you tried to express any private emotion, what always came out was something cramped, arid, even frightened, the product of generations and generations of repression and prohibitions," Amos Oz wrote in his memoir of life in Jerusalem in the 1940s (Oz, 2002, p. 15). But withdrawal into the clinic, behind closed doors, prevented psychoanalysis from contributing to intellectual discourse, where it could have served as an antidote to the semi-messianic rhetoric then prevailing. And, paradoxically, its capacity to contribute to the liberation of the individual was lost in the one place where it became part of the public discussion, in the kibbutzim.

Max Eitingon: a final encounter

By 1943, after ten years of activity in Jerusalem, Eitingon could celebrate his sixtieth birthday and take pleasure in the eminent figures who wished him well. They included members of most of the Yishuv's different and often opposing ideological and intellectual factions. Few felt threatened by the Berlin analysts, or considered psychoanalytic theory to be overly critical or subversive.

This book is about psychoanalysis's migration from Central Europe to Palestine, not about the life of Max Eitingon. But, clearly, his personality and efforts were critical in shaping psychoanalysis in the Yishuv and in modern Israel. It is doubtful whether any of the other psychoanalysts who found their way to Palestine better exemplified the Central European psychoanalytic ethos while, at the same time, embodying all the tensions inherent in the encounter between it and the Eastern European Zionist ethos. The recreation and maintenance, in Jerusalem under the British Mandate, of the model of an integrated clinic and teaching institution must also be credited to the man who had, thirteen years previously, founded the Berlin Institute and established its training programne. Earlier historians of psychoanalysis have tended to view Eitingon as a drab organisational man bound by fondness and unconditional loyalty to Freud. This portrayal, which could perhaps be justified in depicting his first twenty years of psychoanalytic activity, is too simplistic a way to look at his final ten years—a period that has largely been ignored by these writers.

Eitingon's attitude toward Freud was adulatory, even in terms of the almost cult-like lionisation of great men that was common in those days. This reverence was expressed in no small measure on the material level: Eitingon sent Freud his favourite cigars, expensive books, and elaborate flower arrangements, and frequently offered to cover the deficit of the psychoanalytic publishing house in Vienna and the Berlin Institute. Freud depended on subsidies from Eitingon during the harsh years that followed the First World War, and, at Freud's request, Eitingon also lent money to Lou Andreas-Salomé, who had lost all her holdings in the October Revolution in Russia. Eitingon's decision to move to Palestine was the first sign that his agenda was not identical with Freud's. The historical situation in which he decided to make the move was, no doubt, "extenuating circumstances" that enabled him to maintain his seniority in the now decentralised psychoanalytic movement. But, in taking his leave of Europe, he also distanced himself from Freud, who grew suspicious of the interest in psychoanalysis outside the boundaries of "the old continent". Add to this Freud's reservations about the Jewish people's national aspirations, and the cooling of the relationship between him and Eitingon becomes comprehensible.

Eitingon, who in his youth liked to cavort about Europe ostentatiously, became in his maturity an enigmatic figure who conducted all his business under a heavy cloak of secrecy. Everyone knew that he had a huge amount of money and that his family's leather and fur business required him to cultivate friends in high places in Soviet Russia. In 1937, he was implicated in a mysterious Stalinist espionage episode that included the abduction of a White Russian general by two Soviet agents. The two were put on trial in Paris in 1937, and the French press reported about a shadowy Russian–German millionaire who frequented the corridors of Soviet power. It might well be that his disputable family relation to General Leonid Alexandrovich (Nachum Isaacovitch) Eitingon—Stalin's homicidal super-spy who, among other things, was responsible for the murder of Trotsky in August 1940—lent added force to the rumours that Max Eitingon had a hand in Soviet espionage. The fact of there being yet another Nachum Isaacovitch Eitingon in the Family (Motty Eitingon's brother, who ran the Polish operation of the Eitingons from Lodz until 1934) could also contribute to the confusion.[3] Since no new evidence regarding Max Eitingon's involvement in this affair has turned up since then, I conclude, as have others, that this is simply a rumour that does not want to die (cf. Schröter, 1997; Wilmers, 2009). But there can be no question that an author of a Cold War spy novel would think that the mysterious Jewish–Russian immigrant psychoanalyst, son of a Russian fur magnate and anonymous donor to the local Communist party, would be perfect for the role of the Stalinist agent. In fact, the abduction of the veteran General of the Civil War became, in 1943, the subject of Vladimir Nabokov's first story in English. When Jones heard that Eitingon's name had come up in the trial of the spy ring, he wrote dryly that he would be delighted to believe what the Paris papers were writing about Eitingon, but it was not at all clear whose side he should be on in this story (Jones to Eitingon, 8 December 1938: ECI). Taking sides and betrayal were leading tropes in the twentieth century. Freud's taciturn helmsman, at once an illustrious loyalist and industrious "side taker", was destined to get mixed into this saga.

As Freud got older, something in Eitingon's enigmatic personality apparently began to trouble him as well. Eitingon's decision to move to Palestine, and the enthusiastic letters in which he suddenly discovered the virtues of Zionism, made him an easy mark for Freud's animosity. Eitingon frequently travelled to Europe, never missing a single one of the annual psychoanalytic congresses. But his correspondence with Freud grew sparser in the years 1934–1939. Freud made no response to his disciple's reports on the Arab Revolt that broke out in 1936, or to the concerns he raised about Britain's White Paper of 1939, which imposed restrictions on Jewish immigration to Palestine. The two men were no longer attuned to the same events. By this time, Freud already had another correspondent in Palestine, Arnold Zweig. Zweig revered Freud no less than Eitingon did, but, unlike the latter, he was extremely critical of the Zionist project. "I don't care any more about 'the land of my fathers'. I haven't got any more Zionistic illusions either," Zweig wrote to Freud at the time that Eitingon was sending Freud and his daughter excited letters about the establishment of the Palestine Psychoanalytic Society and about blossoming citrus trees (letter dated 21 January 1934, in Freud & Zweig, 1970, pp. 55–58). "[Y]ou ought to be able to be alone for a while . . .", Freud told Zweig, "In Palestine at any rate you have your personal safety and your human rights" (dated 21 February 1936, ibid., pp. 122–123). The letters exchanged by Zweig and Freud, in many ways the most interesting and important correspondence conducted by Freud during the final years of his life, were published in the 1960s in both English and German, but in a partial and censored version edited by Ernst Freud. In one of the letters not included, Freud gave free rein to the doubts that he had about Eitingon, who had just reminded him that they had known each other for thirty years (Wolf, 1993). Zweig enquired of Freud about the financial position of his wealthy friend, because he, Zweig, wanted to refer to him an acquaintance who was in financial difficulties. He also expressed his concern that Frau Eitingon had left Jerusalem suddenly for a long visit with her family in Paris. Freud wrote an uncharacteristically detailed response:

> With regard to our friend Eitingon . . . it's not at all a simple matter.
> A few weeks ago he reminded me that we have known each other for

30 years, that is, he has remained loyal to me for such a long time. But I still don't know much about him. To the best of my knowledge, he has no money of his own, but he belongs to the Eitingon tribe, and as heir he has a part of his family business in America. But the New York firm is currently managed by a nephew [Moti] whom he dearly loves and esteems as a commercial genius. . . . Our friend loves to help others with money and in all other ways, but for whatever reason it always ends up that he receives no gratitude and his beneficiaries drift away from him. Sometimes he can suddenly turn stingy. In general, one can say that he does not get on with people, that is, one can discern in him a surfeit of good-heartedness that originates in an unsuccessful attempt at compensation.

There is much to say about Frau Eitingon . . . I am not fond of her. She has a feline nature, and I, as is well known, do not like cats. One could not say that she lacks grace and charm, but she's no longer a young kitten. She is older than he and all that interests her enjoying herself for the rest of what remains of her life. Everything that was once human in her has not developed, or perhaps was used up. She was apparently once a well-loved actress with a husband and two children, one child died and the second, I believe, disappeared into Siberia. Our friend clearly won her thanks to neurotic conditions of love. She evinces not a trace of interest in his affairs, his friends, or his ideals. What she displays toward me is pure hypocrisy. She is jealous of everything that prevents him from being in her full possession. I doubt if he is of any significance to her other than as a butler who opens the door for her to all sorts of foolish luxuries and who complies with her every whim and moods. . . . Is there any reason for such a washed-out woman to have a chest containing hundreds of pairs of evening shoes, no less and no more, as she herself displayed to me? No, I don't think Frau Eitingon will ever leave her husband. She has no one else who could look after her and prance around her in the way to which she is accustomed. . . . In going away, she wants to get him to come after her, but if he remains firm she will return. She does not wish him ill. She is not strong enough for that. (Freud to Zweig, 10 February 1937, in Freud & Eitingon, 2004, pp. 976–978).

Freud's wicked letter did not long remain in Arnold Zweig's desk on Mount Carmel. Following Freud's death, Eitingon, at the request of Anna Freud, began systematically collecting her father's letters, and, in 1940, he asked Zweig to send all his letters from Freud so that copies could be made (Eitingon to Zweig, 24 January 1940, 9 February

1940: AZA).[4] Zweig long pondered over whether to add this letter to
the packet he sent, and tried to prepare Eitingon for the considerable
anguish that it was likely to cause him, saying: "Our friend was just
like Moses. In his love and in his wrath. That's the way it is". But
Eitingon insisted. He wished to comply with the younger Freud's
request precisely. Zweig gave in and sent him the letter.

It hardly needs to be said that the letter caused Eitingon great
pain. It is more difficult to understand his decision to destroy the original while, nevertheless, sending Anna a copy that he himself typed
up, omitting his own name and that of his wife. The only way he could
have guaranteed that this insulting letter would reach its destination
was to do that which must have been most difficult for him—to
destroy a Freud manuscript. Eitingon, who kept all of Freud's letters to
him, religiously purchased all of Freud's first editions in every possible language, and kept every scrap of paper that Freud handed him,
burnt with his own hands Freud's letter to Arnold Zweig.

Three months later, Zweig's conscience was still troubling him for
having passed on Freud's abusive letter:

> The parting from this letter was hard, but in the end I decided that
> perhaps a day would come after our deaths in which this letter would
> be published with many others of its type. Then they will be read by
> someone like Adam [Zweig's son] who will stand up and say, hey,
> Frau Mira was not like that. (Zweig to Eitingon, 16 May 1940, ibid.,
> pp. 978–979)

Eitingon thanked Zweig for the comforting words:

> I do not think at all about what generations to come will think of this
> letter. Then, like now, I suffice myself with the fact that we loved this
> exceptional man. He also erred when he doubted Mira's love for him.
> But that, too, is of no importance compared to the fact that he was
> there and was worthy of our love. (Eitingon to Zweig, 26 May 1940,
> ibid., p. 979)

Max Eitingon died in Jerusalem in July 1943 of heart failure and
was buried on the Mount of Olives. Seven years after his death, the
Israel Psychoanalytic Society published a memorial volume, a modest
but very moving historical document that marked the end of the
formative stage of psychoanalysis in Israel (Eitingon, 1950).

Max Eitingon: "Neither Orthodox Jews nor Arabs are suitable in any way for psychoanalysis."

During its first decade, the Jerusalem Psychoanalytic Institute established its position, both in Yishuv society and in the international psychoanalytic community, as a teaching, research, and clinical institution that carried on the traditions of Berlin and Vienna. Eitingon's controversial decision to move to Palestine, seen at the time almost as an act of betrayal, turned out to be a source of comfort for Anna Freud in the years following the war, when it seemed as if the various psychoanalytic societies in Europe and America had lost any connection to the Central European intellectual tradition.

After Eitingon's death, Mira, his wife, deeded the Institute building and its contents, free of charge, to the Psychoanalytic Society. Ilja Schalit and Moshe Wulff sought also to keep Eitingon's library in the Institute's possession (Schalit to the International Psychoanalytic Association, 5 July 1944). It was one of the best libraries in the country, containing over 8,000 volumes. But they did not succeed

(Klausner, 1944); Eitingon's exceptional library is now part of the National Library of Israel. Symbolically, at least, one could see these attempts to purchase the library for the Israel Psychoanalytic Society as the organisation's first test after the death of its founder. But, in the post-war world, the task was beyond the capabilities of Eitingon's heirs, who were not well connected with the American psychoanalytic institutes and, thus, could not raise funds from them. The only person who came to their aid was Anna Freud. She had no illusions, reminding Schalit and Wulff that after years of taking in immigrants and endless tensions caused by political developments during the war, most of the well-established psychoanalytic societies were inclined to see to their own affairs rather than display solidarity with Central European psychoanalysts and their memories of Berlin and Vienna:

> May I tell you what made me pessimistic about your appeal? I took a similar step after my father's death, asking several people in America for help toward finishing the new edition of the collected papers, which were destroyed in Vienna, or for bringing out a complete English edition of my father's work. I received only refusals from everywhere (except from the princess [Marie Bonaparte]) and I really became convinced that the societies, under present conditions, have very little desire to undertake any common endeavor, or to make sacrifices of this kind. Many members of the various societies did a great deal to help emigration and immigration of members six years ago. It looks as if that has exhausted their interest in helping. But I may be too pessimistic and I hope to hear from you that the plan has succeeded. In the past we used to look to Dr. Eitingon himself for help in such matters, and he always understood the value of a project.

> The society here [in Britain] is in a sad state and it is difficult to foretell what will happen in the future. Ernst Jones has now resigned his office, having retired to the country, and remains only honorary president. Edward Glover has left the society altogether in protest against its teaching activities, which have developed nearly exclusively along Melanie Klein's lines, with disastrous results for theory and technique. I, along with the small group of continentals with me, have withdrawn from cooperation with the [British Psychoanalytic] Society, though we have to remain members at the moment. It really means that we live without a society and try to work scientifically among ourselves. I look to the future, and the return of the princess, to build up something again. All that makes it all the more necessary to save

and safeguard whatever institutes we still have. (Anna Freud to Wulff, 10 December 1946: ECI; original German version reproduced in Rolnik, 2008b)

"We are here as guests of this country and we were not brought here to create trouble," Anna Freud said to Barbara Lantos at the beginning of the "Controversial Discussions", a series of meetings held by the British Psychoanalytic Society in which the followers of the Viennese school and those of Melanie Klein battled, mainly over the question of who would control the training of candidates in the British Society (King & Steiner, 1991, p. xi). When Sigmund Freud's daughter said she was waiting for the return of the princess—of Marie Bonaparte—she seemed not to be thinking of another rescue operation, but rather a yearning for the *"ancien régime"*, a time in which princesses and kings' daughters held absolute sway in the psychoanalytic movement. The letter testifies to Anna Freud's longing for Eitingon's entrepreneurial skills; to her pessimism about possible coexistence between Freudians and Kleinians in the British Society; and to her eagerness, or, indeed, actual plans, to establish a new psychoanalytic institute. Her plea to Schalit "to save and safeguard the institutes we still have" is a clear indication that, from the point of view of quite a few émigré analysts, whose lives were shaped by the experience of separation and loss, after the Second World War, "good old" Freudian psychoanalysis was alive and well and living in Palestine.

Notes

1. The issue was raised in connection with the status of lay analysts, which the British authorities indeed seemed inclined to favour in comparison with medical analysts, presumably on the score of lessened competition with the medical profession (Jones to Eitingon, 5 June 1936: ECI).
2. The original letter reads: "Ich glaube wirklich, wenn man in so kritischen Momenten die Menschen einfach im Stich läßt, dann muß etwas passieren und dann ist man mitschuldig. Erinnern Sie sich noch: Es ist schade um die Menschen!"
3. Motty Eitingon—since the 1920s the family's admired go-getter and cash supplier—was intermittently a favourite target for FBI investigations on

account of "penetration and possible use of American fur industry by Soviet agents". In 1946, his fur empire collapsed and he filed for bankruptcy. His last claim for property, it was said, was tucked away somewhere in Palestine. Nachum Eitingon, once Stalin's mastermind liquidator, has been denounced as a "Zionist plotter" during the "Doctors Plot", which marked the zenith of Stalin's paranoia and party purges. He spent many years in a Soviet prison and was posthumously "rehabilitated" shortly after the Soviet Union had ceased to exist (Wilmers, 2009, pp. 365–441).

4. After Freud's death, Eitingon put a note in the *Palestine Post* (11 January 1941) requesting recipients of letters from Freud to send the letters to him so that copies could be made from them.

CHAPTER FIVE

Homegrown psychoanalysis

"For some reason, people think that their children receive more love here than anywhere else, but the truth is that nowhere do children cry as much as they do in this country"

(Karl Josef Friedjung, 1942)

Under the British Mandate, the Yishuv underwent a swift process of social and political consolidation. It set up national governing institutions and formulated policies in many areas, among them public health. The influx of Jewish capital and scientific knowledge in the service of constructing the "national home" promised by the terms of the Mandate allowed the highly organised Jewish community to establish and maintain a comprehensive and sophisticated system of healthcare services with only limited financial support and supervision from the Mandate administration.

During the three decades of British rule that preceded independence, the Yishuv's mental health system consisted of a few psychiatrists, two state-run psychiatric hospitals, two philanthropic institutions and a small number of private ones. In the absence of a psychology faculty at the young Hebrew University, the Psychoanalytic

Institute took upon itself not only to disseminate psychoanalysis and provide therapy for those who did not need to be hospitalised, but other tasks as well. It sought to upgrade the professional competence of doctors, educators, and social workers, three key professions in Yishuv society. The psychoanalysts made their presence felt from the start in the fields of education and public mental health, also known as "mental hygiene",[1] but their entry into the mental health system was slow and their influence minimal, despite the fact that most of the members of the Palestine Psychoanalytic Society during these thirty years were psychiatric physicians by training. Furthermore, in later years, when psychoanalysts ascended to key positions in the state of Israel's psychiatric system, their approach was, by and large, not fundamentally different from other mental health professionals who had taken an active part in redefining social problems as problems that endangered the national enterprise of building a Zionist home.

The central pillars of the Jewish healthcare system during this period were the Hadassah Medical Organisation, founded by the American Zionist women's organisation Hadassah in 1921, and Kupat Holim, the health services organisation founded in 1911 by the Histadrut, the labour federation established by Jewish agricultural settlers. Hadassah and Kupat Holim undertook a massive effort to educate the Jewish public in health and hygiene.

The hygiene discourse encompassed not only concrete ways of coping with the issues of sexuality, delinquency, prostitution, and crime, but also the structuring and validation of the ideals and psychological, moral, and cultural criteria that shaped the self-image of those in the centre—that is, "outside the margins". The relationship between scientific and popular images of childhood and forms of political thought, feeling, and belief is much debated by historians. However, studies of childhood in the days of the *Yishuv*—on education, youth movements, and writing for children—expose the national indoctrination methods that were practised on children outside the family framework, for completing the process of the nationalisation of childhood. The use of children as captive performers of national loyalty, and to mobilise sentiments of national identity, seems to have been prevalent throughout Europe in the nineteenth century and was not a peculiar feature of Zionist culture. Just as Zionist youth who immigrated to Palestine embodied the idea of the New Jew, children and young people who drifted away from the Zionist ideal could threaten the nation's future. Coping with the problem of neglect and delinquency was viewed as one of the key social issues faced by Yishuv society during the years when the country, and Tel Aviv in particular, took in immigrants at an enormous rate. When the first Central European psychoanalysts arrived in the Yishuv, a process of "transferring ownership" of the treatment of juvenile delinquency from law enforcement officers to therapeutic professionals went into high gear. The abandoned, or wayward, young person was depicted as precisely the negation of what Zionism sought to produce—productive young men and women embodying the ideal of the New Jew (cf. Ajzenstadt & Cavaglion, 2002; Razi, 2009, 2010; Spector & Kitsuse, 2000; Steedman, 1995).

The fresh breeze carried in by Freud's students was evident, for example, in an affidavit that the senior educator David Idelson submitted to a British magistrate regarding the case a teenage delinquent accused of raping a young girl. The suspect, Idelson wrote to the judge, came from a normative family in Tel Aviv, worked in construction, took an interest in Hebrew literature, and was politically active. He had committed a shameful act "only because of a peculiar mental state". The high point of Idelson's psychologistic line of defence came when he recommended that the judge not cause the girl to reveal the rape publicly, since "according to psychological theory, at this age remorse and moral inhibitions grow in strength. . . . The most important thing for the girl is the moral constraint-modesty—which will preserve her from licentiousness in the future" (Idelson to the Magistrate Court of Tel Aviv-Jaffa, 20 November 1934: TLCA).

One of the first issues that the Yishuv's psychoanalysts had to face was the training of therapists. They sought a middle road that would allow them maximum autonomy in training new practitioners, but which would not arouse the ire of doctors and educators, two professions that were both organised and well represented in the Yishuv leadership. This required the members of the new profession to be especially cognisant of the hopes of the shapers of pedagogic policy. The Yishuv's psychoanalysts' increasing involvement in various educational and "mental hygienic" frameworks inevitably reawakened the question of the legitimacy of lay analysis—the practice of psychoanalysis by people without medical training. Eitingon's first report to the International Psychoanalytic Association shows how quickly and urgently this dispute came to the fore, threatening to create a rift between the larger psychoanalytic movement and the local psychoanalytic community:

> All the signs indicate, and I say this with all necessary caution, that we will be able to train certified teachers for pedagogical–therapeutic work, that is, as psychoanalysts for children. The question of analysis by those who are not physicians is an extremely complex issue here, and we request that we be allowed to address the issue as we see fit, and I repeat, this is a very difficult question. I hope that two years from now we will be able to offer a detailed report on our achievements in this area. (Eitingon's report on the first year of activity of the Jerusalem Psychoanalytic Institute, Spring 1934: ECI)

Not all of Eitingon's colleagues agreed with him on this matter. "Within ten years at the most our Society will be flooded with pre-school and school teachers who have 'undergone analysis'", warned Gershon Barag in an agitated letter in which he complained about the weakness of the organisation's ties to the medical establishment and the rapid growth in the number of members who lacked medical training (Barag to Schalit, 9 November 1943: ECI). Adhering to Freud's well-known position that physicians should not be given preference over the members of other professions, Eitingon ran a tight ship and fended off every proposal that would have given preference to medical doctors for psychoanalytic training (cf. Wallerstein, 1998).

But applications kept coming in. When a certain Dr Rudolphson, who was employed at that time by Kupat Holim, the medical services branch of the Histadrut labour federation, applied for membership of the Society, Eitingon responded that, despite his advanced age—forty-five—he would be required to undergo training analysis before his application could be considered. Wilhelm Nofen of Oslo, who wondered whether to travel to Jerusalem to receive psychoanalytic training from Eitingon, enquired in 1934 what the cost would be. More surprising were the two applications that arrived from Egypt: a Dr Ziwar of Alexandria wished to join the Society and wrote that there was great interest in psychoanalysis at King Farouk University, where he taught. Abdul Hamid, undersecretary to the president of Egypt's National Appeals Court, wrote from Cairo to apply for membership. He offered a list of the works by Freud and Freud's students that he had read avidly in recent years. All these applicants were politely turned down (Eitingon to Schalit, 4 April 1943; Nofen to Eitingon,

28 December 1934; Ziwar to Eitingon, 23 August 1943; Wulff to Ziwar, 19 September 1943; Abdul Hamid to Friedjung, 22 April 1943: ECI).

The discourse on mental hygiene was conducted within the Psychoanalytic Institute, not only outside it, as can be seen from the titles of lectures offered there during the first twenty years of its operation: "The child in communal kibbutz education"; "On the sexual problem of the Yishuv child"; "On adjustment to reality as an educational goal"; "Individual psychoanalytic observation and its importance for the construction of communal education"; "Revolution and drive"; "Psychoanalytic and educational research on wayward children" (Rolnik, 2004).

Shaping a "healthy nation" was not just an end in itself—it was a precondition for performing the physical task of building a Jewish national home. Physicians sometimes discussed sickness in terms of the loss of labour power necessary for the success of Zionist colonisation, and at other times in terms of waste of national funds. Dr Mordechai Brachyahu, a former student of David Eder, the British psychoanalyst who left Palestine in 1923, had founded the education department of the Jewish National Council, the Yishuv's governing body. He had an uncanny talent for connecting seemingly trivial problems of public health with the success of the entire Zionist endeavour. A case in point was the battle he waged against bad teeth and "quick and insufficient mastication". "The annual loss to the Yishuv economy caused by bad teeth and food not fully exploited because of dental disease is estimated at 220,000 Palestinian Pounds", he maintained, wondering "How many farms, how many magnificent schools could we have founded each year had we known how to keep our teeth healthy, how to chew correctly, and thus economize on the cost of food and take full advantage of it?" (cited in Hirsch, 2009, p. 581).

While not a member of the Palestine Psychoanalytic Society, Brachyahu was a key figure in the Yishuv's psychoanalytic discourse, in the Institute, in its professional and popular literature, in his translation of Freud's *The Interpretation of Dreams*, and in the work of psychoanalysts in the Mental Hygiene League he headed.[2] "The high road to healing the nation's psyche is long and full of ruts", he wrote in his memoirs (Brachyahu, 1960, p. 65). He liked to compare the maturation of the Jewish people to a child's mental development:

> Just as when we fashion the life of the state, we see the distress of creation, when the impelling forces sometimes overwhelm the

consolidating ones, when political parties overindulge in polemics and cannot overcome their partisan drives, and so weaken the forces of solidarity and unity, so the same thing happens when a personality comes into being, during the adolescent period, which is generally a period of distress, of erratic behavior, of progress and regression. (Brachyahu, 1947, p. 153)

Brachyahu used insights from psychoanalysis to liberate sexual energies and channel them into communal advancement. A staunch Freudian with a puritanical streak, he mobilised the psychoanalysts for his mental hygiene project. Some of them turned into agents of his

Mordechai Bracyahu: "Just look how the lover appears in contemporary films."

endeavour, which stressed the importance of giving psychoanalytic training to physicians who worked in schools. At the end of the 1930s, five physicians with such training were employed at the Jerusalem Psycho-Hygienic Station (Hirsch, 2000).

Psychoanalytic theory, and in particular Freud's early works on infantile sexuality, provided Brachyahu with the scientific sanction he needed to conflate education, Zionism, and mental health. This paved the way for making hygiene an integral part of Zionist ideology. Paralleling the individual schoolchild's traumatic, fearful past to the Jewish nation's past in the Exile enabled Brachyahu to imbue the school doctor with the standing of one who knew, inside out, the life circumstances of each child. This meant that the doctor knew how to liberate the psychic forces concealed within the child and to harness them to the needs of the national collective. The school and preschool doctor thus sought to become intimately acquainted with the psyche of each child. Training in psychiatry and teaching was considered an advantage for the job, and, upon taking up his position, the school doctor was expected to undergo, in addition, training in psycho-hygienics. Doctors in the hygiene department also had to undergo psychoanalysis and take part in seminars held at the Psychoanalytic Institute (Cavaglion, 2000). Brachyahu's amalgamation of the individual's mental plight with the Zionist cause was evident to anyone who entered his consulting room. A huge map of Palestine hung on the wall facing the analytic couch (Dr Itamar Levi, personal communication).

Oriental voluptuousness

From the start, the Zionist manifesto that calling on all the world's Jews to come to the Land of Israel contained a certain equivocation. Zionist writing stressed the healing and liberating power of *aliyah*, immigration to the Jewish homeland. Yet, at the same time, the Yishuv leadership engaged in selection and classification to identify candidates fit to take part in the Zionist project. This was reflected in the Yishuv's educational, hygienic, and psychiatric discourse from the 1920s onward. It prescribed aesthetic and normative behaviours for the construction of a new and better Jewish identity. But, beyond that, it played a central role in the creation of groups and how they were defined in opposition to other groups. The scientific debate over the question of whether Jews displayed a distinct psychopathological profile, as described in Chapter One, continued in the Yishuv, but with some differences. Jews from Eastern Europe (collectively referred to as *Ostjuden*) were traditionally contrasted to those from Western Europe. In Palestine, the line was drawn between Jews who had come from Europe and the Old Yishuv—the Jews who had lived in Palestine before the Zionist influx. A line was also drawn between Jews and Arabs, and, after the establishment of the state, between Jews who had arrived from Europe during the Yishuv period and Jewish immigrants from the Islamic world. On the one hand, psychiatrists sought to distinguish between Zionist immigrants and the Old Yishuv in order to validate the Zionist settlement project. On the other hand, since the ongoing historical connection between Jews and the Land of Israel was central to the Zionist claim for legitimacy, they wished to stress the common genetic origin of all the Jews who had been exiled from their historic homeland and dispersed to the four quarters of the earth. There was, thus, a constant tension, in the local psychiatric and hygienic discourse, between the view that mental illnesses were illnesses of civilisation, the view that they expressed cultural primitiveness and backwardness, and the view that they were maladies associated with specific ethnic subgroups within the Jewish population (Hirsch, 2009; Zalaschik, 2005).

In other words, the East–West distinction remained a central organising principle in the Yishuv's hygienic discourse, but its referents changed: instead of Eastern *vs.* Western Europe, it became Europe *vs.* the Orient. Thus, newcomers from both Eastern and Western Europe were referred to as "immigrants from Europe" and contrasted to "all 'those' non-Europeans"—both Arabs and "Oriental" Jews. As Henrietta Szold, the founder of Hadassah, wrote to Max Eitingon,

> A child of a Persian or Yemenite family coming to Palestine into our Ashkenazic–Zionist milieu is virtually precipitated forward at least five centuries. The same child, as well as the Ashkenazic child suffering the privations of extreme poverty, fleeing from the repressions of the single-room home of a large family into the street, drops into the arms of the Arab voluptuary. (Szold to Eitingon, 14 December 1934: ECI)

This condemnation of Oriental "voluptuousness" and diaspora-born underdeveloped attitude towards parenting, concepts that were

translated into a professional discourse in which the hygiene department's experts decided on the fitness of parents to raise their children,
sometimes condemned children to grow up far from their homes. In
Brachyahu's paternalistic ideological approach, it was better to
remove "problem" children from their parents' influence. The mental
hygiene discourse often voiced extreme eugenic ideas like those common in late nineteenth-century Europe. The official journal of the
Hebrew Medical Association, *Harefu'ah*, at times published hair-
raising polemics. Mordechai Brachyahu speculated on whether legislation should be passed to require every couple to undergo a psychiatric examination prior to marriage, in order to determine their mental
fitness to be parents. A Dr Rabinowitz proposed disseminating
eugenic ideas by forbidding marriage to people "of the said type",
and a Dr Einhorn advocated "sterilizing the mentally ill and potential
criminals". Martin Pappenheim, who had managed to establish
himself as a local authority on mental hygiene affairs despite his initial
difficulties following his arrival in 1933, maintained that the eugenic
sterilisation of the mentally unfit was no less a responsibility of the
state than defence or tax legislation (Ajzenstadt & Cavaglion, 2002;
Pappenheim, 1936; Weiner, 1984). Erwin Hirsch, a psychoanalyst from
Stuttgart, joined the debate on the connection between mental illness
and immigration immediately after arriving in Palestine. He reached
the conclusion that the patient's attachment to his therapist, which
was the principal factor in the treatment of psychological ailments,
did not exist in Palestine. The problem was, he said, not only that the
therapist did not understand the language and culture of the primitive patient. The members of the Old Yishuv, he said, were suspicious
of the doctor. As Rakefet Zalashik wrote in her study of the origins of
Israeli psychiatry, the Zionist position, which stressed the historic
connection between Jews and the soil and the blood relation of all
Jews, prevented Jewish psychiatrists from turning, upon their arrival
in the Yishuv, to colonial psychiatrists guided by a conception of
racial hierarchy that viewed the native population as inferior and
primitive (Zalashik, 2008).

The discourse that associated both mental illness and parental
dysfunction with specific ethnic and cultural roots was compatible
with the modern welfare tradition imported from Europe, of an ever-
increasing intervention on the part of the authorities in the private
space (cf. Rose, 1990). But, whereas in Europe the class context was

decisive, and working class families were the main target for intervention in the name of bourgeois values and by representatives of the bourgeoisie, in the *Yishuv* there emerged an additional specific ethnic and cultural context. Thus, the perception of institutions as an alternative to the dysfunctional urban family fitted the socialist and Marxist distrust of the family, as was manifested in the kibbutzim at the time, and even echoed its principles of communal education. The aspiration to limit the roles of the families and usurp the care, and mainly the education, of children was also compatible with the perceptions that had emerged in the early Zionist utopias, which imagined the future society as one in which raising and educating children would be in the hands of the society, as a necessary condition for the revolution in the life of the Jewish People (Razi, 2010).

A large part of Brachyahu's work was aimed at shaping knowledge and power relationships in the field of education. He placed psychiatrists loyal to Freudian doctrine at the apex of his pyramid. Max Eitingon, Martin Pappenheim, and Moshe Wulff for a long time enjoyed the status of being psychiatrist–psychoanalyst *über*-advisers to Brachyahu's staff. In this capacity, they collated the information gathered for them by school nurses and used it to instruct school doctors. The school nurse also visited the homes of pupils and served as a kind of envoy of the school system to the child's family. This intrusion went beyond simply inspecting the material conditions and sanitation of the home in which the children grew up. It was intended to supervise the shaping of these impressionable psyches. Brachyahu and his agents used what they asserted were objective medical models to define concepts of good parenting and norms and deviations in children's mental and emotional development. Most of the recommendations made by the hygiene department were rational and sensible, but they were pervaded by the tones of dogmatism and omniscience with which Brachyahu conducted the hygienic discourse. The department's long reach stretched even into the bedrooms of parents and the loins of teenagers. And the hygiene department peered into the most private corners of the home through the eyes of the children.

Masturbation by teenagers discomfited Brachyahu and his staff in no small measure. They were careful not to condemn it openly, but offered parents advice on how to wean their children from the practice, prescribing washing in cold water, avoiding spicy foods, putting children to sleep with their hands on top of the blanket, and making sure that their beds were neither too soft nor too warm. And, most of all, "it is highly advisable that anyone who engages in masturbation consult with an expert, a physician–psychologist . . . who is the only one who can save the young person" (Brachyahu, 1947, p. 114). On the other hand, psychoanalysts sought to demonstrate their progressiveness by intimidating parents who took outdated and hostile approaches to self-stimulation. David Idelson warned parents who ignored the psychoanalytic recommendation not "to touch the child's sexual organs during cleaning and washing". He cautioned that a child touched in this way would grow up to be "disturbed, drunken, and even an opium-smoker" (Idelson, 1940). Basing their practice on Freudian doctrine in almost precisely the same way as Soviet psychoanalysts and sexologists, Idelson and Shmuel Golan claimed that parents relive the unconscious conflicts of their own childhood and implant in the younger generation their own unconscious wishes and inhibitions. The nation required that the child be liberated from the clutches of the sexual conflicts imposed by sanctimonious Diaspora-born parents. Brachyahu, for his part, cautioned parents that the spirit of the times subverted the healthy psychological development of young people because it gave free reign to aggression and sadism. The retreat from the demands of the culture into the demands of the sexual drive, as portrayed in Hollywood films, was bound to make the love of Jewish youth mundane and prosaic, not romantic enough for his tastes:

> Just look how the lover appears in contemporary films, pouring out his heart to his beloved; he wears a straw hat, has a cigarette in his mouth, and he waves a light cane; he is easygoing and cheerful, ready to enjoy the world; he wears insubstantial sporting clothes, as if he had gone out for a walk in the morning breeze, and he himself is limber and light, as is his beloved, and his feelings are insubstantial as well. Since he easily gets what he wants, he doesn't need to make an effort and exert his psychic energy. . . . It looks as if the tree of life in our age is turbulent and shaken to its roots and can produce only a small yield of healthy fruit. (Brachyahu, 1947, p. 166)

Masturbation was also a central subject in the reports that Joseph Karl Friedjung submitted to his employers. Friedjung, a paediatrician who had been a member of the Vienna Psychoanalytic Society since

1909, was assigned by Eitingon and Henreitta Szold to serve as a psychiatric consultant to the Youth Aliyah organisation following his move to Palestine in 1938 (cf. Gröger, 1986; Gumbel, 1965; Hitschmann, 1931; Mühlleitner, 1992; Reichmayr & Wiesbauer, 1979; Woolf, 1946). Youth Aliyah conducted a massive rescue operation in Europe and brought some 22,000 Jewish children to Palestine to save them from the Nazis. Friedjung carefully recorded his 423 visits to different groups of children under the organisation's care, and his individual talks with 2,291 children aged fourteen to eighteen (Friedjung, 1950). The attitudes of the counsellors who worked with these youths ranged from sweeping acceptance and unbounded permissiveness to preaching ascetic self-denial. Friedjung wondered how to fight the "pseudo-revolutionary conservatism" that had taken root among Yishuv educators. From his point of view, the situation required nothing less than a single-minded effort to accomplish "broad psychoanalytic reeducation". The first change he proposed manifested itself in instructions to Youth Aliyah counsellors and staff to be more available and approachable to teenage boys and girls. Only a counsellor who displayed a sincere interest in his charges could earn their trust. Counsellors should initiate talks on sexual matters with the entire group and respond to any requests for private conversations. For the first time, masturbation was to be spoken of openly. Friedjung was particularly concerned about "partially virgin girls", meaning those who had engaged in sexual relations in which their partners reached orgasm but they did not, "with all the neurotic implications of the matter". Friedjung also considered groups which included a "Don Juan", or the female parallel, which he called a "Messalina" (after the promiscuous wife of the Emperor Claudius). The behaviour of such boys and girls generally led to unrest in the group. Girls, who generally matured sexually before the boys in a given cohort, often entered into relationships with older boys, leading to rivalry and intense jealousy between different age groups. Sometimes, this led to the creation of two antagonistic camps within a given group, with boys and girls on either side of the divide.

Friedjung reported on the particular difficulties of immigrants from Southeast Europe, especially boys from Hungary and Romania. They had been accustomed to satisfy their urges by going to prostitutes. Friedjung explained to Youth Aliyah counsellors that in the culture in which these boys had grown up the taboo against masturbation had been particularly strong. Parents and teachers in these countries thought it legitimate for boys to patronise brothels. Now, in their new society in Palestine, they had sexual abstinence imposed on them, and the result was aggressive behaviour toward any girl they encountered. Friedjung taught counsellors to be attentive to the transference relationships between counsellor and children, and of the processes occurring within the group in response to the acts of the counsellors. He used as an example a particular group in which youths had displayed intense jealousy and hostility toward a formerly popular woman counsellor. The change occurred when the counsellor became pregnant. The group could be expected to take its anger out against the baby when it was born, or against one of the younger boys in the group, displacing the jealousy and the urge for revenge on to them. Thus, he recommended that it would be best to train volunteers who were married and already had at least one child. Such counsellors would, first, have an easier time developing paternal or maternal emotions toward their charges and, second, the latter would not feel that their counsellor's new spouse or child was depriving them of attention. Such counsellors would be better at providing the emotional needs of adolescent immigrants, he reasoned.

The seasoned left-wing Viennese paediatrician and psychoanalyst made no secret of his disappointment at the state of Yishuv education. In passionate articles he published in the German-language *Orient*, he voiced his opinion that, in terms of psychological misery, Jewish children in Palestine were no better off than their Diaspora brethren:

> For some reason, people think that their children receive more love here than anywhere else, but the truth is here that nowhere do children cry as much as they do here. In the past it was customary to measure the cultural level of a people according to its consumption of soap, but I would propose measuring it by the quantity of needless tears shed by children. The necessary conclusion is that we have not yet emerged from our pre-cultural stage. (Friedjung, 1942a, p. 5)

And in another article he complained,

> [O]ur children grow up incapable of recognizing authority. They display no respect for adults, for the weak, and for the needy. Their relations with each other are characterized by violence, as are their attitudes toward object and animals. (Friedjung, 1942b, p. 8)

Arnold Zweig voiced similar concerns regarding the emerging psychological profile of Yishuv youth, in an especially fiery introduction he wrote to Brachyahu's book on the subject of juvenile delinquency.

Oedipus at the kibbutz

The individualistic thinking of Sigfried Bernfeld and Martin Buber was a seminal influence on HaShomer HaTza'ir, the youth movement whose 500 members first arrived in the Yishuv in the 1920s as part of the Third Aliyah. But members of the movement who arrived in the 1930s as part of the Fifth Aliyah did not view themselves as part of a revolutionary youth movement of an individualistic cast. By that time, the movement was well on its way to replacing its earlier free-spirited romantic character with a Marxism that was becoming, in some parts of the movement, increasingly doctrinaire. As a result, the new immigrants identified with a movement with a monolithic set of principles dictated largely by the pro-Soviet orientation of the HaShomer HaTza'ir leadership in Galicia. During the years in which the movement developed this party line, which it called "ideological collectivism", psychoanalytic theory as understood by the movement became instrumental, a tool to be used in the service of ideology, losing the romantic tint given to it by Meir Ya'ari and his associates in its early years. The emphasis that its first educators had placed on revolutionary Eros was replaced by a new emphasis—the use of sexuality in the service of the revolution. Infantile sexuality came to be viewed as an object for intervention and for changing human nature. Bernfeld himself, who had in the past viewed the youth culture as an end in itself, revised his position at the end of the 1920s and argued that it was necessary to actualise the revolutionary potential of youth and harness it to the class struggle (Bernfeld, 1928). In the 1930s, Bernfeld's historical role as a mediator between psychoanalysis and the Zionist youth movements came to an end, and the latter found for themselves psychoanalysts of a more unambiguous political and programmatic cast. To grant binding functional validity to the somewhat amorphous Freudian influences that had pervaded HaShomer HaTza'ir since its founding, the shapers of its educational philosophy decided to issue a series of translations that would allow the movement's educators to learn about psychoanalysis. Freud's book, *The*

Future of An Illusion (1927c), and the venerable psychoanalytic work by Fritz Wittels, *Set the Children Free* (1933), were intended to be the first two psychoanalytic works to be published by the HaShomer HaTza'ir press (Tzvi Zohar to Eliezer Hacohen, 30 March 1930: SHA).[3] Zohar, a representative of the movement, met in 1929 with Paul Federn, secretary of the Vienna Psychoanalytic Society, and reached an agreement whereby the Society would give 1,000 schillings toward the translation project. The rendition of psychoanalytic literature into Hebrew, the movement's members promised Federn, was not a commercial enterprise, but, rather, an educational and cultural project (Zohar to Paul Federn, 31 October 1929, 17 September, 1930: SHA).

Some two years after returning to Palestine from Berlin, where he attended courses at the Psychoanalytic Polyclinic, became acquainted with the analytic movement leading theoreticians, and underwent analysis by Moshe Wulff, Shmuel Golan reported to Eitingon that eighty HaShomer HaTza'ir educators were in the psychoanalytic training programme that he and Wulff had started. The participants were divided into two working groups, one of German speakers, the other of Russian speakers, both of whom attended weekly lectures by Wulff on Freudian theory (Shmuel Goldschein (Golan) to Eitingon, 8 July 1933: ECI). Another enthusiastic fan of the efforts of HaShomer HaTza'ir educators to integrate the teachings of Freud and of Marx in their educational frameworks was Otto Fenichel, who routinely attached Golan's reports to the circulars he disseminated among his immigrant left-wing psychoanalyst colleagues. "The psychoanalysts had nothing to complain about" with regard to their private clinics, Golan claimed—they had plenty of work. But what about their responsibility to society? Did they intend to continue to avoid the task of building Zionist Jewish society in Palestine? He complained that Eitingon and his colleagues were not committed to fully integrating their work into the Yishuv's public life. His grievances about the fledgeling psychoanalytic institute in Jerusalem evinced not only the ideological isolation he felt in his contacts with most of his German-speaking colleagues there, but also the contempt displayed by members of HaShomer HaTza'ir for the nationalist sentimentalism of the Fifth Aliyah immigrants:

> Here in the Land of Israel, matters look the way I thought they would—the psychoanalysts who have arrived here are "undergoing

privatization." The level of the Psychoanalytic Society, which has been paralyzed for half a year for objective reasons, was even beforehand most doubtful. The sudden awakening of pseudo-national sentiments and justifications has been expressed in its move toward "Judaism," which has led to several lectures in the "religious" area—which ostensibly sought to cast light on religion's role in the emergence of neurosis. Nothing new has been said there. I fruitlessly tried to elicit a discussion of more fundamental issues. But the worst of all is that the only person who is capable of saying something about it, Dr. Wulff, displays his personal protest by remaining silent (there is tension between him and Eitingon). . . . Mr. Eitingon has nothing to say, Prof. Pappenheim says a few words here and there, and the others, Dr. Barag, Mrs. Brandt, Dr. Hirsch, are new and I do not know them. Current and fundamental problems of psychoanalysis did not come up at all in the discussion. (Golan to Fenichel, 6 September 1936: Fenichel 1998, pp. 193–195)

It is not hard to understand Golan's loneliness, as well as his anger at the fact that Palestine, which seemed at first to offer the Freudians a large range of sociological and anthropological opportunities to make a close examination of the dialectics of the psyche and society, became a gathering place for Berlin psychoanalysts who, from Golan's point of view, were interested only in plumbing the unconscious. Yet, despite his objections to the nature of the Jerusalem institute's scientific gatherings, a not insignificant number of meetings were in fact devoted to issues that were high on the agenda of HaShomer HaTza'ir educators. In her summation of the Institute's first seven years of activity, Margarete Brandt saw fit to note that only a small number of those who had applied to the Institute for psychological help lived in communal frameworks. She concluded from this that communal kibbutz life offered a defence against competition and loneliness, and that it could also purge the immigrant who became part of his age group's society in such a commune of the anxiety produced by parental authority. Many neurotics, Brandt argued, who probably could not have withstood the tribulations of "normal life" without psychoanalytic care, had, after immigrating to Palestine, found happiness in kibbutzim (Brandt, 1941). A similar position on the advantages of kibbutz life would later be taken by another member of the Psychoanalytic Society, Hillel Klein, in the context of the psychic morbidity of concentration camp survivors. Living in a kibbutz, Klein argued, enabled survivors to reinvest in the community, particularly by making real the rebirth fantasies so commonly seen among this group, and by providing mechanisms capable of transforming "survival guilt" into a virtue. The real need to fight to defend themselves and their communities helped them avoid internalising the aggression they had experienced. Klein stressed the sense of historic continuity that the survivors developed, and maintained that kibbutz life offered, more than is generally realised, continuity with a person's past and ideals (Klein, 1972).

Golan's claim about the "privatization" of psychoanalysis and the Jewish nationalist tint of the Berlin psychoanalysts' scientific meetings was not only a portrayal of the Psychoanalytic Society in Jerusalem, but also an indication of the field's very different agenda in the HaShomer HaTza'ir kibbutzim. This first Zionist youth movement, which, when founded in Vienna, had promoted the vitalistic, non-ideological youth culture typical of its time and place, now had a complex and all-inclusive ideological and cultural doctrine instilled by teachers, counsellors, educators, and a single psychoanalyst. They sought to shape the image of the child from the day of his birth through maturity. At a meeting of the movement's educators in 1929, the claim was made that parents tended to treat their children "subjectively", using a combination of fear and over-indulgence to socialise them. Parents should not be allowed to treat their child "as if he were their toy", argued Golan, who tended to view parents' wishes for close relations with their children as a manifestation of neurotic narcissism. Some of his colleagues went so far as to claim that the maternal instinct was a consequence of capitalist materialism that should be eradicated so that the child could be placed in the hands of society (Cavaglion, 2004; Liban, 1999; Liban & Goldman, 2000; Rolnik, 1998).

Golan, the architect of the movement's communal education system, oversaw some 400 children in thirty settlements. In preparation for bringing out a pedagogical journal with a psychoanalytic orientation, he translated Fenichel's essay of 1967[1934], "Psychoanalysis as the nucleus of a future dialectical–materialistic psychology". Golan became aware of the amazing power that the group had over the individual while he was still in training at the Berlin Psychoanalytic Institute. Freud's book *Group Psychology and the Analysis of the Ego* (1921c) enabled him to understand the ties of love that bound the individual to the group and the individual's ability to give up, for the general good, love of an object and self-love. Yet, even at this early stage, Golan believed that Freud had erred in maintaining that the individual's drives and urges were the only significant factors in the relationships between individuals and groups. Freud, he believed, had neglected the importance of economic and material causes. It was precisely this shortcoming that Golan and his educator colleagues sought to rectify in the spirit of HaShomer HaTza'ir's ever-growing allegiance to the Soviet Union. Collectivist educational ideas had, of course, already influenced the new progressive educational move- ment and Austrian Social-Democratic thinking, as implemented by Siegfried Bernfeld and his associates at the Baumgarten Children's Home in Vienna, founded in 1919. But, by the time HaShomer HaTza'ir's educators sought to implement psychoanalytic ideas in the communal educational system of the kibbutzim, they already had before them the Soviet model of Anton Semenovych Makarenko, which stressed the elasticity of human consciousness (Peled, 2002). It was not long before Golan found the area in which he could make a significant contribution to the psychoanalytic theory of neurosis. The challenge he took up was what happens to the Oedipus complex in the process of communal education.

Kibbutz children spent most of their days with female care-givers, counsellors, and teachers, living, playing, and sleeping in children's homes. They generally spent only two hours a day with their parents. Golan came to the conclusion that, under these conditions, parents had much less influence on children than did other educational figures, and that seemed to him sufficient "to produce a fundamental change in the Oedipal situation". Love for parents was not dimin- ished, he argued, but the role of the father changed and the child displayed more love for him than for his or her mother. The father's relations with his children also changed, as he displayed more of his maternal, gentle side. The fact that the power to discipline the child was removed from the parents and transferred to the staff of the chil- dren's homes improved relations between parents and children, according to Golan. Parents displayed more tenderness, sometimes even over-indulgence. They also made no educational demands of their children, demands that required the exertion of effort to satisfy, and, as a result, parent–child relationships were "less ambivalent", Golan maintained. There were also other consequences of having

children sleep outside their parents' home and of communal education. He argued that such children lacked any real experience with the
"primal scene", the name Freud gave to the child's witnessing, or
fantasising of, sexual relations between his parents, which the child
interpreted as an act of violence. Furthermore, he said, kibbutz children's sexual education and development were "much less influenced
by the typical Oedipal situation" than was the case in "bourgeois
families". "Healthy country life" gave children the opportunity to
observe animals, providing them with the sexual information they
hunger for during the Oedipal period. During this same period,
younger children receive explanations of sex from older children, who
play a larger educational role than do adults. Golan had no doubt that
his findings showed that the Oedipus conflict was, in fact, socially
determined and that this "weakened the Freudian view" (Golan to
Fenichel, undated, included in Fenichel's circular letter, 15 October
1938: Fenichel, 1998, pp. 193–195).

Otto Fenichel, who was known as "the encyclopedist of psychoanalysis", welcomed Golan's investigation of the Oedipal complex in
kibbutz society. He, too, believed that there was no longer reason to
debate whether the Oedipus conflict was universal and biologically
determined or, rather, a reflection of a specific social and historical
reality. His socialist views did not permit him to ascribe the Oedipus
conflict to biology, because socialism presumed that human nature
was malleable. Fenichel's encouragement was of huge importance to
Golan, who had just been accepted into the Palestine Psychoanalytic
Society and seen the suspicion with which his teachers, Moshe Wulff
and Max Eitingon, greeted any attempt to revise the theory of drives.
Fenichel himself warned Golan against dismissing the importance of
the family. The influence of society on the individual psyche concerned Fenichel beyond the Oedipal context. He was also critical of
the tendency of Central European psychoanalysts to disregard external factors, preferring the "realist" approach of the American school,
which had no problem recognising that economic forces were seminal
influences on the individual.

The book *Sex Education* that Golan co-authored with Tzvi Zohar,
the movement's leading educator, displays the tension between their
desire to meld Bernfeld's ideas with the ideological collectivism that
gradually took hold of their movement's agenda. The two authors
noted the central place of the sexual issue in the labour and kibbutz

movements, "which have seen the synthetic education of the individual as ensuring the creation of new forms of life for the Hebrew worker in the Land of Israel". The kibbutz movement had a role in that synthesis, by inculcating new ways of life based on psychoanalytic discoveries about human sexuality. It was the kibbutz movement, they stated, that took it upon itself "to sustain in practice forms of family life, education, and sex education that conform to the socialist ethic and innovative education" (Zohar & Golan, 1941, p. 5).

Liberating the young Jew from the chains of petit-bourgeois sexuality was not a goal in and of itself. Whenever HaShomer HaTza'ir educators mentioned sexuality, they connected it to the group. The most efficient way to transfer to the individual the power of the group was to turn the most private sphere, sexuality, into a target of group intervention. Removing the dividers between the individual and the group in the area of sexuality in the form of talking about it openly, or "confessions", to use the HaShomer HaTza'ir term, was a means by which educators could mould the individual into the utopian new man they sought to create. This new man would be liberated from the bounds of his biological urges and shaped entirely by society.

The autonomy enjoyed by kibbutz teenagers also played a central role in creating a firm connection between sexuality and ideology. Golan and Zohar themselves pointed out the ostensible paradox inherent in their desire to create an independent youth society within the kibbutz framework. They were well aware that the appearance of autonomy was meant, in fact, to enhance young people's identification with the ideological collective for which they had been trained. "The term 'identification' expresses the most important principle in the process that now interests us and is in fact the Archimedean point of the educational enterprise in every generation" (ibid., p. 166). Educators harnessed the sexual turbulence of adolescence to reinforce the movement's control over the psyches of its teenage members. They sought to ensure that these young people did not find other ways of sublimating the biological–social conflicts that troubled them, leaving open only those solutions that were ideologically acceptable. Paradoxically, it was psychoanalysis, which placed the individual at the centre, that showed the movement's educators the psychological way for them to achieve almost complete control over the individual psyche. They did not need the usual repressive methods of the totalitarian state. Instead, they could achieve this innocuously by creating an autonomous youth enclave that served as an arm of society reaching into the consciousness of the adolescent.

Historians of the kibbutz movement as well as psychoanalysts have written extensively about the family structure promulgated by the movement's educators and about the faulty interpretation to *sublimation* of the sexual drive, a concept that was particularly popular amongst the advocators of the communal showers that were the rule for boys and girls, up until late adolescence, at most kibbutzim (cf. Berman, 1988; Bettelheim, 1969; Golan, 1959; Nagler, 1963; Rabin, 1965; Rapaport, 1958; Safir, 1983; Spiro, 1958; Yitzhaki, 1989: for a recent personal account of growing up in a kibbutz, see Ne'eman, 2011). But this Freudian catchword, used in both Soviet sexology and in the pedagogical discourse of HaShomer HaTza'ir from their earliest years, is not sufficient to explain the profound connection between the sex education of the individual as a psychological programme and the shaping of the new man of the kibbutz in its ideological sense. The connection between sex and society needs to be sought in the group dynamic put into operation by the shapers of communal education when they linked sex education to the movement's collectivist goals. The movement's sexual discourse was effective because it blurred, among children, the distinction between their interiority and the wishes and goals of the group. Sexuality served principally as a window through which to peer into and penetrate the individual psyche.

The desire of young immigrants to tie their personal sexual liberation to the national cause was not compatible with the pedagogical ideology of Marxist educators. Thus, they had to forgo, for example, any display of solidarity with Wilhelm Reich, who preached the utter sexual liberation of youth. In his book, *The Invasion of Compulsory Sex-Morality* (1970[1931]), Reich sought to show that sexual repression served the existing capitalist regime. As long as the regime continued to repress young people's sexuality it could be sure that they would not assert their independence. He added a scientific-medical dimension, arguing that masturbation, so prevalent among young people, was no different, from a physiological standpoint, than adult sexuality. The division between physical sexual maturity and social psychic maturity is artificial, he argued, and served only to police young people's permitted channels of sexual gratification (Reich, 1931).

Golan and Zohar were in fundamental agreement with Reich, which made the internal discussion of the latter's works into an especially sensitive issue. Reich's final break with Freud, which culminated in his expulsion from the psychoanalytic movement, centred on the former's political radicalism. By 1934, neither Jones nor Eitingon would risk inviting Reich to Britain or Palestine for fear he might bring along his predilection for associating psychoanalysis with Communism. His fixation with the political and social aspects of psychoanalysis, and particularly the role of psychoanalysis in bringing about a sexual revolution by openly criticising the structure of the modern bourgeois family, is still a subject of historiographic debate (cf. Chasseguet-Smirgel & Grunberger, 1986; Corrington, 2003; Fallend & Nizschke, 2002; Rolnik, 2008a; Scharaf, 1983).[4] In his letters to Fenichel, Golan described his doubts about whether he should "make a scandal" in response to Eitingon's hostility to Reich, but in the end he decided to adhere to the views of Freud and Eitingon. The formulators of communal education firmly opposed Reich's claim that society paid a heavy price in the form of neurosis for repressing sexuality. The approach taken by HaShomer HaTza'ir educators to collective education needed, despite its radicalism and utopian streak, to serve the movement's purposes. This meant that they could not adopt, wholesale, pedagogical models developed in Europe. From their point of view, the sexual liberation of youth was far from being a goal *per se*. Their ultimate purpose was to preserve the collectivist ideological framework. Had they been tempted to adopt Reich's simplistic parallel between capitalism and sexual repression, they would have had difficulty adapting psychoanalytic theory to their constructivist aims of building a New Man. The wish to eliminate the tension between the ideals of the individual and society by transforming the individual into a "society of an individual" is the key to understanding their reading of psychoanalytic theory at this time, and their instrumental approach to sexuality. The centre of gravity of kibbutz preoccupation with sexuality was, therefore, not the question of whether to encourage abstinence or sexual liberation. Rather, by "elucidating" the sexual question, the movement's educators achieved their principal goal of moulding the new man to feel autonomy and freedom while remaining entirely open to the ideological intervention by which society shaped the individual to its needs. The neo-romantic new man who served as a primary model for the young members of HaShomer HaTza'ir during the 1920s enabled them to adopt Freud's teachings with their neo-romantic individualistic cast. In contrast, the kibbutz man of the 1940s was a test case of bringing Freudian theory within Soviet parameters, which stressed the constant presence of society within the individual psyche. However, the movement was growing ever more distant from its Central European roots as it turned its gaze eastward to "Great Russia". As a result, among the second generation of HaShomer HaTza'ir educators psychoanalysis had much less cachet. As one critic of "Freudian pan-sexuality" wrote,

> Freud produced his theory in the face of patients who needed help, without class distinction and without any connection to the problems of life and the particular struggles of workers. And what was his ideal of the normal human being to which he wished to bring the patient? He wanted to transform these suffering, pathological creatures into normal, healthy citizens and bring them into the bosom of their petit-bourgeois class or to the camp of Social Democratic laborers of the "golden" age of the Weimar Republic. (Cited in Zohar, 1940, p. 17)

In the 1950s, HaShomer HaTza'ir began to make formal decisions that testified to the desire of many of those involved in determining its educational policy to divest themselves entirely of psychoanalytic theory, on the grounds that Freud's "non-dialectic" position focused on unconscious psychic conflicts. Freud's Marxist disciples liked his critique of religion, but they had trouble with the death drive hypothesis that Freud advanced in 1920. The introduction to the Hebrew translation of *Three Essays on the Theory of Sexuality*, issued by the HaShomer HaTza'ir press in 1954, states that the concept of the death drive was a byproduct of Freud's bourgeois education and should not be viewed as a fundamental part of his theory.

While HaShomer HaTza'ir's members were happy to employ Freud's subversive doctrine against the world they rejected, they could not bear to apply it to their own society. Their dilemma was how to adhere to a Freudian perspective without subjecting their own utopian views to Freudian analysis (Liban & Goldman, 2000). A case in point is the reception of the Hebrew translation of *Totem and Taboo*.

Members of the herd

The call to strip Freudian theory of its bourgeois elements appeared in a number of critical responses to the Hebrew publication of *Totem and Taboo.* An article in one of the labour movement's most important periodicals called upon Hebrew readers to "review and scrutinize sociological psychoanalytic research and draw from it all that is important and helpful to our proletarian world-view" (Ben-Shaul, 1939). Nevertheless, Yehuda Dvir-Dwosis, the translator, viewed *Totem and Taboo* as a platform on which an entirely different agenda could be played out. He believed it was important to provide Freud's text with a foundation in Jewish sources, and notified Freud of his intention to add to the translation a number of references to biblical and Talmudic literature, which he argued would "strengthen and corroborate your claims, and occasionally cast them in a new light" (Dvir-Dwosis to Freud, 30 November 1938: AFM).

Freud, it should be said, was sceptical from the start about Dvir-Dwosis's choice of this work. He recommended that Hebrew readers first be given a chance to read his *Introductory Lectures on Psychoanalysis*, which was based on a series of two-hour talks he gave at the University of Vienna between 1915 and 1917. This would initiate both doctors and lay people to the fundamental principles of the field. The published *Introductory Lectures* had enormous success, with fifty thousand copies sold in German during Freud's lifetime. Freud also suggested that Dvir-Dwosis consider translating his three "speculative, difficult, but intriguing" works, *Beyond the Pleasure Principle* (1920g), *The Ego and the Id* (1923b), and *Civilization and Its Discontents* (1930a). All these, he thought, were more important than *Totem and Taboo* (Freud to Dvir-Dwosis, 1 January 1936: AFM).

Dvir-Dwosis's decision to ground his Hebrew translation of the latter work in Jewish texts is not itself surprising. Many Zionist intellectuals viewed the revival of the Hebrew language as a necessary foundation for Jewish national life. Translators of great works of world literature into Hebrew at this time habitually searched out and used words and idioms from the Jewish canon. But Dvir-Dwosis's initiative contradicted, to a certain extent, the view taken by Freud in the introduction he provided for the Hebrew edition. There he stated that his view of the origin of morality and religion should not be tied to the Jewish tradition specifically. Rather, he meant it to be based on objective and universal scientific principles devoid of any ethnic or religious presuppositions:

> [A] book, moreover, which . . . deals with the origin of religion
> and morality, though it adopts no Jewish standpoint and makes no

exceptions in favor of Jewry. The author hopes, however, that he will
be at one with his readers in the conviction that unprejudiced science
cannot remain a stranger to the spirit of the new Jewry. (Freud,
[1930]1939, in Freud, 1913, *S.E.*, *8*: 15)

Dvir-Dwosis peppered his published version with pedantic translator's notes that sought to collate nearly every paragraph of Freud's
with a biblical verse.[5] At one point he offered a counterpoint of some
twenty footnotes one after the other:

> In the Torah, a sacrifice is called "bread of God": "They shall be holy
> . . . for the offerings of HaShem made by fire, the bread of their God,
> they do offer" (Lev. 21:6); as do the prophets: "when ye offer My
> bread, the fat and the blood" (Ez. 44:7); and the altar is called "the
> table of God": "The altar . . . of wood . . . 'This is the table that is before
> HaShem' (Ez. 41:22); "You offer polluted bread upon my altar. . . . You
> say: 'The table of HaShem is contemptible'". (Mal. 1:7). (Freud[1913]
> 1939, pp. 154–165)

Dvir-Dwosis did not just hijack Freud's essay for his own ideological ends or to offer biblical citations in support of Freud's arguments.
In some places he debated with the author in his footnotes. For example, where Freud wrote that "In later antiquity there were two classes
of sacrifice: one in which the victims were domestic animals of the
kinds habitually used for eating, and the other extraordinary sacrifices
of animals which were unclean and whose consumption was forbidden", Dvir-Dwosis added a footnote:

> There was never, of course, a place for such things in the Israelite reli-
> gion. The Torah stresses and repeats: "When any man of you brings
> an offering unto HaShem, you shall bring your offering of the cattle,
> even of the herd or of the flock" (Lev. 1:2); "You shall therefore sepa-
> rate between the clean beast and the unclean, and between the unclean
> fowl and the clean; and you shall not make your souls detestable by
> beast, or by fowl, or by any thing wherewith the ground teems"; (Lev.
> 20:25); or "And if it be any unclean beast, of which they may not bring
> an offering unto HaShem" (Lev. 27:11), and in many other verses.
> (Ibid.)

In contrast to *Group Psychology and the Analysis of the Ego*, which
was published a decade earlier, during a nadir in the Yishuv's literary
scene, the Hebrew translation for *Totem and Taboo* came out when

Jewish intellectual life in Palestine was at a high point. The events in Europe caused a resurgence in Jewish settlement that went beyond just an increase in immigration. The process of building the nation and Yishuv society accelerated both on the ground and ideologically.

The Bible teacher who read *Totem and Taboo* through the lens of scripture in order to stress that its author's thinking was fully in accord with Jewish tradition used Freud to promote his own agenda. So did the editors of *Orient*, the German-language periodical published in Palestine under the editorship of Arnold Zweig and Wolfgang Yourgrau. *Orient* published the works of well-known German–Jewish writers and poets who lived in Palestine at the time, including Else Lasker-Schüller, Zweig, and Max Brod. But *Orient* also took a firm position on the question of the superiority of Central European culture, and sought to instil in its readers identification with, and pride for, Germany's cultural heritage (Gordon, 2004). Freud's introduction to the Hebrew edition of *Totem and Taboo* was a prize catch for the journal's editors, who published it in an issue devoted to Vienna. The conundrum of Freud's Jewish identity and the reservations about political Zionism he expressed in the piece fit perfectly with the image of the German-speaking intellectual that *Orient* proclaimed and defended. The declaration by the famous doctor of the mind that Jewish nationality and religion had nothing to do with his Jewish identity offered intellectual and emotional solace for those who sought to preserve their German–Jewish identity in the face of Germany's declaration of war against the Jews (Gordon, 2004, p. 78).

One of the sternest critics of the translation, the writer and journalist Israel Cohen, wondered whether psychoanalysis reinforced people's allegiance to the existing regime or made them critical of the prevailing order. He was very certain of the answer:

> Every element in psychoanalysis is a living contradiction of the existing regime. . . . The restoration of the individual's importance, which is the psychoanalytic therapeutic goal, is possible only in an economic and social order in which there is no high and low, poor and rich, those who eat their fill and the hungry, rulers and subjects. . . . We must first cure the rot that comes from society or that has become second nature to the psyche because of society's corruption. Remedying that corruption helps psychoanalysis, making it a revolutionary tool for the revitalization of man and society. (Cohen, 1936, p. 6)

Cohen was devoid of the utopian illusions that shaped the psycho-analytic reading prevalent in HaShomer HaTza'ir and among the Freudian left, which aimed its principal critique at the depression of the patriarchal family (cf. Lasch, 1989), but he also muted the social pessimism implied in Freud's works. The socialist world-view of these readers of Freud did not automatically make them adherents of his theory. For example, Eliezer Yaffe, who had arrived as part of the Second Aliyah, wrote sarcastically about Freud's theory of drives and mocked the anthropological findings that he cited in *Totem and Taboo*. His critique of the book (1934) was published in *Gazit*, an important literary periodical that appeared over a period of fifty years, and which at the time was supported financially by Eitingon (Eitingon to Gavriel Talpir, 3 September 1939: GAL). Most of Yaffe's vitriol was directed at the ethnological–anthropological foundation on which Freud based his conclusions about man's subliminal urge "to murder his father and copulate with his mother". Eliezer Yaffe of Nahalal, a founder of this first of the semi-communal types of settlement called the *moshav ovdim*, wrote as a Jewish farmer who had better and more authentic experience of the world than did the assimilated Viennese professor (Yaffe, 1947). In contrast with the learning and detachment of the city-dwelling doctor, Yaffe offered unmediated contact with nature and its creatures. He recommended to Freud to go out to pasture and observe herds of cattle.

> Freud (like most scientists) forged his theory within the walls of a big city and did not sufficiently peruse the life of the herds of beasts and animals that live like the flocks of primeval man; but, had he looked only at the herds of cattle he would have discovered very many diffi-culties for his theory in general and certainly for the matter of the Oedipus complex. (Yaffe, 1934)

Yaffe opened his article by describing a herd of cows grazing in a meadow. One of the young beasts is in heat and the old bull had his eye on her—but then a young bull suddenly approaches and he, too, wants to mount the cow:

> Springtime, a local herd of cattle grazing in an ancient forest. The herd consists of several dozen cows and mature calves, and a single stocky and belligerent bull (like the father in the primeval human herd). The herd also includes a few young bulls and adolescent calves (like the

sons in the primeval human herd). The old bull is preoccupied at this moment with a cow in heat, but even though she is in heat she keeps trying to get away from the old guy, whether deliberately, in order to arouse him, or perhaps because she has set her eye on a younger male, or perhaps simply because the old guy is bothering her more than she wants. Or perhaps that's just the way females are. A few young bulls follow the old one around and try from time to time to mount a cow in heat, if the old bull's attention can be diverted, and it sometimes happens that the old guy goes after one of the young ones and gives him a good thrashing for having dared to go near one of his females, and then another young bull will immediately jump on the old guy's lover; and before the old bull has an opportunity to carry out his deed against the first uppity youngster, he has to turn his horns toward another, and in the meantime a third quickly grabs his lover, and he, too, gets what he has coming to him from the old bull's horns. (Ibid. p. 25)

Yaffe goes on to chronicle how one of the "sons" defeats the old bull and copulates with the cow, and how he loses sight of his younger brother, himself a rebel of no small proportions, who also manages to mount the favourite cow of the now deposed old bull. Afterwards, the old bull makes an alliance with his eldest son and together they defeat the upstart:

And another question: when the violent son overcomes the violent father, does he really want to copulate with his old mother, just so Freud and his theory be proven true about the Oedipus complex? Would he not rather lust after his nubile sister, and so bestow us with an Amnon complex? [In the Bible, Amnon, a son of King David, lusts after and rapes his sister Tamar.] Or were our primal forefathers such blockheads that in the dark of the night (since there still wasn't any electricity), while our primal father mated with one of the females, they couldn't find any way to copulate with one of the other females in their band and so cool off their blood, so as not to reach the boiling point and murder our primal father in revenge?

Eliezer Yaffe's resounding critique of the Freudian version of the rule of the father should be understood in the context of his view of the relations between the Hebrew pioneer and his land, a view that places the mother at the centre. According to Yaffe, even more than the man wants to suckle, the land wants to nurse him. "The greatest sin on this earth", he wrote in an article with the title "Separated", "is that man does not cling to the bosom of Mother Earth in order to drink the bounty that will turn bitter if she has no one to suckle" (Yaffe, 1947, vol. 2, p. 305). He also proclaimed: "When I see a man working the soil in his field, I see the image of an infant grasping his sleeping mother's breast, trying to attach his lips to her nipple" (ibid., p. 306).

The patriarchal bias so characteristic of Freud's thinking was also criticised by psychoanalysts. Gershon Barag, who received his medical and psychoanalytic training in Europe, published his article "On prostitution" just a short time after joining the Palestinian Psychoanalytic Society. In that work he linked the sexual behaviour of the prostitute to female divinity (Barag, 1936; Gumbel, 1958). Barag saw the key to the understanding of the phenomenon in a narcissistic phantasy according to which father, mother, and child are united in one person. In 1946, he advanced this idea in another connection, in "The mother in the religious concepts of Judaism" (1946). There he showed that, even in Jewish monotheism, the purest form of a father religion, vestiges of former mother goddesses are to be found. Moreover, every god figure seems to exhibit both male and female features. This leads him back to the phantasy of the unity of father, mother, and child, and eventually to the suggestion that a characteristic attribute of the Semitic religions can be seen in this very union of male and female in one god. Thus, the roots of monotheism lay not only in the Oedipal rebellion against the primal father, but also in the fantasy of fusing with the mother.

Notes

1. "Mental hygiene" (or "psychic hygiene") was a term that mental health professionals began using in the mid-nineteenth century to designate a broad domain of knowledge, technologies, and practices associated with the promotion of mental health. The hygienic repertoire offered models for the right way to wash, sleep, eat, dress, work, organise time, and much more.

2. Brachyahu's Hebrew translation for the *Interpretation of Dreams* has only recently been replaced by a new translation.

3. Zohar was sent as a representative of the movement to the "World Congress on sexual reform" which took place in Vienna in 1930.

4. Responding to Siegfried Bernfeld's query as to whether he should accept a paper which Reich submitted for publication, Freud wrote:

    The practical Marxist (The Bolshevik) is a man who presume to be in possession of a revelation, a Khalif who rules by the Koran, and therefore someone who in principal stands in opposition to science ... to such a person our journals should therefore remain out of reach. (Freud to Bernfeld, 22 May 1932: Bernfeld Collection (FCLC))

5. These unauthorised footnotes bring to mind Freud's (1892–1894) critical footnotes which he, without permission or warning, inserted in his translation of Jean-Martin Charcot's *Lecons du Mardi a la Salpetriere* (cf. Roith, 2008).

CHAPTER SIX

A psychoanalytic midrash

"And then his [Freud's] students and their students and the disciples of his disciples have come and added exaggeration to hyperbole: a gaggle of babblers have, evoking the 'ineffable name' of their 'rabbi,' broken brazenly into the home of the writer, cutting into and poking through the soul of his works, turning over and upending all that is sacred and intimate, in order to uncover and reveal the root of the 'libido,' the sexual urge, which is, ostensibly, the ultimate source and motivator of all motivations. And some do this with a kind of lustful appetite in order to satisfy the licentiousness and filth that abides within them"

(Chaim Nachman Bialik, 1931)

Unsurprisingly, many of Freud's critics in Palestine had a penchant for speculating on the relationship between the Jewish origins of the creator of psychoanalysis and his theories. Some even went so far as to claim that his concept of repression should be viewed as an acknowledgment of his faith.

The members of the committee that in 1942 awarded the Tchernikovsky translation prize to the Odessa-born Zvi Wislavsky for his Hebrew rendering of *The Psychopathology of Everyday Life* (1901b) emphasised that the excellence of his translation of Freud's book lay in its use of the language of the Mishnah and midrash, creating an illusion that "one of our ancients" wrote the original.[1] The committee's statement displayed the prevailing tendency of Yishuv writers to view Freud's theory as a manifestation of his Jewish origin, a proclivity already evident in Dvir-Dwosis's translations. The desire to impart Freud's teaching to Hebrew-language readers in a prophetic-biblical style, like Dvir-Dwosis's translations twenty years previously, and to turn him into a kind of ancient prophet, reached its climax during the 1940s, a formative period for Hebrew culture. The purpose was to make Freud's works part of the Hebrew literary canon, rather than something created outside it. True, since the publication of *Moses and Monotheism*, Freud's works remained controversial in the Yishuv and were not given easy acceptance, even after being "converted" by their translators. In fact, to Hebrew readers, it seemed that the doctor from Vienna who coined the term "repression" had already given away, in *The Psychopathology of Everyday Life*, his neurosis regarding his Jewish descent.

When the translation came out, the poet Shin Shalom (Shalom Yosef Shapira) published an angry article with the headline "Freud's repressed Judaism". Shalom wrote of Freud's "repressed fundamental experience", manifested in his theory of self-disclosure and confession. He described how he himself broke free of the "initial intoxication" he had felt upon making an acquaintance with Freud's theory, which gave the concept of repression a central place. Shalom related that he had eventually reached the conclusion that he had to judge Freud according to his own standards. Was it just a coincidence that the creator of psychoanalysis was a Viennese Jew of the generation of assimilation, who hoped to find a solution for his own ills in the obliteration of his Jewish self? Shalom had no doubt that the repressed Judaism of Freud and his generation was the root experience behind his theory:

> The generational cry of the anguished Jewish nation that was compelled to repress and conceal its birth and its explicit name, its desire and its mission, in order to give in to the forceful ruling gentile reality of the world and all that is in it is what gave rise to the crushing and broad wings of this theory. Herzl, a member of Freud's generation and a party to his fate at first, was in fact the great discoverer and

great redeemer of that repressed fundamental experience that Freud
himself, originator of the theory of repression, could not comprehend.
(Shalom, 1942, p. 318)

Herzl and Freud, each in his own way, were products of the
repression experienced by the Jewish people. But while the former
emancipated the Jews from being ruled by gentiles, Shalom maintained, Freud's theory was an expression of the way in which the Jews
repressed their true desires. *The Psychopathology of Everyday Life*, in
Wislavsky's translation, provided Shin Shalom with the proof that a
repressed Jewish experience lay behind Freud's doctrines. His central
piece of evidence was one of the examples Freud offered in his book,
a conversation he has with a young Jewish friend about the "social
state of the people that we are both sons of". According to Shalom,
this young Jew's words indicate Freud's own repressed desire to
speak of what oppressed him, of his country and homeland. Shalom
found in Freud's text the tragedy of the Jews of the West and of the
entire Diaspora, which "is compelled to repress its connection to itself,
to fear both the priest and the warrior . . . and to cast the newborn son
into the Nile". Elsewhere in the same work, Shalom finds additional
support for his claim about Freud's Jewish secret. Freud ascribed a
question to one of the subjects of his study: "Was the faith of your
fathers an obstacle to obtaining the bride you desired?" Shalom rendered it: "Were you forced to conceal and repress the faith of your
fathers?" The answer was obvious: the secret of Freud's life and work
was the secret of the covert Jews of all generations, from the Con-
versos of Spain and Portugal to the assmiliationists of Berlin and
Vienna—the so-called "Germans of the Mosaic persuasion" (ibid.
p. 319).

Shin Shalom's angry tirade about Freud's repressed Judaism was
written at the height of the Second World War, at a time when many
of the Yishuv's leaders and intellectuals found it difficult to shed their
ambivalent attitude toward the Jewish immigrants from Central
Europe. They felt a need to leaven their display of empathy and solidarity with no small amount of condemnation for the extent to which
German-speaking Jews had assimilated into German cultural life. But
the watershed in the way the Yishuv's intellectual circles of the 1930s
and 1940s related to Freud was the latter's last great work, *Moses and
Monotheism*, a volume that seemed to be aimed at reminding the

Yishuv readership that the intellectual horizons of the originator of psychoanalysis, and the pressing needs of his fellow Jews, whether Zionist or non-Zionist, could never sit well together.

Impossible confession

Freud has an assured place in the history of ideas and of science as a man of intellectual courage who turned his back on essentialist views of humanity and on the Darwinistic, biologistic, and racist theories that reigned supreme in the psychiatric thinking of his time. He founded a science of subjectivity based on investigation of the dynamic but universal psychological mechanisms that lie behind human differences and mental diversity. Yet, paradoxically, in the 1930s, just when the explosive political potential of ethno-psychological and neo-Lamarckian views became apparent, Freud once again took up the idea of the hereditary transmission of character traits, leaving his heirs an enigmatic legacy in the form of the eerie theory of Judaism that he offered in his book *Moses and Monotheism* (1939a). Few texts in his oeuvre have proved as enduringly controversial as the work in which he applied the psychoanalytic tools he had developed over forty years to an examination of the iconographic representative of the Jewish ethos—Moses, the greatest of the prophets.

Freud's book on Moses is, without question, many things at once. It addresses the psychology of religion and biblical criticism. It is also a novel that rewrites a myth, a historical work on the emergence of the psychoanalytic idea, a monograph on the origin of neurosis in the individual and in society, as well as a political manifesto and a metaphorical biography. Noting all these elements in *Moses and Monotheism*, Grubrich-Simitis (1997) termed it a "daydream". Edward Said (2003), for his part, aptly characterised the book with a musicological term, calling it a *Spätwerk*, a late composition, the kind that the composer leaves incomplete and which he writes largely for himself, leaving incompatible elements as they are—temporal, fragmentary, unpolished.

For those who had followed the author's intellectual development, the book was not a big surprise. Interesting testimony that has not yet been cited in the large body of work on Freud's depiction of Moses can be found in an article published in 1950 in a Hebrew journal by Chaim Bloch (Blach), who studied Hasidism and Kabbalah.[2] Bloch reported a meeting with Freud twenty-five years earlier at which they discussed Moses's origin and what might happen should Freud publish his thoughts on the matter:

> Twenty-five years ago I told Sigmund Freud, the eminent scholar, that his study of Moses and the Torah are abominable sacrifices to the anti-semitic demon. . . . I pleaded with him not to mow down what he had already planted, that the life of the Jewish people depended on him, and I warned him that the end would be that our people's enemies would place him among the traitors and informers. (Bloch, 1950, p. 101)

This was Bloch's opening to an account of his two encounters with Freud, during which Freud initially expressed his willingness to write an introduction to a book Bloch had written. But the first meeting ended in a major altercation, with Freud stalking out of the room in anger. Their conversation had turned to Judaism and Hasidism, Freud impressing Bloch with his knowledge. The former then produced two typewritten manuscripts and asked for his guest's opinion.

"My heart went hollow and my hair stood up", Bloch recalled, "when I saw the headings 'Moses was an Egyptian born and bred,' 'Moses's Torah is the creation of Egyptian magi,' 'The Jews killed Moses,' no less. I read a few pages and my eyes filled with tears" (ibid., p. 102).

Bloch's account of his meeting with Freud claims, in other words, that, around 1925, Freud already had in hand a manuscript that included the thesis that Moses, the great prophet of the Jews, was an Egyptian who was murdered by the Israelites. If true, this is evidence that *Moses and Monotheism*, the composition of which has always been dated to the years 1933–1938, was, in fact, written almost ten years earlier. Bloch wrote that he told Freud that publication of the manuscript would be disastrous for the Jews, and Freud replied that "The truth causes neither a disaster nor danger." Bloch iterated that "Every man creates whatever truth he likes for himself and that there is no truth in the world as great as silence. The antisemites will lick their fingers when they read your studies." Freud responded that "he was repelled by the idea that we are chosen and superior to other nations", and held forth on his negative opinion of religion. To support his claims, he quoted from Theodor Herzl's Zionist novel *Altneuland*. He also cited the claim made by the writer Max Nordau, Herzl's partner in the founding of the Zionist movement, that the Holy Scriptures are a pile of superstitions and traditions from Egypt. Freud linked his manuscript with Nordau's writings:

> I will not deny that when I read [Nordau's] book on consensual lies and his sentence on the Holy Scriptures, I decided to take up this problem. After all, it cannot be claimed that Nordau harmed our nation! To the best of my knowledge the Jews admired Nordau when he was alive and honor his memory after his death. Nordau did not offer any proof of his statement that the Torah contains Egyptian traditions, but rather based his arguments on common sense alone. I have based my conclusions on evidence that no eye has yet seen. (Ibid., p. 105)

At this point, the argument grew heated. Bloch claimed that Nordau had repudiated his statemen ts about the Bible and had regretted allowing himself to be carried away by gentile biblical critics. Freud claimed that Nordau had never recanted. Bloch adduced evidence in support of his claim, a conversation Nordau had with Reuven Breinin, a Zionist journalist and critic, during which he acknowledged that he had been mistaken. Freud produced a letter he had received from Nordau in which the latter congratulated him for "your courage to uncover the truth about Moses and his Torah" and complained that the newspapers had spread a rumour that he had told Breinin he regretted what he had said about the Holy Scriptures. In the letter, Nordau denied the allegation categorically. Freud also showed Bloch the most recent edition of Nordau's book *The Conventional Lies of Our Civilization* (1913) to demonstrate to Bloch that its author had not revised his critical attitude toward the Bible. Bloch's transcription of the conversation indicates that the argument went on for quite some time. Bloch expressed his reservations, censured Freud, pleaded with him to file away his study of Moses—all to no avail. Freud even argued that his new findings were not based on vague ancient sources of the type cited by the Hebrew author Micha Josef Berdichevsky, but, rather, on new evidence that could not be denied.

The Conventional Lies of Our Civilization, which condemns religion as a falsehood, was published in 1883 and was a great success (Gilman, 1993b). The title does not appear in the bibliographies of any of Freud's works, nor was it in the library Freud brought to London. Yet, if we take Bloch's report at face value, Freud was acquainted not just with Nordau's book but also with Berdichevsky's writing on the subject. This is a new and interesting claim, especially in light of the fact that neither is cited anywhere in the writings of Freud published so far. Freud was almost certainly referring to Berdichevsky's great work *Sinai and Grizim*, in which he sought to prove that a critical reading of the Bible, Mishnah, Tannaitic, Talmudic, and rabbinic literature throughout the ages reveals an unending conflict between centres of power and spiritual leaders. It is hard to resist the temptation to speculate about why Freud chose not to cite Nordau's and Berdichevsky's studies in support of his ideas. The most obvious answer is that the writings of these two men were part of a scholarly discourse of a particularistic Jewish nature debated within the context of the Zionist movement. Citing them would have directed the debate over the figure of Moses from its innovative psychoanalytic context and restricted it to its traditional theological and historical aspects. Freud certainly must have known, however, that, in the final analysis, this strategy would not safeguard his book from a "Jewish offensive".

When Bloch saw that his claims had been countered, he tried another strategy. "'The measure that a man uses to evaluate others is used to evaluate him'", he told Freud, quoting a passage from the Mishnah. "Thousands of years from now some investigator will appear who will provide murky evidence that Prof. Sigmund Freud, originator of psychoanalytic science, was an Egyptian and his teachings are Egyptian, and the members of his generation killed him."

Freud was not alarmed by the possibility that some future scholar might similarly conjecture that he, the founder of psychoanalysis, was not really Jewish. "And so what if they do?" he replied. "May it be— the principal thing is that my theory endure." Furthermore, in his earlier work *The Moses of Michaelangelo* (1914b), it is already apparent that one thing that attracted Freud to the figure of the prophet and to identify with him was the fact that Moses reached the highest spiritual level within reach of humankind: the ability to set aside his personal emotions for the good of, and in the name of, the goal to which he had dedicated himself. Freud's equanimity induced Bloch to offer a less scholarly and more sarcastic rejoinder: "Have you also examined the list of births and deaths in Egypt so that you have unimpeachable evidence that Moses was of Egyptian extraction and that the Jews killed him?"

Freud felt the sting. "I won't write the introduction to your book and I don't want to see you again," he snapped and strode out of the room. Bloch was left in shock. When the two ran into each other on the street a few years later, Bloch was surprised to discover that Freud had forgotten the episode; neither did he even recall that they had ever met. He asked Bloch to remind him what their conversation had been about and why it had ended so badly. Bloch recounted the story and Freud recollected the conversation. "I remember your insolence, and I indeed don't want to see you again," he said, and walked off. (Ibid., p. 107.)

*   *   *

Much of the literature on *Moses and Monotheism* mentions that a draft of the manuscript included a subtitle: "A Historical Novel". Freud's letters to Arnold Zweig and Max Eitingon show that the subtitle was Eitingon's suggestion, one of many he offered as "safety measures" intended to minimise the uproar that the book could be expected to set off among its Jewish readers.

> Since we live at a time so close in its spirit to the time of the Inquisition, it would be legitimate to take the same precautions taken in that time. Let's equip *Moses* with a subtitle that will appease its dangerous opponents, such as for example "A Historical–Psychological Novel." We know, after all, the amount of truth that novels conceal. One thing is certain—as opposed to Arnold Zweig's advice, I believe that publishing this work privately or anonymously will not provide sufficient protection. And another thing about which we can undoubtedly be certain: the work must come out in the framework of the [psychoanalytic] publishing house. . . . Still, the idea of publishing a book by you in Palestine, privately, is a wonderful and entertaining idea. Unfortunately, however, I must oppose the idea. It is simply not practical. (Eitingon to Freud, 14 October 1934, in Freud & Eitingon, 2004, p. 881)

Eitingon was apprehensive about how reaction to the book would affect the acceptance of psychoanalysis in the Yishuv. Rumours about Freud's plan to publish a book about Moses had already spread through Palestine's Jewish community. Yehuda Dvir-Dwosis, who had translated other works by Freud, wrote to him to ask,

> In light of the great travails of the Jewish people in these times, has the time not come to answer the question with which you concluded the introduction to the Hebrew edition of your *Introductory lectures on*

Psychoanalysis: What is it that makes me Jewish? (Dvir-Dwosis to Freud, 30 November 1938: courtesy of Ora Rafael)

In his reply to Dvir-Dwosis, Freud dispersed some of the clouds of mystery that surrounded what he had written eight years previously:

> I have nothing to add or revise in what I wrote then. The mysterious sentence to which you refer relates to the question about the way in which our common tradition manifests itself in our psychic life—a complex problem of a purely psychological nature. . . . My next book, about Moses and monotheism, will be issued at the beginning of the year in English and German. Of course its translation into the Holy Tongue will gratify me greatly. It is an extension of the subject discussed in *Totem and Taboo*, applied to the history of the Jewish religion. I ask that you take into account that the material in this work is particularly likely to offend Jewish sensibilities to the extent that these [sensibilities] are not interested in submitting themselves to the authority of science. (Freud to Dvir-Dwosis, 2 December 1938: AFM)

And, on 28 June 1938, Freud wrote to "Meister Arnold" (Zweig), evidently his favourite émigré interlocutor during the 1930s: "Could you imagine that my arid essay could, even if it were to fall into the hands of a man whose heritage and education had made him into a believer, unsettle his faith?" (Freud & Zweig, 1970, p. 163).

The responses to *Moses and Monotheism* from intellectuals and psychoanalysts around the world spanned the spectrum. But the book clearly reverberated particularly strongly in the Yishuv years before it became a popular subject for debate in the historiography of psychoanalysis. The reactions came in the form of letters and critical articles written by scholars, personal letters from psychoanalysts to Freud, and a lively public debate carried out in the press. There was even one public letter written by a citrus grower, which he published in the country's most important literary magazine.

Yisrael Doryon, a Jerusalem-based writer and physician who was then working on a book on the Austrian philosopher Josef Popper-Lynkeus, immediately wrote to Freud to report that he had discovered an identical idea—that Moses was an Egyptian—in Lynkeus's book *The Fantasies of a Realist*. Freud related to Doryon that it was a great honour to discover that he owed his idea about Moses's Egyptian origins to Lynkeus. He was unable to tell Doryon with certainty "exactly how Popper-Lynkeus's *Fantasies*" had found its way into his work, but he reminded Doryon that the innovativeness of his book on Moses lay not in its conclusions, but in the way he reached them (Doryon to Freud, 15 September 1938; Freud to Doryon, 7 October 1938: FCLC). Indeed, the matter of Moses's true identity is not central in the work. Its principal contribution lies in the role played by Moses in bringing the monotheistic doctrine to the Hebrews, and the way that that belief shaped Jewish identity. Freud used the figure of Moses to iterate his claim that racial and intellectual differences, not Jewish religion and practices, stood between the Jews and their Christian environment. These differences kept the Jews distinct from all other nations in a way that does not permit complete integration, but only superficial cultural assimilation.

Why did Freud devote his final strength to a speculative thesis about the extraction of the leader of the Hebrews and the implications of Moses's life for the destiny of his people? One of the answers to this question can be provided by another Jewish thinker, who also viewed Moses as a critical nexus of mythos and logos, rationalism and religious faith. In many ways, Freud's answer is surprisingly like that of Ahad Ha'am, the founder of spiritual Zionism. Both men maintained that religion and tradition should be examined scientifically in order to uncover the deepest levels of the human psyche's thinking, feeling, and imagination. If this is done consistently, without anti-religious prejudices, we will be able to uncover the depths of human truth that were, in ancient times, revealed to humankind as divine truth. Ahad Ha'am's essay on Moses, like Freud's work on the same figure, shows him at the peak of his creative powers. It opens by making a distinction between archaeology and history. In his view, archaeology is the study of "material truth", the truth Freud sought in his book. But, wrote Ahad Ha'am, the biblical figure of Moses should not be seen as a "true" archaeological figure. In his view, it made no difference whether or not there actually was an ancient leader named Moses. The Moses of the Bible was a mythological figure who reflected the Jewish nation's ideal view of itself. The fact that he was not an archaeological figure did not in any way diminish the figure's tremendous influence. The prophet as portrayed in the people's imagination, fixed in the nation's collective consciousness, was more real than any archaeological figure. It shaped Jewish experience and its historical path:

Surely it is obvious that the real great men of history, the men, that is, who have become forces in the life of humanity, are not actual, concrete persons who existed in a certain age. There is not a single great man in history of whom the popular fancy has not drawn a picture entirely different from the actual man; and it is this imaginary conception, created by the masses to suit their needs and their inclinations, that is the real great man, exerting an influence which abides in some cases for thousands of years—this, and not the concrete original who lived a brief period in the actual world, and was never seen by the masses in his true likeness. (Ahad Ha'am, 1912, p. 306)

The most salient characteristic of Moses, according to Ahad Ha'am, is that he is a "man of truth" and a "man of extremes". In other words, he is a person who saw life as it really is, who adhered to the path he believed in, and who rose above his selfish interests in order to realise his sublime values. The sublime validity of these values derives from their objectivity, the fact that they express a realistic and precise view of the world. Divine truth is simple, absolute, objective truth. It is not the truth of an individual, but, rather, the truth for everyone. Ahad Ha'am even provided a Freudian psychological explanation for Moses's experience of revelation at the burning bush. He argued that the voice Moses heard, the voice of God, was the voice of the national spirit that Moses bore in his heart from the time of his forgotten childhood, which was later, following his education in Pharaoh's palace, covered up and shunted aside in his adult life. This repressed memory suddenly surfaced in Moses's psyche in the wake of two incidents. The first was when he killed the Egyptian taskmaster he saw beating a Hebrew slave, and the second was when he encountered two Hebrews fighting each other. In the latter instance, when Moses told them to stop, one of them castigated Moses for murdering the Egyptian and trying to conceal his crime. As a result, Moses fled for his life. He tried to forget what had happened but did not succeed. His flight weighed on his conscience. But then came the most important event of all: he awakened from his "fainting fit [and] temporary loss of consciousness" and understood that he had fled not from his personal destiny but rather from that of his people (cf. Schweid, 1985, 2008).

In the monologue with which he concludes his book, *Freud's Moses: Judaism Terminiable and Interminable*, Yosef Hayim Yerushalmi (1991) wrote that the theory of Oedipal morality that Freud put in final form in his book on Moses is incontrovertible proof of Moses's "non-Jewish" origin. The interminable repetition of the repressed, Yerushalmi argued, is the precise opposite of the Jewish telos that looks to a specific future. Yerushalmi's sweeping conclusion was that Freud hoped that psychoanalysis would gradually become an alternative Jewish religion, devoid of all transcendental, metaphysical, and irrational components. Yerushalmi's somewhat hyperbolic interpretation of Freud's Moses brings to mind Eissler's (1965) mortifying conclusion that the birth of the State of Israel was a direct consequence of Freud's successful analysis in *Moses and Monotheism* (cf. Friedlander, 1978 p. 32).

More recently, in *On the Psychotheology of Everyday Life: Reflections on Freud and Rosenzweig* (2001), Santner has taken a less radical approach to the psychoanalytic project, one that reconciles it with the philosophy of Franz Rosenzweig, a German–Jewish philosopher of the early twentieth century. Santner proposed that these two post-Nietzschean thinkers were classic representatives of secular theology. If there was any inherent Jewish dimension to psychoanalytic thinking, it was reducible to the concept that psychic healing is a type of Exodus from Egypt, in a more general way—it means giving up the national project and the search for a "home" (Santner, 2001).

Edward Said reached a similar conclusion in his book, *Freud and the Non-European* (2003). For Said, Moses became paradigmatic for the encounter with the Other, or, to use Said's post-colonial language, with the "non-European". Both Moses, the founder of Jewish self awareness, and Freud, the founder of psychoanalysis, should, thus, be placed among those "non-Jewish Jews" (Deutscher, 1968) such as Spinoza, Marx, and Heine, who operated simultaneously from within and outside their Jewish identities. These writers, Said argued, not only stress the universal imperative within their self-conception as Jews, but also mark that intermediate space in which the concept of identity manifests itself in general. Said countered the common claim that Freud's search for his roots in a tribe that adopted Moses as a leader was no more than an expression of Freud's yearning to return to his and his parents' childhood home and to the Jewish tradition he had shed during his adult life. And, in doing so, Said did more justice to Freudian psychoanalysis's complex view of humankind. Freud's Jewish identity, like Moses's, was, according to Said, a partial, broken identity that acknowledged that the psychology of the individual, like that of the collective, contains within it heterogeneous and fortuitous elements that have their source in influences lying outside consciousness and personal history. The paradox in the Freudian conception of identity derived from the inability of a whole and integrated identity to be achievable via a search for the like. Rather, it was actually arrived at, ironically, through the incorporation of the foreign, different, stressful, and unpleasant within the boundaries of the self. In other words, identity is the reward of those who are prepared to apply the concept of identity also to cultural and emotional elements that constantly subvert the sense of a cohesive identity and homogenous solidarity. Identity is possible only if we acknowledge the presence of the foreign (or the Other) within us. When Freud sarcastically declared that he intended to get at the truth behind Moses's "true identity", even if it meant undermining his people's "national interests", he might have thought that his claim would help mitigate Zionism's solipsistic tendencies. That such tendencies existed was proved by the Yishuv's reaction to the book.

The Jewish offensive

A few months after Freud received Dvir-Dwosis's letter, Max Eitingon reported to him that the Yishuv was awash with rumours about the content of his new book, and that he had gained opponents even though none of his critics had read it in its entirety. Shortly after the publication date, Eitingon met for the first time with Martin Buber, whom he considered one of the most influential critics of psychoanalysis on the Yishuv's intellectual scene. Following the meeting, he notified Freud that, while he thought he had got through his incisive conversation with the philosopher with his honour intact, there could be no doubt that psychoanalysis in Palestine had a determined nemesis in Buber. While Freud's assumptions about the aetiology of the dream or on totemism were unacceptable to Buber, he saw no need to voice his views. But when it came to *Moses and Monotheism*, Buber informed Eitingon that he "could no longer remain silent", and that he intended to come out with a public statement condemning the book (letter dated 16 February 1939, in Freud & Eitingon, 2004, pp. 918–920). Buber and "his sanctimonious pronouncements" against the psychoanalytic theory of dreams did not cost Freud any sleep.

"*Moses* is much more vulnerable and I am prepared for the Jewish attack on it", he assured Eitingon (letter dated 5 March 1939, ibid., pp. 920–921). In 1945, when Buber published his own book on Moses, he rejected the approach of Bible scholars who cast doubt on the historicity of this Hebrew leader and wrote "that a scholar of so much importance in his own field as Sigmund Freud could permit himself to issue so unscientific a work, based upon groundless hypotheses, as his Moses and Monotheism (1939), is regrettable" (Buber, 1958, p. 7).

Eitingon himself had a hard time with *Moses and Monotheism*. Apparently, he read drafts of the manuscript prior to publication. His letter of thanks to Freud betrays the bewilderment of even Freud's most loyal admirers, especially his disciples in Palestine, over this work. Eitingon's ambivalence was evident between his lines of praise. He seems to have realised that the book could shut the door on his teaching psychoanalysis at the Hebrew University. Establishing a chair in psychoanalytic studies now seemed further away than ever.

> There is something exceptionally symbolic in the fact that your book on Moses arrived here on the Passover holiday, about which the Haggadah relates that God took the Jews out of Egypt "with a strong hand and an outstretched arm" [Eitingon wrote this phrase in the original Hebrew, but in German letters]. One can somehow sense the analogy in your book. Piercing logic, and a charm that cannot be withstood. That is how you bring the reader close to you in the final section, repeating for him the difficult arguments you make in Part II. It is a fine book. (Eitingon to Freud, 11 April 1939, in Freud & Eitingon, 2004, p. 923)

To write these flat lines of thanks, Eitingon had to muster not only all his love for Freud, but also the best verbal acrobatics that both languages, German and Hebrew, could offer. Two weeks later he informed Freud that "some excitement" was evident in the public's reaction to the book (letter dated 30 April 1939, ibid., pp. 924–925). In May 1939, the Palestine Psychoanalytic Society convened a special meeting at which its members heard a lecture on the volume by Erich Gumbel, the Jerusalem Psychoanalytic Institute's first graduate and Eitingon's senior student (Gumbel to Freud, 22 May 1939: AFM). The task of surveying this complex work was not an easy one. Even readers accustomed to reading Freud found that this book upset them. In his speech at this exceptional meeting, Eitingon intimated that the time might come when people would be sceptical of Freud's Jewish origins (Eitingon, 1950).

Moshe Wulff was the first member of the Society to publish his impressions of the work. He noted that the book's structure and the wealth of subjects addressed made it much different from the rest of Freud's writings. While in his other books Freud had conveyed to his readers a feeling that he was totally on top of the subject at hand and that the main issues he faced as a writer were stylistic and aesthetic, in *Moses and Monotheism* Moses had "overwhelmed" Freud and suppressed his organisational and conceptual abilities. "I must acknowledge", Wulff wrote, "that I have never been so profoundly affected by a work of Freud's as I have been by this one"(Wulff, 1950).

The Hebrew press seethed and only with difficulty was able to provide space for all those who wanted to fulminate about the book. "Freud's war against Moses!" shouted a headline in the religious Zionist daily *Hatzofeh* (Kaminka, 1939). Moses defenders came from all walks of life: a citrus farmer, Nachum Perlman, was deeply affected by Freud's book. He sought to link his critique to the campaign then under way to persuade Jews to buy goods grown or manufactured in the Yishuv. Did the campaign, he queried, relate only to material items, or should not Jews also boycott intellectual and spiritual imports which undermine Jewish national interests? In an open letter to Freud published in the Yishuv's leading literary magazine, *Moznayyim*, headlined "Professor Freud and buying local", Perlman rebuked those who allowed themselves "to cast into the depths of the sea our spiritual possessions and, in spiritual matters, to open all gates wide to concepts entirely foreign to Judaism" (Perlman to Freud, 2 July 1939: AFM). Perlman did not simply write his open letter to Freud in Hebrew. He translated it into German and sent it directly to Freud, adding a covering letter:

> I presume to address you, sir, as I do below, despite being no more than a layman with regard to your scientific profession. I write from the point of view of a Jew who has lived in the Land of Israel for the last thirteen years, not by coincidence, but because he feels that the continued existence of the Jewish people is something valuable for all of humanity. But because I am, sir, as I have already said, no more than a layman, I do not permit myself to critique your book *Moses* but only to ask you one question. You must certainly know, sir, that at this time a large number of our brethren view the results of Biblical criticism as

the actual content of the Jewish people's literature, without thinking through to themselves that in doing so they are cutting off the branch on which they sit, a thing that is on the one hand consistent, since it is known that we, the Jews, are "air people." . . . But not only does the reading public welcome this science, so do intelligent people and well-known Jewish writers among those who steer them, without considering the fact that all the archaeological excavations that have been conducted so far that contain any sort of indication regarding the Torah all confirm the words of the Bible and prove the flimsiness of Biblical criticism. (Perlman to Freud, 2 July 1939: AFM)

Was not affirmation or repudiation of Biblical criticism by Jews intended, whether they were aware of it or not, to justify their betrayal of the foundations of the Jewish religion and the Torah's commandments, Perlman asked Freud. He answered the question himself: "I believe that you, Herr Professor, are the best man to offer a full answer to my question, and I believe that in answering this question you will have the privilege of doing more for Jewish existence than you did with your book *Moses*" (ibid., the original letter is reproduced in Rolnik, 2010).

Raphael DaCosta of Jerusalem also wrote to Freud after reading the book. Unlike Perlman, he enjoyed it immensely. Nevertheless, he was of the opinion that the evidence Freud had adduced was insufficient. Freud based his claims on the thesis that the figure of Moses was actually composed of two different men, each of whom represented a distinct set of beliefs. This had to be the case, Freud maintained, because the differences between the two deities represented in the Torah are so huge that it would be difficult to conceive that they had been put forward by a single priest. DaCosta wrote that he would have accepted this proposition had it not implied that the Israelites had chosen the wrathful Egyptian priest. The other priest, the merciful man from Midian, was not appointed to represent Aton, the civilised sun god (DaCosta to Freud, 23 April 1939: AFM). Freud took the reservations of this Jerusalem reader seriously, and seems even to have regretted his speculative proposal that the biblical Moses was actually a composite of two men, a "good" priest and a "bad" priest. He replied to DaCosta:

There is indeed a difference in the natures of the two figures called Moses that I am unable to explain, but it could be said that the matter is not of great significance. We know very little about the second

Moses, who is of course an invention of mine, and I could have made do without the comment about his even-temperedness. (Freud to DaCosta, 2 May 1939: AFM)

Another point DaCosta made to Freud concerned the implications the book should have for the Jewish view of the world. He asked Freud whether the two beliefs, in religious truth and in scientific truth, were mutually exclusive. In other words, is there a way to reconcile rationalism with faith? Would Freud permit his fellow Jews to maintain their theological truth along with material truth, or did he insist that historical truth, which he recreated in his psychoanalytic studies, replace religious truth?

In *The Future of an Illusion*, Freud had already taken a firm position on the order of precedence of varying truths. He claimed that religious thinking of all kinds was simply the civilised incarnation of infantile sexuality, and that religion was tantamount to a neurosis that needed to be overcome. Freud repeats this position in *Civilization and Its Discontents* (1930a). But Freud's work on Moses seems to have led him to a somewhat more nuanced view, implying a certain revision of his conception of religious faith. In *Moses and Monotheism*, he acknowledged two truths, one religious and subjective, and the other archaeological and objective. He did not present these as contradictory, but rather as two positions that a person can move between. In the newer work, Freud gave historical truth itself the special status of being able to include several truths. It did not derive from an unambiguous rational decision of any type, but, rather, from an ongoing process of give and take that also allowed phantasmic, mythological, and subjective elements to play a role in a dynamic representation of reality. The grafting of religious and historical truth to each other (in the absence of the ability to recreate lost material truth in the positivist sense) constituted one of the most important goals of the psychoanalytic project. The ability to tolerate doubt did not deprive Freud of the right to feel that he was persuaded of the truth of his conclusions. Freud repeatedly addressed the question of certainty *vs.* scepticism throughout *Moses and Monotheism*, and, in doing so, stressed for his readers the convoluted nature of psychoanalytic epistemology. As Blass (2003) has pointed out, from a clinical point of view this is the book's kernel. It is in this later work of his that Freud gave final expression to the dialectic view of the concept of "truth" in its unique psychoanalytic form. He stressed the tentative and speculative nature of his account, but did not let this prevent him from recognising that he was approaching the truth. His reply to DaCosta shows that as soon as he reached conclusions about historical truth, he could not put in its place another truth simply because the latter was worth believing in from a religious point of view. Freud wrote to DaCosta:

> I am amazed at the way you succeed in bringing together the findings of scientific investigation and belief in the accuracy of the biblical account. I myself would be incapable of such acrobatics. But who gave you the right to grant the Bible a monopoly on the truth? All you are saying is that I believe because I believe. (Letter dated 2 May 1939: AFM)

The question, then, is what is the nature of that truth that Freud proclaims? He opens his book hesitantly, qualifying his assertions, but, as the book proceeds, he seems to become more and more certain of himself, until, by the end, he states his thesis unambiguously. Did Freud convince himself on purely scientific grounds, or was he asserting a belief? After all, the scholar must have no less faith in historical and scientific truth than the religious person has in biblical truth. Freud tried to resolve this paradox by skipping back and forth between two of his favourite genres, the historical novel and the clinical case study. It becomes clear to the reader that *Moses and Monotheism* is neither a positivist historical account nor speculative psychology. Rather, it is a readers' response text devoted to examining the theory of psychoanalytic epistemology and the persuasive force that the truth—whether about the identity of the Hebrew leader or about the true value of the autobiographical memory that emerges during psychoanalytic treatment—can elicit from the person who seeks it. Freud thought that the historical novel genre could enable him, even though he viewed himself neither as a historian nor as a novelist, to address the question of the identity of this biblical figure in accordance with the rules of the clinical case study, in which the act of reconstruction is accomplished through the integration of historical evidence into the subjective narrative. Freud's biography of Moses can, thus, be seen as the last case study left to us by the creator of psychoanalysis.

Evidently, Freud's essay on Moses has been reading its readers long before the emergence of reader response literary criticism. Its particular effect on Israeli psychoanalysts as an "interpretative community"

(Fish, 1980) should one day make for a fascinating study in its own right.[3] For now, let it take us to the early days of psychoanalytic literary criticism—the last locus of psychoanalytic discourse in modern Hebrew culture that will be examined in this book.

Hebrew literature on the couch

> They take a poem by Bialik or a story by Brenner and render it into its constituent parts, until they get down to the 22 letters [of the Hebrew alphabet] from which they are composed, and then they meticulously search, by light of some psychoanalytic assumption, motifs and symbols and intimations in that heap of bones.

So Israel Cohen (1942), one of the Yishuv's leading writers, criticised those of his colleagues who had taken up psychoanalysis as a fashionable way of pursuing literary studies.

Psychoanalytic literary criticism has a long history, dating back to just before the beginning of the twentieth century. Freud himself was the first to try his hand at it, in a letter to Wilhelm Fliess, dated 15 October 1897, in which he discussed *Oedipus Rex*. Freudian ideas made their way into literary criticism in the UK, the USA, and France only after psychoanalysts of differing theoretical persuasions, such as Ernest Jones, Marie Bonaparte, and Jacques Lacan, had already used it to decipher an author's biography, or to expand and validate psychoanalytic theory (cf. Berman, 1993; Holland, 2000). In Palestine, however, the incorporation of Freudianism into literary criticism was rapid and took a somewhat different course.

I have argued that the image of the Zionist revolution's New Man was influenced by the view of man that could be discerned in Freud's writings. Many of the protagonists in modern Hebrew literature appear to have been born into the world of Freudian interpretation. The fact that a literary character dreams, lusts, fantasises, wrestles with psychic conflict, or even loses his mind, is not sufficient to prove that the author subscribes to Freud's theories. Drives, frustrations, identity crises, broken souls, childhood psychic wounds, and unfulfilled sexual wishes have all been part of modern Hebrew literature from its birth in the nineteenth century. But, to judge by the swiftness with which psychoanalytic methods were adopted by the Yishuv's best literary critics, it seems reasonable to assume that Hebrew writers were making conscious use of Freudian paradigms. Freud's thinking was already integrated into Zionist theory, whether it addressed the national rebirth or the identity crisis of young Jews. So, it is hardly surprising to find evidence that it was used by the writers of the modern Hebrew renaissance that was an integral part of the national revival (cf. Zakim, 2006). Yet, paradoxically, sometimes a psychoanalytic reading of the works of these writers helped save their characters from being straitjacketed into Zionist readings, although at other times it served to bind them within those same constraints.

Ya'akov Beker's essay "Rabbi Nachman of Breslau: a psychoanalytic study" (1928) marked the first instance of a genre that would, for decades, fill Yishuv and Israeli literary journals. Immediately after publishing this study, Beker applied the method to solving the riddle of the life and work of Chaim Nachman Bialik, the Hebrew national poet, by tracing his "psychosexual development" Beker found that "Bialik's libido was, during his childhood, the crucial period of his mental development, indisputably auto-erotic and narcissistic, and that his libido was forcefully and decisively fixated in the course of his intellectual and creative development" (Beker, 1931, p. 13). Unlike people who have undergone proper psychosexual development, Bialik's libido became fixated and he was, thus, unable to establish a robust and heartfelt libidinal relationship with any other person: "There is no connection or contact between Bialik's libido and the external world: an unseen barrier divides it from the outside" (ibid.).

Using Freud's theories, Beker was also able to analyse the image of the beloved woman in Bialik's poetry. Like previous writers on Bialik, he also sought to explain the lack of harmony between flesh and spirit in Bialik's oeuvre. But, unlike others, he refused to attribute the poet's "ambiguous love" to the world of the Eastern European yeshiva. Underneath Bialik's work, Beker asserted, was an unconscious lust for his mother. This forbidden love prevented him from actively giving his love to other women. Becoming close to a woman deprived the poet of his narcissistic pleasure and his world came crashing down on him. The love Bialik expressed in his poems was, thus, indistinct, passive, idealised, and masochistic. Beker saw the poet's mother between the lines of "The Scroll of Fire," one of Bialik's major works, concluding that this poem was the most powerful and profound expression of the Oedipus complex in all of world literature. And the Oedipus complex, he maintained, was both "the pillar of fire and the pillar of smoke in the soul of humankind and its culture". Bialik obtained Beker's essay for his library. The poet directed a critique of psychoanalysis at Freud and also against Dov Sadan, who, from the 1930s onward, was the Yishuv's leading practitioner of psychoanalytic literary analysis:

> Exaggeration and hyperbole can falsify even the most sublime and purest idea. Something like this has happened with Freud's important theory of the psyche, which has opened a way into the hidden parts and obstructed recesses of the soul so that light may be cast on its dark corners and the flaws in the human spirit corrected. But the primary and fundamental purpose of this system is to cure the psyche. Yet now a scholar has come and sailed far from his own field into the field of the creations of the spirit and of faith and taken the staff of his criticism and the scalpel of his analysis toward the past as well, unsettling the great men of spirit who have lain in their graves for generations. And then his students and their students and the disciples of his disciples have come and added exaggeration to hyperbole: a gaggle of babblers have, evoking the "ineffable name" of their "rabbi," broken brazenly into the home of the writer, cutting into and poking through the soul of his works, turning over and upending all that is sacred and intimate, in order to uncover and reveal the root of the "libido," the sexual urge, which is, ostensibly, the ultimate source and motivator of all motivations. And some do this with a kind of lustful appetite in order to satisfy the licentiousness and filth that abides within them. And when one attempts to argue and complain about this sacrilegious groping, they immediately retort with scientific self-importance: "You have so-and-so's complex! Your wounded yearning for respect speaks from your throat," and so on and so forth. The truth is that few possess that rare ability to enter into the writer's secrets, adhere to his spirit and to delve into his words, only those of great talent and transcendent purpose. (Bialik, cited in Ovadyahu, 1969, pp. 129–130)

One can understand Bialik's anger at having fallen victim to such psychologistic rummaging that reduced his work to a reflection of a single psychoanalytic complex. But Beker's analysis, while simplistic, helped universalise Bialik's work and to extricate it from the prevailing view that his poems could only be understood in the context of Zionism and the Jewish national and literary revival. Later writers on Bialik, such as Baruch Kurzweil, Dan Miron, Menachem Peri, and Michael Gluzman, would refine the psychological approach begun by Ya'akov Beker and Dov Sadan during the poet's lifetime (cf. Gluzman, 2005; Rolnik & Simkin, 2005).

Bialik also spoke harshly of Sadan's psychological analysis of his work, charging that he "has gotten caught up with a certain extreme school of psychological analysis and prying that leads to one-sidedness and pedantry" (cited in Ovadyahu, 1969, p. 110). Yet, Sadan was not deterred by Bialik's censure and went on to provide his readers with further analyses of works by Tchernikovsky, Bialik, and Brenner, using insights derived from Freud's theory of drives. Sadan's "psychoanalytic exegesis", as he referred to it in one of his manuscripts, was mostly directed towards the psychology of his favourite writer, Y. H. Brenner (Sadan, 1996). Sadan sought to use psychoanalysis to liberate the Hebrew literature of his generation, which had been mobilised to serve the interests of the Jewish collective. His goal was show that Hebrew writers had individual and idiosyncratic voices that gave expression to their inner worlds. But, when he donned the garb of the psychoanalyst and attended to the hidden repressions and desires of Hebrew writers and their characters, he tended to locate the source of the individual's repression not in his biography or in his world of unconscious fantasy, but, rather, principally in the historical plight of his people. Sadan proposed a distinction between two types of writers: those who confess and those who conceal. He maintained that Mendele Mocher Sfarim, a seminal Hebrew writer of the nineteenth century, was an observer who had a technique for encoding his hidden experiences, whereas Brenner was one of the "confessional youths" who reveal their unconscious. Sadan viewed Bialik as a figure who integrated both of these literary typological categories. Sadan's psychoanalytic reading of Brenner enabled him, for example, to argue that the "central character" in Brenner's work was a man caught in difficult emotional circumstances who cannot be understood without knowledge of his generation's historical situation:

> A young Jewish man tormented by the world and its anguish, whose memories are like a succession of agony and melancholy, who has salvaged from the world of his childhood tiny specks of light that were overwhelmed by a surfeit of darkness: his soul flutters between a feeling of guilt and sin and between a desire for purity and clarity, his soul is burdened and despondent, his gait is stooped with apprehension and inner timidity, the bridges between him and the rest of the world and other people are unsteady, his attention is directed to his

own trembling and he delves deep into it in order to know himself; he is not daunted by any cruelty to himself. It is a soul that broods over its own convolutions within the tragic maze of its generation, and it is no more than shards of cries for redemption and wholeness, for a steady bridge between it and all else—the world, experience, life, and in the absence of redemption it is tempted by ways out, mostly suicide and madness. (Sadan, 1996 p. 159)

Brenner's novels and short stories portrayed the conflict with which life in the Land of Israel confronted the Zionist settlers who arrived in the first decades of the twentieth century. After all, every person who sought personal redemption by joining a national move-ment that promised its members that "in the land of our forefathers' delight will all our hopes be realized" had to subordinate his deepest personal dreams to the demands of the collective. The letters Brenner wrote when he came to Palestine and as he tried to adjust to it reveal that he hoped that the Land would heal his physical, gender, and sexual anguish. He was disabused of these hopes a short time after arriving, but both his hopes and his disappointments motivated him to devote himself intensively to writing about the emerging New Jew of the Land of Israel. His subject matter, and the fact that he was murdered in the Arab riots of 1921 and became the emerging society's first literary martyr, turned him into one of the most admired figures of the pioneer era (Gluzman, 2007; Shaked, 1996).

At about the same time, the Hebrew poet Avraham Shlonsky, who, after arriving in Palestine as part of the Third Aliyah, became one of the most influential figures in the Yishuv's, and later Israel's, cultural and intellectual life, sought an explanation for a recurring and alarm-ing dream in which mice played a central role. He wrote,

For many years a single nightmare, which came in two versions, would not let go of me. Either a needle was stuck in the black of my eye, in the pupil, right in the middle of the hole in the eye, or a mouse was gnawing at my Adam's apple, and again, at the middle of my neck at the Adam's apple. And the mouse was very small. I have no idea what the Freudians would say. (Shlonsky, 1943, cited in Halperin, 2011, p. 117)

He gave poetic expression to his horror dream in his poem of 1932, "Mice in the Night". A draft of the poem kept in his archive makes it possible to link the dream mouse gnawing at Shlonsky's throat not just with the terrifying thoughts of pogroms that plagued him but also with the guilt feelings that gnawed at his conscience for having fled the European city of his birth "like a mouse from a sinking ship". The poet felt that he had abandoned his brothers and sisters to suffering in the Exile and that he should have stayed behind and watched over them, since they were "the apple of his eye" (Halperin, 2011, p. 117).

Shmuel Yosef Agnon, the seminal Hebrew writer who would later win the Nobel Prize, also began to take an interest in Freud's teachings in the early 1930s. His writings, his personal life, and readings of his works all testify to this.

Agnon's influential novella, *In the Prime of Her Life* ([1923]1983), establishes a plot pattern that can be regarded as a distinctive national paradigm. It links two dysfunctional generations through the figure of a shared lover, a person who is carried over from one generation to the next as a troublesome inheritance. Yael Halevi-Wise has suggested that, except for this preoccupation with national redemption, *In the Prime of Her Life* replicates Freud's famous patient "Dora" in *Fragment*

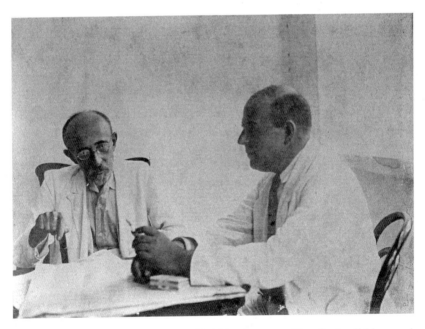

Bialik and Ahad Ha'am: "A gaggle of babblers have, evoking the 'ineffable name' of their 'rabbi,' broken brazenly into the home of the writer."

of an Analysis of a Case of Hysteria (1905e). In Freud's story, Dora's syphilitic father engages in an adulterous affair with Frau K. In Agnon's novella, Tirza's heartsick mother hankers after her first love, Akavia Mazal. Sexual desire for a parental figure, which Freud encourages Dora to acknowledge and possibly even act upon, is actually consummated in Agnon's story when Tirza marries her mother's beloved and conceives his child (Halevi-Wise, 2008). Sexual ambivalence and identity are also central to the emotional trauma of Hirshl, the protagonist of another Agnon novella, *A Simple Story*([1923]1985). According to Nitza Ben-Dov (1993), Dr Langsam, a distinctively non-Freudian soul doctor, "cures" Hirshl by restoring his ability to communicate his love to others and to come to accept that in this world one's romanticised fantasies are not fully realised.

Agnon's acquaintance with Freud's work apparently goes beyond formal declarations. His wife was treated by Eitingon, with whom Agnon himself had become acquainted during the time he spent in Leipzig. Psychoanalytic influence on his work is apparent as early as his short story collection, *The Book of Deeds*, published in 1931, in which he adopted a modernist, surrealist style and offered a dream-like plots in which events occur one after the other without any causal relationship between them and without making any attempt at a realistic portrayal of the world. The story of the love of Hirshl and Blume that is at the centre of *A Simple Story* clearly shows Agnon's familiarity with Freud's writing. The conflict between the individual and society at the centre of the novella is not conducted solely on the conscious level; it also takes place in the shadows of the unconscious. Repression destabilises the protagonist's peace of mind, attacks his manhood, and, in the end, pushes him into madness (Laor, 1998, p. 258).

Dreams also have a large role in Agnon's work. In fact, an Agnon story is always enigmatic. It takes place on multiple levels and invites interpretation and decoding, just as a dream does. Feldman (1987) examined the latent and the manifest in Agnon's *A Guest for the Night*, and Schreibaum (1993), a clinical psychologist, offered evidence that most of the stories in *The Book of Deeds* originated as dreams. He initially referred to them as such, but later rewrote and adapted them to obscure their dream markers, and he published them without any indication of their dream genesis. Whether these were actual dreams during sleep or daydreams, Freud's influence on Agnon is manifested precisely in the writer's exceptional ability to blur the line between reality and imagination and between different states of consciousness. An excellent example of a characteristic Agnon story based on a dream is "Another *Tallit*", which appeared in a Max Eitingon memorial volume published by the Israel Psychoanalytic Society in 1950 and was included in Agnon's *Book of Deeds*. The story is dedicated "to the soul of R. [Reb, an honorific term] Mordechai Eitingon, may peace be on him". In the introduction to the volume, Moshe Wulff relates that the story was based on a childhood memory that Agnon often spoke of to Eitingon. Whether this was an actual memory or a poetic one, it seems to have been of a dream, and the story is written as though it were. The narrator seeks to pray in a house of study with his father, but he arrives late, and the rest of the story shows him trying to find a place for himself. In the process he undergoes weird experiences and has baffling visions in and outside the house of study. He meets a group of odd-looking strangers who do not make room for him; he follows a boy who offers him a jar of fruit juice to drink; and the study house's furnishings metamorphose so that it resembles, for an instant, the venue of a licentious musical performance. When, finally, he seems to have found his place and can join the worshippers, the *tallit*, the prayer shawl that he finds there, turns out to be defective, one that a man is forbidden to wrap himself in to pray. It is a *tallit* used as a shroud for a dead man.[4] A mysterious figure whispers something of tremendous meaning into the protagonist's ear, seemingly linking the fear of death expressed in the dream with his wish to once again meet his dead father:

> When I stood to wrap myself in the *tallit*, I saw that one fringe was missing. The same one from whom we divert our attention but whose attention is never diverted from us came and whispered to me, a three-fringed *tallit*. I began to consider what this was meant to tell me. Don't I know that a three-fringed *tallit* is defective? Or did he wish to remind me of a forgotten teaching. (Reproduced in Eitingon, 1950, pp. 56–58).

The writer and critic Israel Cohen emphasised to his readers that Freud himself had been supremely cautious in using his psychoanalytic insights to analyse artistic works. He avoided employing his method as an oracle, on the ground that psychoanalysis was unable to reveal the mysteries of an artist's soul. He reminded literary commentators that "analysis is a kind of dialectic" and that, as such, it needed "two present [individuals] in give and take with each other, with one serving to stimulate the other":

> Were a person to come to a psychoanalyst and say to him: take this sheaf of papers, containing my dreams, imaginings, and wishes, just as I have written them with my own hand, please decipher them— would that not be laughable? That sheaf of papers would contain more raw material [metallic ore, in Freud's words] than the carefully composed works of a great creative artist, in which the psychoanalytic elements are barely apparent. That being the case, how can a literary critic arrive at literary and psychic truth using this organically flawed method? (Cohen, 1942, p. 316)

Beyond this theoretical and methodological difficulty in using psychoanalysis to extract literary truth, literary critics lack the necessary training for the task. To be qualified to psychoanalyse others, a person had to undergo psychoanalysis himself. Cohen wrote,

> It is a self-evident demand in this complex profession, in which the most important thing is the capacity for coming together with another's psyche, *einfühlung* [empathy], and as one might presume, the great majority of critics have not experienced 'self-analysis' of this sort, so they are explicitly forbidden to analyze others. (Ibid.)

Cohen was not dismissive of the evidence critics cited to confirm a hypothesis or to identify effects of childhood. In general, this evidence was carefully culled. But even were they true, they would be useless in determining the value of the literary work itself. As a result, heaps of father complexes and neuroses and "imaginary hypotheses on infantile wounds that had never scarred over were accumulating in Hebrew literary criticism" (ibid., p. 317). The practice of literary criticism that was emerging in this way reflected, as far as Cohen was concerned, a kind of esoteric doctrine that shed more darkness than light.

"A totem clan is created"

Such was the title of the only clinical article in the memorial volume that the Israel Psychoanalytic Society dedicated to its founder in 1950. The author of the article, Aharon Isserlin, joined the Society in 1941 and received his training from Moshe Wulff.[5] It is ironic that the clinical article chosen for inclusion in a volume meant to sum up the formative years of Israeli psychoanalysis was intended, according to its author, to demonstrate the common roots of the tribal totemic thinking of primitive aborigines and modern culture (Isserlin, 1950). Isserlin demonstrated his claim with a case study from his analysis of an unmarried young Jewish man of Eastern European extraction. He had immigrated to Palestine and suffered from an obsessive neurosis. During the analysis, Isserlin reached the conclusion that the patient had always had a totem with the non-specific name of *hayyah*—a Hebrew word that means "living thing", or "beast". The unconscious fantasy behind the choice of the totem, like that behind the obsessive symptoms from which he suffered, was that he himself was the offspring of a *hayyah*. The word is also a common feminine name and was, in fact, the name of the patient's mother. Furthermore, the family name of his paternal grandmother was Wulff. His mother's brother's name was Dov—the Hebrew word for "bear"—and his parents had given his brother the nickname "Monkey". The patient's father had not borne the name of an animal, but, in fact, the patient had never recognised him as his real father. In his childhood fantasy, his uncle, Dov the bear, had sired him. This imaginary incestuous relationship between his mother and her brother served the purpose of satisfying his unconscious wish for an incestuous relationship with his mother, and later with his sister. The most significant figures in the patient's life—the members of his clan—had borne the names of animals, like his brother the monkey and his grandmother the wolf, while he himself was the product of a marriage between his mother the beast and his uncle the bear.

Isserlin reported that bestial symptoms had shaped the everyday life of his patient. His work involved constant contact with the public, and the patient had begun to notice that his attitude towards certain people was determined largely by their names. At first, he did not understand what caused him to feel comfortable and friendly in his relations with people with whom he had only a passing acquaintance, while relations with others he knew much better were typified by a certain harshness. Psychoanalysis revealed that the condition for receiving especially friendly treatment from him was to have an animal name, or one that hinted at the name of an animal. His unconscious would identify as members of his totem clan only those people who had such names. Since animal names are quite common among Jews, it quickly emerged that his clan was very large, with far too many members for him to be able to ignore in his work as a public servant. He noticed, for example, that he would give a man named Silverstein ordinary treatment, but that he would give special treatment if he was approached by a man named Levinstein—a name that includes the word *lavi*, a Hebrew word for "lion". Such a person would benefit from the same special treatment that he gave to people whose names were manifestly animal-like, such as Katz (which sounds like the Yiddish word *ketz*, meaning cat), Adler (the German word for eagle), and Hirschfeld (containing the German word *Hirsch*, meaning deer).

In *Totem and Taboo*, Freud stated that the practice of exogamy—the practice of marrying outside the clan, because of a taboo against sexual relations with a female of the same clan—was an inseparable part of totemism. Isserlin's neurotic patient practiced exogamy in an unusual way. He avoided appearing in public with women with whom he had a sexual relationship, even with those with whom he wanted only a sexual relationship. It also emerged that this unconscious taboo against sexual contact with women with whom he had been seen in public was also connected to their names. Among the women with whom he appeared in public, the name Rachel—a Hebrew word for "ewe"—occurred with high frequency. Others bore the names Tzipora (bird), Devorah (bee) and even his mother's name, Hayyah. But he slept with none of these women. The incest taboo was, thus, expressed by this man in two ways: first, through his childhood fantasy that he was the child of his mother and his uncle, and second, through his taboo against sex with women who bore animal names. His totem clan included all those forbidden women who belonged to the name group to which his mother and sister belonged.

Notes

1. Prize committee discussions, not dated, and letter of Mayor Israel Rokach to Wislavsky, 29 January 1945 (TACA). Max Eitingon wrote the introduction to the Hebrew translation.
2. Rabbi Chaim Bloch (Blach) emigrated from Galicia to Vienna in 1915. There he published extensively on Jewish legends and became known for

his interviews and correspondence with famous Jewish scholars. In 1938, he immigrated to New York, and became known for his essays against Zionism. His report about his meeting with Freud could not be authenticated by other sources.

3.   Such a study might also address, among other things, the conspicuous absence of Freud's essay on Moses from most Freud seminars that are being taught in the Max Eitingon Institute for Psychoanalysis in Jerusalem.

4.   Agnon's story brings to mind Freud's "The theme of the three caskets" (1913f), which also concerns the fear of death.

5.   Ahron Isserlin's brother, Max Isserlin, was a student of Kraepelin, Bleuler, and Jung, established the first hospital of child psychiatry in Munich, and emigrated to the UK in 1933.

Epilogue: dynamite in the house

"Withdraw your libido from your fatherland in a timely fashion and shelter it in psychoanalysis, or else you will have to feel uncomfortable"

(Sigmund Freud, 1918)

The Jewish experience in Europe at the turn of the nineteenth century played a central role in engendering three of the twentieth century's great intellectual movements: socialism, Zionism, and psychoanalysis (cf. Diner, 2003; Slezkine, 2004). Yet, only one of them, psychoanalysis, remained at the turn of the twentieth century, faithful to European universalism. The first encounter between psychoanalysis and Yishuv society was in part a re-enactment of the encounter between psychoanalytic theory and Russian Marxism, and in part a continuation of the encounter between the youth culture of Central Europe and German neo-romanticism. Even if the introduction of Freudian theory in the Yishuv involved a certain measure of selectivity, of over-simplification, or of vulgarisation, the most critical possible account of psychoanalytic practice in the Zionist milieu must recognise that above and beyond the rational justification for its implementation as a therapy, the rapid acceptance of Freudian theory conflated both a psychological need and a national political agenda. People sought to rescue personal identity from the intersecting ownership of communal memory and ideology, and to grant new and personal meaning to the doubts and fears that seemed so nauseatingly replete with ideological and historical import. "There is something ridiculous about an ancient nation," writes Israeli novelist A. B. Yehoshua, "that is still, after some 3,300 years, hammering so intensely and so obsessively at the enigma of its identity, tirelessly searching for more and more explanations, definitions and versions of it"(Yehoshua, 2005). Freud's explorations of the "true identity" of Moses, leader of the Jewish nation, address this very conundrum. Identity, Freud told us, whether historical or psychological, of an individual or nation, is the product of mixture and borrowing, and always includes splits and repressions. Freud's fractured Jewish identity could thus serve, if not as an example, then at least as a metaphor for the yawning abyss separating the ideal of pure identity that nurtured the Zionist project and the psychoanalytic project, born in the Diaspora. Unlike the Zionists, Freud never rejected the Jew of the Exile, and, unlike the socialists, he never rejected bourgeois life. He did not pretend to be designing a "new man", much less a "new Jew". Ironically, in this sense, the philo-psychoanalysis of the Yishuv's immigrant society, despite its contradictions and paradoxes, testified to the immensity of anxieties, anguish, and doubts that were the lot of those who tied their personal redemption to reborn Jewish nationalism in the Land of Israel. Zionism, to put it simply, might not have agreed with Freud's theory, but very badly needed it.

The formative years of psychoanalysis in the Yishuv, and later in the state of Israel, were informed by migration, separation, and loss, continuity and new beginnings. But, beyond that, they serve the cultural and intellectual historian as a slate on which the meeting between these three intellectual movements, these three modern European radical interpretations to history, can be juxtaposed and reinterpreted. If the historical interpretation of the past creates the conditions for self-understanding, then contemporary Israeli psychoanalytic discourse can offer us still more food for thought on the relationship between science and history, between therapy and ideology, between political culture and analytic theory. The juxtaposition of history and theory offers new angles of interpretation and poses new questions.

Could it be that the redemptive fantasies of Zionist culture, its rejection of diasporic Jewish existence, and its dialectics of "true" *vs.* "false" Jewish identity have correlates in contemporary psychoanalytic discourse? Does Israeli psychoanalysis's favouring of clinical notions such as "trauma", "corrective emotional experience", or "true self" reflect the peculiar Israeli experience and self-understanding? Have Israeli clinicians grown ever more "traumacentric" in their under-standing of their patients' mental pain? Can the violent realisation of the Zionist dream imbue with historical meaning the shift in Israeli psychoanalytic culture whereby the Freudian Law of the Father is being de-emphasised and replaced by the powerful fantasy of a fusion with the Mother? In short, do Zionism, the Israeli experience, the Holocaust, the Arab–Israeli conflict, or social violence in general affect the way psychoanalysis is understood and practised in Israel today?

Freud's recommendation to Ferenczi, that his libido seek refuge in psychoanalysis marked the emergence of a tradition in which analytic identity and solidarity was expected to encourage the disintegration of ethnic, national, and political bonds (letter dated 27 October 1918, in Freud & Ferenczi, 1993–2000, pp. 304–305).[1] This "neutral" analytic stance towards politics was shared not only by Jewish analysts who, disillusioned by assimilation, had a particular interest in stepping outside history. Four years earlier, at the beginning of the First World War, Ernest Jones wrote to Freud that "if the future of psychoanalysis had to be weighed with the future of my own country, I should side with the former" (letter dated 15 December 1914, in Freud & Jones, 1993, pp. 307–308). Such statements should not be read as gestures of loyalty or expressions of partisanship. In the early twentieth century, psychoanalysis was viewed by many of its followers—Jews and non-Jews alike—as an antidote to the discontents of the modern political subject.

Shortly after the Great War, in his essay *Beyond the Pleasure Principle* (1920g), Freud postulated the existence of a death drive alongside the sexual drive. Not for the first time, it looked as if a new development in Freud's thinking might shatter the framework of his previous work. The nature of the psycho-sexual unconscious, the backbone of Freudian theory, was suddenly open to question. By closely observing the reactions of traumatised individuals who survived a perceived or an actual threat, Freud reached the conclusion that the re-experiencing of trauma originates from the drive to return to an inanimate state. For

Freud, the individual's reaction to trauma indicates that traumatic re-enactment is not a simple memory. Moreover, it is not an expression of a menacing experience. Instead, it expresses the person's longing for that experience. It is this yearning that prompts the mind to internalise the stimulus and repeat it. It is, in a way, an attempt to master what was never fully experienced and inscribed, an attempt to confront the ghostly presence of a threat that has passed. This new theoretical building block had vast repercussions in the psychoanalytic community. Being a Freudian became much more complicated than it had been when the theory of the libido had been the bond that held Freudians together. Melanie Klein, who made the death drive the basis of her theory of the mind, later recalled that shortly after Freud published his essay, Max Eitingon alluded to it as "putting dynamite to the house, but", he added, "Freud knows what he is doing" (Klein, cited in King & Steiner, 1991, p. 89). The death drive did not gain much acceptance among the diehard Freudians of the first and second generation. In fact, it took another world war to secure the centrality of the dual theory of drives in post-Freudian psychoanalytic discourse.

In the wake of the Holocaust, large numbers of survivors of death, forced labour, and other kinds of concentration camps immigrated to Israel, as did others who had survived by escaping, hiding, or joining partisan groups. This tremendously varied, yet on the whole deeply traumatised, population formed a large and decisive group in Israeli society. They spanned all walks of life. Their traumatisation presented Israeli mental health professionals with a real challenge: to understand their pathology, symptoms, and adaptation in ways that reached beyond well-worn concepts and to offer help and therapeutic understanding with newly fashioned tools. In the 1950s, in the context of the discussion of the suffering of Holocaust survivors, psychoanalytic thinking could be discerned in the local psychiatric discourse. Gradually, clinical and theoretical writing on the Holocaust's direct and indirect effects on the survivors, and on the members of the second and third generations, became the speciality of a number of Israeli psychoanalysts. One of the first indications of the great interest that Israeli psychoanalysis would develop in the treatment of the Nazis' victims was a short article published by Gerda Barag in 1956, in which she presented three cases of Holocaust survivors who suffered from attacks of losing consciousness. It marked a turning point in Israeli psychiatric and psychoanalytic writing about this subject, because, unlike previous researchers and clinicians, who had hesitated to connect the mental problems of Holocaust survivors with the actual events they had lived through, Barag proposed a causal relationship (Zalashik, 2008, p. 171). Beginning in the 1960s and to the present day, Israeli psychoanalysts have published a large number of articles and books devoted to the psychological effects of the Holocaust and on the clinical treatment of survivors and their children and grandchildren. These works consider the implications of the trauma of the Holocaust for Israeli society, the Israeli–Palestinian conflict, and the relations between Israelis and Germans. It looks as if Israeli clinicians embraced the idea of transgenerational transmission of trauma as a way to counterbalance the general reluctance of Israelis to acknowledge the presence of Jewish history and past in their self-understanding.

Contemporary Israeli psychoanalysis presents an interesting phenomenon. The number of applicants for training slots at the Max Eitingon Institute for Psychoanalysis is steadily rising, as are the number of postgraduate training programmes for psychoanalytically informed psychotherapy. Psychoanalytic literature in Hebrew sells briskly, and a Hebrew-language psychoanalytic journal was recently inaugurated. On top of all this, in 2000 a second analytic institute— the country's first non-IPA affiliated psychoanalytic society—was founded. All the evidence indicates that Israeli society's taste for psychoanalysis is going strong. Psychoanalysis might be in crisis elsewhere in the world, but the crisis has either bypassed or not yet reached the Mediterranean's eastern shore. These facts might be interpreted in different ways, but the least likely explanation is that Israeli society is now in the midst of a collective "soul searching", or that Israelis are now engaged in some sort of a psychoanalytically informed journey into their inner selves. Although the history of psychoanalysis has shown that psychoanalysis can survive, and even flourish, in the most diverse political and economic circumstances, the particular kind of psychoanalysis being practised in Israel today raises serious questions.

Towards the 1970s, Central European Germanic influence on Israeli psychoanalysis gradually gave way to other influences: American ego psychology was followed by British object relations, later replaced by self psychology, and, still more recently, by the Kleinian, relational, intersubjective, French, and Lacanian influences. Just as Israeli society became increasingly pluralistic, variegated, and prone to internal splits, intense ethnic rivalries, and a sense of victimisation, so did the Israel Psychoanalytic Society, now one of the largest societies in the International Psychoanalytic Association (cf. Erlich, 2010). This study has addressed the early history of psychoanalysis in Israel, and, therefore, focused on its links to European history. But no portrait of contemporary Israeli psychoanalysis can ignore the impact of the Arab–Israeli conflict, the ever-longer shadow of the Holocaust on Israel's self-understanding, or the violent stamp of Israel's occupation of the Palestinian population since 1967.[2] The scientific discussions held by the Israel Psychoanalytic Society and the case reports of its graduates demonstrate that the vast majority of younger analysts in Israel today pursue their clinical work on the basis of psychoanalytic models of the mind that emphasise the role of actual trauma in mental life. These paradigms de-emphasise infantile sexuality and, more often than not, avoid the idea of primary innate aggression as implied by Freud's death instinct. The rising popularity of theories which deal with so called "primitive mental states" completes the picture: the imagined patient of Israeli psychoanalysis is the diametric opposite of the "New Man" of the Zionist revolution, a fairly passive individual, mostly reactive to his environment and, therefore, hardly accountable to his interiority and his mind. It is an image that, above and beyond its emphasis on the environmental factors in the patient's life history, tends to address the maternal order in the patient's mental life, an image whose romanticism and mysticism smacks somewhat of late nineteenth-century German neo-romanticism and Gnosticism. Such theoretical and cultural shifts might well be viewed as part of the general trend in today's analytic discourse, frequently associated with the New Age or the postmodern turn of the late twentieth century and, therefore, not specific to Israeli society and its particular analytic culture. But this trend requires historical–social evaluation.

One possible explanation would be that Israel's political culture, in which violence, omnipotence, projective identification, self-idealisation and victimisation take precedence over the assumption of responsibility and the work of mourning, once more invokes some of the neo-romantic sentiment that characterised earlier attempts to juxtapose Zionism and psychoanalysis. Israel's ever-narrowing willingness to critically reflect upon its own contribution to the escalation of the Arab–Israeli conflict might, thus, be linked to the rising popularity in Israel of analytic theories that might best be designated as "traumacentric". Such theorising tends to portray the patient as a passive template on which the atrocities or the shortcomings of his significant others are inscribed, rather then as an active agent. They tend to attribute a patient's emotional suffering to excessive frustration, parental failures, or other concrete adversities. It is a trend that has accompanied a steady decline in interest in the dynamic unconscious and in promoting the patient's sense of responsibility for both the creative and the destructive forces in his psyche. Could it be that this trend is itself multiply determined, and perhaps reinforced, by an Israeli political culture that, while turning its back on the Father's Law, promulgates the notion that all evil comes from outside? Clearly, one must be careful not to draw simplistic analogies between political cultures of blame and analysts' preferences for psychoanalytic models of the mind that emphasise the maternal order or the impact of the environment on mental functioning. A continued threat of annihilation and the ever-longer shadow of the Holocaust are bound to interfere with Israel's willingness to assume responsibility for its growing isolation and keep fuelling its self-justifying politics of omnipotence. It stands to reason that working analytically at the frontier of militant nationalism and religious fanaticism will continue to pose a unique challenge for those seeking to translate their patients' concrete reality into meaningful psychic experience. Psychoanalysts in Israel cannot meet this challenge by adhering to the old Freudian prescription of "withdrawing" their libido from the fatherland. In our times, it takes more than that.

Notes

1. This letter was written shortly after Hungary signed a special truce with the Allies at the end of the First World War. Freud was responding to Ferenczi's lament over the demise and disintegration of the monarchy.
2. For nearly five decades, Israeli analysts have been studying the psychic ramifications of various forms of societal violence as well as political and religious forms of extremism (cf. Bunzl & Beit-Hallahmi, 2002; Erlich, Erlich-Ginor, & Beland, 2009; Klein, 2003; Kogan, 1995; Moses, 1993; Rangel & Moses-Harushovski, 1996; Stein, 2009; Winnik, Moses, & Ostow, 1973).

REFERENCES

Adorno, T. W. (1986). What does coming to terms with the past mean? In: G. Hartmann (Ed.), *Bitburg in Moral and Political Perspective* (pp. 114–129). Bloomington, IN: Indiana University Press.

Adorno, T. W., Frenkel-Brunswik, E., Levinson, D. J., & Sanford, R. N. (1950). *The Authoritarian Personality*. New York: Norton.

Agassi, J. B. (2008). Introduction. In: *The Collected Papers of Martin Buber*, 10: 11–27.

Agnon, S. Y. ([1923]1983). In the prime of her life. In: A. Lelchuk & G. Shaked (Eds), *Eight Great Hebrew Short Novels*. New York: New American Library.

Agnon, S. Y. ([1923]1985). *A Simple Story*, H. Halkin (Trans.). New York: Schocken Books, 1985.

Ahad Ha'am (1912). *Selected Essays of Ahad Ha-'Am*, L. Simon (Ed.). Philadelphia: Jewish Publication Society [reprinted New York: Atheneum, 1970].

Ahad Ha'am (1956–1960). *Collected Letters* (igrot). Tel Aviv: Devir [Hebrew].

Ahimeir, A. (1925). Two theories on sexuality. *Hapoel Hatzair, 47/48*: 4–5 [Hebrew].

Ajzenstadt, M., & Cavaglion, G. (2002). The sexual body of the young Jew as an arena of ideological struggle 1821–1948. *Symbolic Interaction, 25*: 96–116.

Almog, O. (2000). *The Sabra: The Creation of the New Jew*. Berkeley, CA: University of California Press.

Alroey, G. (1999). Suicide in the second and third Aliya periods. *Yahadut Zémanenu: Zionism, the State of Israel, and the Diaspora, 13*: 209–241 [Hebrew].

Alroey, G. (2004). *Immigrants: Jewish Immigration to Palestine in the Early Twentieth Century*. Jerusalem: Yad Izhak Ben-Zvi [Hebrew].

Anonymous (1924). *International Journal of Psychoanalysis, 10*: 101.

Armstrong, R. H. (2005). *A Compulsion for Antiquity: Freud and the Ancient World*. Ithaca, NY: Cornell University Press.

Aron, L., & Henik, L. (Eds.) (2010). *Answering a Question with a Question: Contemporary Psychoanalysis and Jewish Thought*. Boston, MA: Academic Study Press.

Asad, M. (1954). *The Road to Mecca*. New York: Simon and Schuster.

Asad, T. (2003). *Formations of the Secular: Christianity, Islam, Modernity*. Stanford, CA: Stanford University Press.

Aschheim, S. (1982). *Brothers and Strangers: The East European Jew in Germany and German–Jewish Consciousness 1800–1923*. Madison, WI: University of Wisconsin Press.

Ash, M. (1991). Central European emigré psychologists and psychoanalysts in the United Kingdom. In: J. Carlebach (Ed.), *Second Chance— Two Centuries of German-Speaking Jews in the United Kingdom* (pp. 101–120). Tübingen: Mohr (Paul Siebeck).

Ash, M., & Söllner, A. (1996). *Forced Migration and Scientific Change— German Speaking Scientists and Scholars after 1933*. Cambridge: Cambridge University Press.

Avineri, S. (1981). *The Making of Modern Zionism: Intellectual Origins of the Jewish State*. London: Weidenfeld & Nicolson.

Bakan, D. (1958). *Sigmund Freud and the Jewish Mystical Tradition*. Princeton, NJ: D. Van Nostrand.

Barag, G. (1936). Zur Psychoanalyse der Prostitution. *Zeitschrifft für Psychoanalyse, XXII*: 330–362.

Barag, G. (1946). The mother in the religious concepts of Judaism. *American Imago, 4A*: 32–53.

Bargal, D. (1998). Kurt Lewin and the first attempts to establish a Department of Psychology at the Hebrew University. *Minerva, 36*: 49–68.

Bauer, R. (1952). *The New Man in Soviet Psychology*. Cambridge, MA: Harvard University Press.

Becker, R. (1919). *Die Nervosität bei den Juden: Ein Beitrag zur Rassenpsychiatrie für Ärzte und Gebildete Laien*. Zürich: Orell Füssli.

Bein, A. (1952). *The Return to the Soil: A History of Jewish Settlement in Israel.* Jerusalem: Youth and Hechalutz Department of the Zionist Organisation.

Beker, Y. (1928). *Rav Nahman mi-Bratslav: mehkar psikhoanaliti.* Jerusalem : De'ah [Hebrew].

Beker, Y. (1931). *Psychoanalytic Reading of H. N. Bialik.* Jerusalem: De'ah [Hebrew].

Beller, S. (1989). *Vienna and the Jews, 1867–1938: A Cultural History.* Cambridge: Cambridge University Press.

Ben-Artzi, Y. (1997). *Early Jewish Settlement Patterns in Palestine, 1882–1914.* Jerusalem: Magnes Press.

Ben-Dov, N. (1993). *Agnon's Art of Indirection: Uncovering Latent Content in the Fiction of S. Y. Agnon.* Brill's Series in Jewish Studies, Vol. 7. Leiden: E. J. Brill.

Ben-Shaul, Y. (1939). Book review—*Totem and Taboo. Derech Hapoel,* 10 March [Hebrew].

Bentwich, N. (1937). David Eder in Erez Israel. *Hapoel Ha'Tzait, 31–32:* 18–19 [Hebrew].

Berg, N. (2005). Bilder von 'Luftmenschen': Über Metapher und Kollektivkonstruktion. In: D. Diner (Ed.), *Synchrone Welten: Zeitenräume jüdischer Geschichte* (pp. 199–224). Göttingen: Vandenhoeck & Ruprecht.

Bergmann, S. H. (1928). A critic of psychoanalysis. *Hapoel Ha'tzair, 21:* 18–24 [Hebrew].

Bergmann, S. H. (1928–1929). Review of Freud's *Group Psychology and the Analysis of the Ego. Kiryat Sefer, 5:* 302 [Hebrew].

Bergmann, S. H. (1939). Sigmund Freud in Memoriam. *Davar—The Daily Newspaper of the Labor Movement,* 10 October [Hebrew].

Bergmann, S. H. (1985). *Tagebücher und Briefe. Volume I: 1901–1948; Volume II: 1948–1975,* M. Sambursky (Ed.). Frankfurt: Jüdischer Verlag/Athenäum.

Berkowitz, M. (1993). *Zionist Culture and West European Jewry before the First World War.* Chapel Hill, NC: University of North Carolina Press.

Berman, E. (1988). Communal upbringing in the kibbutz: the allure and risks of psychoanalytic utopianism. *Psychoanalytic Study of the Child, 43:* 319–335.

Berman, E. (Ed.) (1993). *Essential Papers on Literature and Psychoanalysis.* New York: New York University Press.

Bernfeld, S. (1928). *Die Schulgemeinde und Ihre Funktion in der Klassenkampf.* Wien: Verlagsbuchhandlung.

Bernfeld, S. (1973[1925]). *Sisyphus or the Limits of Education.* F. Lilge (Trans.). Los Angeles, London: Berkeley.

Bernfeld, S., & Feitelberg, S. (1931). The principle of entropy and the death instinct. *International Journal of Psychoanalysis, 12*: 61–81.

Bettelheim, B. (1943). Individual and mass behavior in extreme situations. *Journal of Abnormal and Social Psychology, 38*: 417–452.

Bettelheim, B. (1969). *Children of the Dream*. New York: Avon.

Bettelheim, B. (1982). *Freud and Man's Soul*. New York: Knopf.

Biale, D. (1997). *Eros and the Jews: From Biblical Israel to Contemporary America*. New York: Basic Books.

Blass, R. (2003). The puzzle of Freud's puzzle analogy: reviving a struggle with doubt and conviction in Freud's *Moses and Monotheism*. *International Journal of Psychoanalysis, 84*: 669–682.

Bloch, H. (1950). Recollections of my meeting and debating with Freud over Moses. *Bitsaron, XXIII*: 101–108 [Hebrew].

Bloom, A. (1987). *The Closing of the American Mind*. New York: Simon and Schuster.

Blüher, H. (1912). *Die deutsche Wandervogelbewegung als ein erotisches Phänomen: Ein Beitrag zur Erkenntnis der sexuellen Inversion*. Berlin: Tempelhof.

Blum, H. (2010). Anti-Semitism in the Freud case histories. In: A. Richards, (Ed.), *The Jewish World of Sigmund Freud: Essays on Cultural Roots and the Problem of Religious Identity* (pp. 78–96). Jefferson, NC: McFarland & Co.

Bohleber, W. (1986). Psychoanalyse in Stuttgart. *Psyche, 5*: 377–341.

Bohleber, W. (1995). Zur romantisch-idealistischen Freudrevision deutscher Psychoanalytiker nach 1933. In: L. Hermanns (Ed.), *Spaltungen In Der Geschichte Der Psychoanalyse* (pp. 153–167). Tübingen: edition diskord.

Bohleber, W. (1997). Die Konstruktion imaginarer Gemeinschaften und das Bild von den Juden-unbewusste Determinanten des Antisemitismus in Deutschland. *Psyche, 6*: 570–605.

Borinski, F., & Werner, M. (1982). *Jugendbewegung: Die Geschichte der Deutschen Jugend 1896–1933*. Frankfurt: Dipa Verlag.

Boyarin, D. (1997). *Unheroic Conduct: The Rise of Heterosexuality and the Invention of the Jewish Man*. Berkeley, CA: University of California Press.

Boyer, J. W. (1995). *Culture and Political Crisis in Vienna: Christian Socialism in Power, 1897-1918*. Chicago, IL: Chicago University Press.

Brachyahu, M. (1947). *The Life of Man*. Munich: ha-Sokhnut ha-Yehudit le-Erets Yiśra'el veha-Joint [Hebrew].

Brachyahu, M. (1960). *Memoirs*. Jerusalem: Achva [Hebrew].

Brainin, E., & Kaminer, I. J. (1982). Psychoanalyse und Nationalsozialismus. *Psyche, 36*(11): 989–1012.

Brandt, M. (1941). Unpublished report on the first seven years of the Jerusalem Psychoanalytic Institute (ECI).

Brecht, K. (1987). Der Fall "Edith Jacobson" Politischer Widerstand, ein Dilemma der IPA. *Psa-Info, 28*: 3–8.

Brecht, K. (1988). Adaptation and resistance. *Psychoanalytic Contemporary Thought, 11*: 233–247.

Brecht, K., Volker, F., Hermanns, L. M., Kammer, I. J., & Juelich, D. H. (Eds.) (1985). *Here Life Goes On in a Most Peculiar Way: Psychoanalysis Before and After 1933.* Hamburg: Kellner.

Brentzel, M. (2002). *Anna O. Bertha Pappenheim: Biographie.* Göttingen: Wallstein.

Brill, A. A. (1943). Max Eitingon. *Psychoanalytic Quarterly, 12*: 456–457.

Brunner, J. (1991). The (Ir)relevance of Freud's Jewish identity to the origins of psychoanalysis. *Psychoanalytic Contemporary Thought, 14*: 655–684.

Brunner, J. (2001). *Freud and the Politics of Psychoanalysis.* New Brunswick, NJ: Transaction.

Buber, M. ([1926]2005). Rede über das erzieherische [A talk on education]. *Werkausgabe Bd. 8 Schrifften zu Jugend Erziehung und Bildung* (p. 136). Gütersloh: Gütersloher Verlagshous.

Buber, M. (1957[2008]). Das unbewußte [The unconscious]. In: *The Collected Papers of Martin Buber, 10*: 215–235.

Buber, M. (1958). *Moses: The Revelation and the Covenant.* New York: Harper.

Buchholz, H. (2008). "Ich wäre mir ohne sie gar nicht denkbar." Wolfgang Hildesheimer und die Psychoanalyse. *Luzifer Amor, 21*(41): 141–152.

Bunzl, J. (1992). Siegfried Bernfeld und der Zionismus. In: K. Fallend, & J. Reichmyers, (Eds.), *Siegfried Bernfeld oder Die Grenzen der Psychoanalyse.* Frankfurt: Suhrkamp.

Bunzl, J., & Beit-Hallahmi, B. (2002). *Psychoanalysis, Identity, and Ideology: Critical Essays on the Israel/Palestine Case.* Boston: Kluwer Academic.

Bunzl, M. (1997). Theodor Herzl's Zionism as gendered discourse. In: R. Robertson, & E. Timms (Eds.), *Theodor Herzl and the Origins of Zionism* (pp. 74–87). Edinburgh: Austrian Studies VIII.

Cavaglion, G. (2000). The institutionalization of knowledge in Israeli sex education programs: a historical review, 1948–1987. *Journal of Sex Education and Therapy, 25*: 286–293.

Cavaglion, G. (2004). The rise and fall of sexual education in Ha'Shomer Ha'Tzair. *Katedra, 113*: 53–82 [Hebrew].

Chasseguet-Smirgel, J., & Grunberger, B. (1986). *Freud or Reich? Psychoanalysis and Illusion.* New Haven, CT: Yale University Press.

Cocks, G. (1985). *Psychotherapy in the Third Reich: The Goering Institute*. New York: Oxford University Press.

Cohen, A. (1983). *The Educational Philosophy of Martin Buber*. Rutherford, NJ: Fairleigh Dickinson Press.

Cohen, I. (1936). Freud and the ruling party. *Davar*, 15 May [Hebrew].

Cohen, I. (1942). Useless labour. *Moznayyim*, 14: 316–317 [Hebrew].

Cohen, U. (2006). *The History of the Hebrew University of Jerusalem*. Tel Aviv: Am Oved [Hebrew].

Corrington, R. S. (2003). *Wilhelm Reich: Psychoanalyst and Radical Naturalist*. New York: Farrar, Straus and Giroux.

Cushman, P. (1995). *Constructing the Self, Constructing America: A Cultural History of Psychotherapy*. New York: Addison-Wesley.

Dachs, G. (Ed.) (2005). *Jüdischer Almanach: Die Jeckes*. Frankfurt am Main.

Damousi, J. (2005). *Freud in the Antipodes. A Cultural History of Psychoanalysis in Australia*. Sydney: UNSW Press.

Danto, E. A. (1998). The Berlin Poliklinik: psychoanalytic innovation in Weimar Germany. *Journal of the American Psychoanalytic Association*, 47(4): 1269–1292.

Danto, E. A. (2005). *Freud's Free Clinics: Psychoanalysis and Social Justice, 1918–1938*. New York: Columbia University Press.

Decker, H. (1977). *Freud in Germany, Revolution and Reaction in Science 1893–1907*. New York: International Universities Press.

Decker, H. (1991). *Freud, Dora and Vienna 1900*. New York: Free Press.

Deutscher, I. (1968). *The Non-Jewish Jew and Other Essays*. New York: Hill and Wang.

Diner, D. (2003). *Gedächtniszeiten. Über jüdische und andere Geschichten*. Munich: CH Beck.

Dotan, S. (1991). *Adumim b'erez Israel*. Kfar Saba: Shavna Hasofer [Hebrew].

Dreyfuss, D. (1936). Über die Bedeutung des psychischen Traumas in der Epilepsie. *Internationale Zeitschrift für Psychoanalyse*, XXII: 249–273.

Edelstein, E. (1982). Heinz Zvi Winnik 1902–1982. *Israel Journal of Psychiatry and Related Sciences*, 19: 183–184.

Eder, D. (1924). Psychoanalysis in politics. In: E. Jones, (Ed.), *Social Aspects of Psychoanalysis: Lectures Delivered under the Auspices of the Sociological Society* (pp. 141–160). London: William & Norgate.

Eder, D. (1927). Kann das Unbewusste erzogen werden? *Allmanach der Psychoanalyse*, 2: 65–75.

Efrati, N. (2004). *The Evolution of Spoken Hebrew in Pre-State Israel, 1881–1922*. Jerusalem: The Academy of the Hebrew Language [Hebrew].

Efron, J. M. (1994). *Defenders of the Race: Jewish Doctors and Race Science in Fin-de-Sie_cle Europe*. New Haven, CT: Yale University Press.

Efron, J. M. (2001). *Medicine and the German Jews: A History*. New Haven, CT: Yale University Press.

Eickhoff, F. (1995). The formation of The German Psychoanalytical Association (Dpv): regaining the psychoanalytical orientation lost in the Third Reich. *International Journal of Psychoanalysis, 76*: 945–956.

Eisenstadt, S., & Noah, M. (Eds.) (1999). *Zionism and the Return to History: A Reappraisal*. Jerusalem: Yad Izhak Ben-Zvi [Hebrew].

Eissler, K. (1965). *Medical Orthodoxy and the Future of Psychoanalysis*. New York: International Universities Press.

Eitingon, M. (1923). *Bericht Über die Berliner Psychoanalytische Polyklinik*. Wien: Internationaler Psychoanalytischer Verlag.

Eitingon, M. (1950). *Max Eitingon: In Memoriam*, M. Wulff (Ed.). Jerusalem: Israel Psychoanalytic Society.

Ekstein, R. (1996). Siegfried Bernfeld: Sisyphus or the Boundaries of Education. In: F. Alexander, S. Eisenstein, & M. Grotjhan (Eds.), *Psychoanalytic Pioneers* (pp. 349–368). New York: Basic Books.

Elboim-Dror, R. (1994). Gender in utopianism: the Zionist case. *History Workshop Journal, 37*(1): 99–116.

Elboim-Dror, R. (1996). He is coming from among ourselves, the new Hebrew person. *Alpayim, 12*: 104–135. [Hebrew].

Elias, N. (1982). *The Civilizing Process*. Oxford: Blackwell.

Erlich, H. S. (2010). Letter from Jerusalem. *The International Journal of Psychoanalysis, 91*: 1329–1335.

Erlich, H. S., Erlich-Ginor, M., & Beland, H. (2009). *Fed with Tears — Poisoned with Milk: The Nazareth Group Relations Conferences*. Giessen: Psychosozial.

Etkind, A. (1994). Trotsky and psychoanalysis. *Partisan Review, 2*: 303–308.

Etkind, A. (1997). *Eros of the Impossible: The History of Psychoanalysis in Russia*. Oxford: Westview.

Even-Zohar, I. (1990). The emergence of a native Hebrew culture in Palestine: 1882–1948. *Polysystem Studies (Poetics Today), 11*(1): 175–194.

Falk, A. (1978). Freud and Herzl. *Contemporary Psychoanalysis, 14*: 357–387.

Fallend, K., & Nizschke, B. (2002). *Der Fall Wilhelm Reich: Beiträge zum Verhältnis von Psychoanalyse und Politik*. Giessen: Psychosozial Verlag.

Farber, M. (1937). Review of Klatzkin. *The Philosophical Review, 46*(1): 91–93.

Federn, E. (1988). Psychoanalysis—the fate of a science in exile. In: E. Timms & N. Segal (Eds.), *Freud in Exile — Psychoanalysis and its Vicissitudes* (pp. 156–162). New Haven, CT: Yale University Press.

Feigenbaum, D. (1929). Psychological problems of infancy and adolescence and their relation to education. *Hed Ha'Chinuch, 11–13*: 1–15 [Hebrew].

Feigenbaum, D. (1936). Montagu David Eder, M.D.—(1866–1936). *Psycho-analytic Quarterly*, 5: 444–446.

Feigenbaum, D. (1937). Depersonalization as a defense mechanism. *Psychoanalytic Quarterly*, 6: 4–11.

Feldman, Y. (1987). The latent and the manifest: Freudianism in *A Guest for the Night*. *Prooftexts: A Journal of Jewish Literary History*, 7(1) (Special Issue on S. Y. Agnon): 29–39.

Fenichel, O. (1967[1934]). Psychoanalysis as the nucleus of a future dialectical–materialistic psychology. *Am. Imago*, 24: 290–311.

Fenichel, O. (1998). *Fenichel Otto, 119 Rundbriefe in 2 Bände*. J. Reichmayr, & E. Mühlleitner, (Eds.), Frankfurt, Basel: Stroemfeld.

Ferenczi, S. (1949[1908]). Psychoanalysis and education. *International Journal of Psychoanalysis*, 30: 220–224.

Fermi, L. (1968). *Illustrious Immigrants: The Intellectual Migration from Europe, 1930–41*. Chicago, IL: University of Chicago Press.

Fish, S. (1980). *Is There a Text in this Class? The Authority of Interpretive Communities*. Cambridge, MA: Harvard University Press

Frank, C., Hermanns, L. M., & Löchel, E. (Eds.) (2008). Psychoanalyse aus Berlin 1920–1933. *Jahrbuch der Psychoanalyse*, 57.

Freud, S. (1892–1894). Preface and footnotes to the translation of Charcot's Tuesday lectures. *S.E.*, 1. London: Hogarth.

Freud, S. (1900a). *The Interpretation of Dreams. S.E.*, 4–5. London: Hogarth.

Freud, S. (1901b). *The Psychopathology of Everyday Life. S.E.*, 6. London: Hogarth.

Freud, S. (1905d). *Three Essays on the Theory of Sexuality. S.E.*, 7: 125–245. London: Hogarth.

Freud, S. (1905e). *Fragment of an Analysis of a Case of Hysteria. S.E.*, 7: 3–122. London: Hogarth.

Freud, S. (1908d). "Civilized" sexual morality and modern nervous illness. *S.E.*, 9: 179–204. London: Hogarth.

Freud, S. (1912–1913[1934]). *Totem and Taboo*: Preface to the Hebrew translation. *S.E.*, 13: xv. London: Hogarth.

Freud, S. (1913f). The theme of the three caskets. *S.E.*, 12: 289–302. London: Hogarth.

Freud, S. (1914b). *The Moses of Michelangelo. S.E.*, 13: 211–238. London: Hogarth.

Freud, S. (1914c). On narcissim: an introduction. *S.E.*, 14: 67–102. London: Hogarth.

Freud, S. (1914d). On the history of the psychoanalytic movement. *S.E.*, 14: 3–66. London: Hogarth.

Freud, S. (1916–1917). *Introductory Lectures on Psychoanalysis. S.E., 15.* London: Hogarth.

Freud, S. (1917e). Mourning and melancholia. *S.E., 14:* 239–258. London: Hogarth.

Freud, S. (1920g). *Beyond the Pleasure Principle. S.E., 18:* 7–64. London: Hogarth.

Freud, S. (1921c). *Group Psychology and the Analysis of the Ego. S.E., 18:* 67–143. London: Hogarth.

Freud, S. (1922a). Dreams and telepathy. *S.E., 18:* 195–219. London: Hogarth.

Freud, S. (1923b). *The Ego and the Id. S.E., 19:* 3–66. London: Hogarth.

Freud, S. (1925c). On the occasion of the opening of the Hebrew University. *S.E., 14.* London: Hogarth.

Freud, S. (1925d). An autobiographical study. *S.E., 20:* 3–70 London: Hogarth.

Freud, S. (1927c). *The Future of An Illusion. S.E., 21:* 3–56. London: Hogarth.

Freud, S. (1930a). *Civilization and Its Discontents. S.E., 21:* 59–145. London: Hogarth.

Freud, S. (1937c). Analysis terminable and interminable. *S.E., 23:* 211–253. London: Hogarth.

Freud, S. (1939a). *Moses and Monotheism. S.E., 23:* 3–137. London: Hogarth.

Freud, S. (1941d[1921]). Psycho-analysis and telepathy. *S.E.,* London: Hogarth.

Freud, S. (1941e[1926]). Address to the Society of B'Nai B'Rith. *S.E., 20.* London: Hogarth.

Freud, S. (1960). *Briefe 1873–1939.* Frankfurt: Fischer.

Freud, S. (1961). *Letters of Sigmund Freud 1873–1939*, E. L. Freud, (Ed.). London: Hogarth.

Freud, S., & Abraham, K. (1965). *Sigmund Freud Karl Abraham Briefe*, H. C. Abraham & E. L. Freud (Eds.), Frankfurt: Fischer.

Freud, S., & Abraham, K. (2002). *The Complete Correspondence of Sigmund Freud and Karl Abraham 1907–1925*, E. Falzeder, (Ed.), London: Karnac.

Freud, S., & Eitingon, M. (2004). *Sigmund Freud–Max Eitingon Briefwechsel, 1906–1939*, M. Schröter (Ed.), Tübingen: edition diskord.

Freud, S., & Ferenczi, S. (1993–2000). *The Correspondence of Sigmund Freud and Sandor Ferenczi.* E. Brabant, E. Falzeder, & P. Giampieri-Deutsch (Eds.), Cambridge, MA: Belknap Press of Harvard University Press.

Freud, S., & Jones, E. (1993). *The Complete Correspondence of Sigmund Freud and Ernst Jones, 1908–1939.* R. A. Pauskaskas, (Ed.), Cambridge, MA: Harvard University Press.

Freud, S., & Jung, C. G. (1974). *The Correspondence Between Sigmund Freud and C. G. Jung*. W. McGuire, (Ed.), Princeton, NJ: Princeton University Press.

Freud, S., & Zweig, A. (1968). *Sigmund Freud Arnold Zweig Briefwechsel*. Frankfurt: Fischer.

Freud, S., & Zweig, A. (1970). *The Letters of Sigmund Freud and Arnold Zweig*, E. L. Freud, (Ed.). London: Hogarth Press and the Institute of Psycho-Analysis.

Friedjung, J. K. (1942a). Und der Aufbau des Menschen? *Orient, 4*: 5.

Friedjung, J. K. (1942b). Reform der Erziehung? *Orient, 8*: 8.

Friedjung, J. K. (1950). 5 years psycho-analytical educational work among Jewish youth immigrants. In: *Max Eitingon, in Memoriam*. Jerusalem: Israel Psycho-Analytical Society.

Friedlander, S. (1978). *History and Psychoanalysis: An Inquiry into the Possibilities and Limits of Psychohistory*. New York: Holmes and Meier.

Friedlander, S. (1997). *Nazi Germany and the Jews. Vol I. The Years of Persecution 1933–1939*. New York: HarperCollins.

Frosh, S. (2005). *Anti-Semitism and Anti-Goyism: Hate and the 'Jewish Science': Anti-Semitism, Nazism and Psychoanalysis*. London: Palgrave Macmillan.

Funkenstein, A. (1991). *Perceptions of Jewish History from Antiquity to the Present*. Tel Aviv: Am Oved [Hebrew].

Galef, H. R. (1976). Dr. Max Stern's 80th Birthday—An interview *The Newsletter of the New York Psychoanalytic Society and Institute* (January): 7–9.

Gast, L. (1999). Fluchtlinien-Wege ins Exil. Psychoanalyse im Exil. *Forum der Psychoanalyse, 15*: 135–150.

Gay, P. (1970). *Weimar Culture: The Outsider as Insider*. New York: Harper Torchbooks.

Gay, P. (1987). *A Godless Jew*. New Haven, CT: Yale University Press.

Gay, P. (1988). *Freud: A Life for Our Time*. London: Macmillan.

Gekle, H., & Kimmerle, G. (Eds.) (1994). *Geschichte der Psychoanalyse in Berlin. Luzifer-Amor, 7*(19). Tübingen: edition diskord.

Gelber, Y. (1990). *New Home. The Immigration and Absorption of Central European Jews, 1933–1940*. Jerusalem: Yad Izhak Ben-Zvi and Leo Beck Institute [Hebrew].

Geller, J. (1995). The conventional lies and paradoxes of Jewish assimilation: Max Nordau's pre-Zionist answer to the Jewish question. *Jewish Social Studies: History, Culture, and Society, 1*(3): 129–160.

Geter, M. (1979). The immigration from Germany in the years 1933–1939. Socio-economic absorption versus socio-cultural absorption. *Catedra, 12*: 125–146. [Hebrew].

Gilman, S. (1986). *Jewish Self-Hatred: Anti- Semitism and the Hidden Language of the Jews*. Baltimore, MD: Johns Hopkins University Press.

Gilman, S. (1991). *The Jew's Body*. New York: Routledge

Gilman, S. (1993a). *The Case of Sigmund Freud: Medicine and Identity at the Fin de Siècle*. Baltimore, MD: Johns Hopkins University Press.

Gilman, S. (1993b). Max Nordau, Sigmund Freud, and the question of conversion. *Southern Humanities Review, XXVII*(1):1–25.

Glover, E. (1945). David Eder as a psychoanalyst. In: J. B. Hobman, (Ed.), *David Eder: Memoirs of a Modern Pioneer* (pp. 89–116). London: Victor Gollancz.

Gluzman, M. (1997). Longing for heterosexuality: Zionism and sexuality in Herzl's *Altneuland. Theory and Criticism: An Israeli Forum, 11*: 145–162 [Hebrew].

Gluzman, M. (2005). Pogrom and gender: On Bialik's *Unheimlich. Prooftexts, 25*(1&2): 39–59.

Gluzman, M. (2007). *The Zionist Body: Nationalism, Gender, and Sexuality in Modern Hebrew Literature*. Tel Aviv: Hakibbutz Hameuhad [Hebrew].

Goggin, J. E., & Goggin, E. B. (2001). Politics, ideology, and the psychoanalytic movement before, during, and after the Third Reich. *Psychoanalytic Review, 88*: 155–193.

Goggin, J. E., Goggin, E. B., & Hill, M. (2004). Emigrant psychoanalysts in the USA and the FBI Archives. *Psychoanalytic History, 6*: 75–92.

Golan, S. (1959). Collective education in the kibbutz. *Psychiatry, 22*: 167–177.

Goldhammer, L. (1958). Herzl and Freud. *Herzl Year Book, 9*: 194–196.

Golomb, J. (2004). *Nietzsche and Zion*. Ithaca, NY: Cornell University Press.

Gordon, A. (2004). *The Orient: A German-Language Weekly between German Exile and Aliyah*. Jerusalem: Magnes Press [Hebrew].

Goren, A. (1982). *Dissenter in Zion: From the Writings of Judah L. Magnes*. Cambridge, MA: Harvard University Press.

Goren, A. (1996). The view from Scopus: Judah L. Magnes and the early years of the Hebrew University, *Judaism, 45*: 203–205.

Gorny, Y. (2001). *Zionism and the Arabs, 1882–1948: A Study of Ideology*. New York: Oxford University Press.

Govrin, A. (2004). *Between Abstinence and Seduction: The Analysis of American Psychoanalysis*. Tel Aviv: Dvir [Hebrew].

Grab, W. (1989). Nicht aus Zionismus, sondern aus Österreich. In: H. Funke (Ed.), *Die andere Erinnerung: Gespräche mit jüdischen Wissenschaftlern im Exil* (pp. 115–148). Frankfurt: Fischer.

Grinberg, L., & Grinberg, R. (1989). *Psychoanalytic Perspectives on Migration and Exile*. New Haven, CT: Yale University Press.

Gröger, H. (1986). Kinderarzt, Politiker, Psychoanalytiker- Zum 40. Todestag von Josef Karl Friedjung. *Sigmund Freud Haus Bulletin, 10*(2): 21–25.

Grosskurth, P. (1991). *The Secret Ring: Freud's Inner Circle and the Politics of Psychoanalysis*. New York: Addison-Wesley.

Grubrich-Simitis, I. (1995). 'No greater, richer, more mysterious subject ... than the life of the mind': an early exchange of letters between Freud and Einstein. *International Journal of Psychoanalysis, 76*: 115–122.

Grubrich-Simitis, I. (1997). *Early Freud and Late Freud: Reading Anew Studies on Hysteria and Moses and Monotheism*. London: Routledge.

Gumbel, E. (1958). Dr. Gershon Barag. *International Journal of Psychoanalysis, 39*: 617–619.

Gumbel, E. (1965). Psychoanalysis in Israel. *Israel Annals of Psychiatry and Related Disciplines, 3*(1): 89–99.

Gumbel, E. (1995). Über mein Leben mit der Psychoanalyse. *Jahrbuch der Psychoanalyse, 34*: 7–63.

Hale, N. G. (1977). *Freud and the Americans*. New York: Oxford University Press.

Hale, N. G. (1995). *The Rise and Crisis of Psychoanalysis in the United States: Freud and The Americans 1917–1985*. New York: Oxford University Press.

Halevi-Wise, Y. (2008). Reading Agnon's *In the Prime of Her Life* in light of Freud's Dora. *Jewish Quarterly Review, 98*(1): 29–40.

Halfin, I. (2003). *Terror in My Soul. Communist Autobiographies on Trial*. Cambridge, MA: Harvard University Press.

Halperin, H. (2011). *The Life and Work of Avraham Shlonsky*. Tel Aviv: Sifroiat Poalim-Hakibbutz Hameuchad [Hebrew].

Halpern, B., & Reinharz, J. (1991). The cultural and social background of the second Aliyah. *Middle Eastern Studies, 27*(3): 487–517.

Halpern, L. (1938). Some data of the psychic morbidity of Jews and Arabs in Palestine. *American Journal of Psychiatry, 94*: 1215–1222.

Hart, M. (2000). *Social Science and the Politics of Modern Jewish Identity*. Stanford, CA: Stanford University Press.

Hartmann, H. (1939). *Ego Psychology and the Problem of Adaptation*. New York: International Universities Press, 1958.

Hartnack, C. (1990). Vishnu on Freud's desk: psychoanalysis in colonial India. *Social Research, 57*(4): 923–949.

Hassler, M., & Wertheimer, J. (Eds.) (1997). *Der Exodus aus Nazideutschland und die Folgen: Jüdische Wissenschaftler im Exil*. Tübingen: Attempto Verlag.

Haynal, A. (1994). Central European psychoanalysis and its move westwards in the twenties and thirties. In: H. Ehleers, & J. Lidi (Eds.), *The Trauma of the Past: Remembering and Working Through* (pp. 101–116) London: Goethe-Institut.

Heid, L. (Ed.) (2005). *"Das nenne ich ein haltbares Bündnis!" Arnold Zweig, Beatrice Zweig, Ruth Klinger Briefwechsel (1936–1962)*. Bern: Peter Lang.

Heller, P. (1992). *Anna Freud's Letters to Eva Rosenfeld*. Madison, CT: International Universities Press.

Hermanns, L. M. (1994). Karl Abraham und die Anfänge der Berliner Psychoanalytischen Vereinigung. *Luzifer-Amor, 12*: 30–40.

Hertz, D. (1983). Pioneers and psychoanalysis: beginnings of the psychoanalytic movement in Eretz Israel. *Israel Journal of Psychiatry and Related Sciences, 20*(1–2): 5–12.

Hess, J. M. (2002). *Germans, Jews and the Claims of Modernity*. New Haven, CT: Yale University Press.

Hildesheimer, W. (1984). Mein Judentum. In: *Das Ende der Fiktionen*. Frankfurt: Suhrkamp.

Hinshelwood, R. D. (1995). Psychoanalysis in Britain: points of cultural access, 1893–1918, *International Journal of Psychoanalysis, 76*: 135–151.

Hinshelwood, R. D. (1998). The organizing of psychoanalysis in Britain. *Psychoanalysis and History, 1*(1): 87–102.

Hirsch, D. (2000). We spread here culture. Unpublished MA thesis [Hebrew]. Tel Aviv University.

Hirsch, D. (2009). "We are here to bring the West, not only to ourselves": Zionist occidentalism and the discourse of hygiene in mandate Palestine. *International Journal of Middle East Studies, 41*(1): 577–594.

Hirschmüller, A. (1998). Max Eitingon über Anna O. (Breuer) in psychoanalytischer Betrachtung. *Jahrbuch der Psychoanalyse, 40*: 9–30.

Hitschmann, E. (1931). Sixtieth birthday of Josef K. Friedjung. *International Journal of Psychoanalysis, 13*: 260.

Hobsbawm, E. (1997). *On History*. New York: The New Press.

Hödl, K. (1997). *Die Pathologisierung des jüdischen Körpers: Antisemitismus, Geschlecht und Medizin im Fin de Siècle*. Wien: Picus.

Hoffer, W. (1981). Siegfried Bernfeld and Jerubaal: an episode in the Jewish youth movement. In: W. Hoffer & M. Brierley, (Eds.), *Early Development and Education of the Child* (pp. 123–144). New York: Jason Aronson.

Holland, N. (2000). The mind and the book: a long look at psychoanalytic literary criticism. *Journal of Applied Psychoanalytic Studies, 2*(1): 13–23.

Hollander, C. (1990). Buenos Aires: Latin mecca of psychoanalysis. *Social Research, 57*(4): 889–919.

Horowitz, D., & Lissak, M. (1978). *Origins of the Israeli Polity: Palestine under the Mandate.* Chicago, IL: Chicago University Press.

Hotam, Y. (2007a). *Modern Gnosis and Zionism: The Crisis of Culture, Life Philosophy and Jewish National Thought.* Jerusalem: Magnes Press [Hebrew].

Hotam, Y. (2007b). *Die Zeitalter der Jugend. Deutsch-Jüdische Jugendlichen in der Moderne.* Tübinegen: Vandenhoeck und Ruprecht.

Hotam, Y. (2008). Nationalized Judaism and diasporic existence. Jakob Klatzkin and Hans Jonas. *Behemoth. A Journal on Civilisation,* 2: 67–78.

Huber, W. (1977). *Psychoanalyse in Oessterrich seit 1933.* Wien—Salzburg: Geyer-Edition.

Idelson, D. (1940). *The Child's Sexual Life.* Jerusalem: Hasefer [Hebrew].

Isserlin, A. (1950). A totem clan is created. In: M. Wulff (Ed.), *Max Eitingon, In Memoriam* (pp. 179–183). Jerusalem: Israel Psychoanalytic Society.

Jacoby, C. (1927). Analyse eines Coitus-Interruptus-Traumes. *Int. Zeitsch. Psycho., XIII*(4): 458–459.

Jacoby, R. (1983). *The Repression of Psychoanalysis: Otto Fenichel and the Political Freudians.* New York: Basic Books.

Jay, M. (1973). *The Dialectical Imagination: A History of the Frankfurt School and the Institute for Social Research 1923–1950.* Boston, MA: Little, Brown.

Jay, M. (1986). *Permanent Exiles: Essays on the Intellectual Migration from Germany to America.* New York: Columbia University Press.

Jones, E. (1943). Max Eitingon. *International Journal of Psychoanalysis,* 24: 190–192.

Jones, E. ([1947]1974). The psychology of the Jewish question. In: *Psycho-Myth Psycho-History, Volume 1* (pp. 284–300). New York: Hillstone.

Jones, E. (1953–1957). *The Life and Work of Sigmund Freud.* Vols1–3. London: Hogarth Press.

Kaderas, B. (1998). Karl Abrahams Bemühungen um einen Lehrauftrag für Psychoanalyse an der Friedrich-Wilhelms-Universität: Quellenedition der "Denkschrift der Berliner Psychoanalytischen Vereinigung betrffend Einführung des psychoanalytischen Unterrichts an der Berliner Universität" und ihrer Ablehnung. *Jahrbuch für Universitätsgeschichte,* 1: 205–232.

Kafka, F. (1982). *Schriften, Tagebücher, Briefe,* J. Born, G. Neumann, M. Pasley, & J. Schillemeit (Eds.). New York: Fischer.

Kaminka, A. (1939). Freud's war against Moses the Prophet. *Hatzofeh,* 17 August [Hebrew].

King, P., & Steiner, R. (1991). *The Freud–Klein Controversies in the British Psycho-analytical Society 1941–1945.* London: Routledge, New Library of Psychoanalysis.

Kirsner, D. (2000). *Unfree Associations: Inside Psychoanalytic Institutes.* London: Process Press.

Klatzkin, J. (1935). *Der Erkenntnistrieb als Lebens-und Todesprinzip.* Zürich: Rascher U. CIE.

Klatzkin, J. (n.d). Triebleben; psychoanalyse. Undated manuscript, 7 pp: Klatzkin Collection, CZA.

Klausner, M. (1944). Bibliothek von Dr. Eitingon. *Mitteilungsblatt, 16l*: 2.

Klee, E. (2001). *Deutsche Medizin im Dritten Reich: Karrieren vor und nach 1945.* Frankfurt: Fischer.

Klein, D. B. (1985). *Jewish Origins of the Psychoanalytic Movement.* Chicago, IL: University of Chicago Press.

Klein, H. (1972). Holocaust survivors in kibbutzim. *Israel Annals of Psychiatry, X*: 78–91.

Klein, H. (2003). *Überleber und Versuche der Wiederbelebung,* C. Biermann., & C. Nedelmann (Eds.). Stuttgart: Frommann-Holzboog

Kloocke, R. (2002). *Mosche Wulff: Zur Geschichte der Psychoanalyse in Rußland und Israel.* Tübingen: edition diskord.

Knei-Paz, B. (1978). *The Social and Political Thought of Leon Trotsky.* London: Oxford University Press.

Kogan, I. (1995). *The Cry of Mute Children: a psychoanalytic perspective of the second generation of the Holocaust.* London: Free Association Books.

Körner, J. (1980). Über das Verhältniß von Psychoanalyse und Pädagogik. *Psyche, 34*: 769–789.

Kramer, M. (1999). The road from Mecca: Mohammad Asad (born Leopold Weiss). In: M. Kramer (Ed.), *The Jewish Discovery of Islam. Studies in Honor of Bernard Lewis* (pp. 225–247). Tel Aviv: The Moshe Dayan Center for Middle Eastern and African Studies, Tel Aviv University.

Kreuter, S. J. (1992). *Mein Leipzig.* Leipzig: Sachsenbuc.

Krüll, M. (1979). *Die Entstehung der Psychoanlyse und Freuds ungelöste Vaterbindung.* Munich: C. H. Beck.

Kuriloff, E.A. (2010). The Holocaust and psychoanalytic theory and praxis. *Contemporary Psychoanalysis, 46*: 395–422.

Kuriloff, E. A. (2012). *Contemporary Psychoanalysis and The Legacy of the Third Reich.* New York: Routledge.

Kurzweil, E. (1996). Psychoanalytic science: from Oedipus to culture. In: M. Ash & A. Söllner (Eds.), *Forced Migration and Scientific Change —German Speaking Scientists and Scholars after 1933.* Cambridge: Cambridge University Press.

Laor, D. (1998). *Agnon: A Biography.* Jerusalem: Schoken [Hebrew].

Laqueur, W. Z. (1962). *Young Germany: A History of the German Youth Movement*. New York: Basic Books.

Laqueur, W. Z. (1974). *Weimar: A Cultural History 1918–1933*. London: Weidenfeld & Nicholson.

Lasch, C. (1989). The Freudian left and cultural revolution. In: J. Sandler (Ed.), *Dimensions of Psychoanalysis* (pp. 123–139). Madison, CT: International Universities Press.

Lavsky, H. (1996). German Zionists and the emergence of Brit Shalom. In: A. Shapira & J. Reinharz, (Eds.), *Essential Papers on Zionism* (pp. 648–670). New York: New York University Press.

Lavsky, H. (1998). *Before Catastrophe—The Distinctive Path of German Zionism, 1897–1938*. Detroit: Wayne State University Press.

Lepenies, W. (2006). *The Seduction of Culture in German History*. Princeton, NJ: Princeton University Press.

Levi, N. (1988). The immigrant physicians from Nazi Germany and their contribution to medicine in Eretz Israel. *Harefuah, 214*: 205–210.

Liban, A. (1999). Freuds Einwanderung nach Eretz Israel. PhD Dissertation, Technische Universität Berlin.

Liban, A., & Goldman, D. (2000). Freud comes to Palestine: a study of psychoanalysis in a cultural context. *International Journal of Psychoanalysis, 81*: 893–906.

Lieberman, E. J. (1985). *Acts of Will: The Life and Work of Otto Rank*. New York: Free Press.

Limentani, A. (1989). The psychoanalytic movement during the years of the war (1939–1945) according to the archives of the IPA. *International Review of Psychoanalysis, 16*: 3–13.

Little, M. I. (1985). Winnicott working in areas where psychotic anxieties predominate. *Free Associations, 1D*: 9–42.

Lockot, R. (1994). *Die Reinigung der Psychoanalyse: Die Deutsche Psychoanalytische Gesellschaft im Spiegel von Dokumenten und Zeitungen 1933–1951*. Tübingen: edition diskord.

Loewenberg, P. (1970). A hidden Zionist theme in Freud's 'My Son, the Myops . . .' dream. *Journal of the History of Ideas, 31*(1): 129–132.

Loewenberg, P. (1971). Sigmund Freud as a Jew: a study in ambivalence and courage. *Behavioral Sciences, 7*(4): 363–369.

Lohmann, H. M. (Ed.) (1984). *Psychoanalyse und Nationalsozialismus. Beiträge zur Bearbeitung eines unbewältigten Traumas*. Frankfurt: Fischer Taschenbuch.

Lück, H. E. (1997). Der Exodus und die Folgen für die Psychologie. In: M. Hassler, & J. Wertheimer (Eds.), *Der Exodus aus Nazideutschland und die Folgen: Jüdische Wissenschaftler im Exil* (pp. 73–90). Tübingen: Attempto.

Makari, G. (2008). *Revolution In Mind: The Creation of Psychoanalysis*. New York: HarperCollins.

Margalit, E. (1971). *Hashomer Hazair—From Youth Community to Revolutionary Marxism (1913–1936)*. Tel Aviv: Tel Aviv University Press [Hebrew].

Marinelli, L. (Ed). (2001). *"Meine . . . alten und dreckigen Götter". Aus Sigmund Freuds Sammlung*. Frankfurt: Stroemfeld.

Marinelli, L., & Mayer, A. (2003). *Dreaming by the Book: Freud's "The Interpretation of Dreams" and the History of the Psychoanalytic Movement*. New York: Other Press.

Massen, T. (1995). *Pädagogischer Eros: Gustav Wyneken und die Freie Schulgemeinde Wickersdorf*. Berlin: Rosa Winkel.

Masson, J. M. (1985). *The Complete Letters of Sigmund Freud to Wilhelm Fliess, 1887–1904*. Cambridge, MA: The Belknap Press of Harvard University Press.

May, U. (2008). Psychoanalyse in Berlin: 1920–1936. *Jahrbuch der Psychoanalyse, 57*: 13–39.

McGrath, W. J. (1974). *Dionysian Art and Populist Politics in Austria*. New Haven, CT: Yale University Press.

Meisel, P., & Kendrick, W. (Eds.) (1985). *Bloomsbury/Freud: The Letters of James and Alix Strachey 1924–1925*. New York: Basic Books.

Miller, M. (1990). The reception of psychoanalysis and the problem of the unconscious in Russia. *Social Research, 57*(4): 875–888.

Miller, M. (1998). *Freud and the Bolsheviks*. New Haven, CT: Yale University Press.

Mintz, M. (1995). *Pangs of Youth—Hashomer Hazair 1911–1921*. Jerusalem: Hassifriya Haziyonit [Hebrew].

Moses, R. (1992). A short history of psychoanalysis in Palestine and Israel. *Israel Journal of Psychiatry and Related Sciences, 29*(4): 229–238.

Moses, R. (Ed.) (1993). *Persistent Shadows of the Holocaust: The Meaning to Those Not Directly Affected*. Madison, CT: International Universities Press.

Moses, R. (1998). A short history of psychoanalysis in Palestine and Israel. *Journal of the American Academy of Psychoanalysis, 26*: 329–341.

Mosse, G. L. (1980). *Masses and Man*. New York: H. Fertig.

Mosse, G. L. (1985). *Nationalism and Sexuality. Middle-class Morality and Sexual Norms in Modern Europe*. Madison, WI: University of Wisconsin Press.

Mosse, G. L. (1996a). Central European intellectuals in Palestine. *Judaism, XLV*(2): 131–142.

Mosse, G. L. (1996b). *The Image of Man: The Creation of Modern Masculinity*. New York: Oxford University Press.

Mühlleitner, E. (1992). *Biographisches Lexikon der Psychoanalyse—Die Mitglieder der Psychologischen Mittwochsgesellschaft und der Wiener Psychoanalytischen Vereinigung 1902–1938*. Tübingen: edition discord.

Müller, T. (2000). *Von Charlottenburg zum Central Park West: Henry Lowenfeld und die Psychoanalyse in Berlin Prag und New-York*. Frankfurt: Edition Déjà Vu.

Myers, D. (1995). *Re-inventing the Jewish past: European Jewish intellectuals and the Zionist Return to History*. New York: Oxford University Press.

Nagler, S. (1963). Clinical observations on kibbutz children. *Israel Annals of Psychiatry & Related Disciplines*, 1: 201–216.

Nagler, S. (1965). Obituary. Dr. Fanya Lowtzky. *Israel Annals of Psychiatry and Related Disciplines*, 3: 285–286.

Naiman, E. (1997). *Sex in Public: The Incarnation of Early Soviet Ideology*. Princeton, NJ: Princeton University Press.

Ne'eman, Y. (2011). *We Were the Future*. Tel Aviv: Ahuzat Bayit [Hebrew].

Neiser, E. M. J. (1978). Max Eitingon. Leben und Werk. Inaugural Dissertation, Universität Mainz.

Neumann, B. (2007). *Being-in-the-Weimar-Republic*. Tel Aviv: Am Oved Publishers. [Hebrew]

Neumann, B. (2011). *Land and Desire in Early Zionism*. Waltham, Massachusetts: Brandeis University Press/University Press of New England.

Niederland, D. (1985). Deutsche Ärzte-Emigration und Gesundheitspolitische Entwicklungen in "Erez Israel" (1933–1948). *Medizinisches Journal*, 20: 149–184.

Niederland, D. (1988). The emigration of Jewish academics and professionals from Germany in the first years of Nazi rule. *Leo Baeck Institute Year Book*, 33: 285–286.

Niederland, D. (1996). *German Jews—Immigrants or Refugees? A Study of Migration Patterns between the Two World Wars*. Jerusalem: Magnes [Hebrew].

Nordau, M. (1913). *Die conventionellen Lügen der Kulturmenschheit*. Leipzig: Elicher.

Nordau, M. (1955). *Zionist Writings*. Jerusalem: World Zionist Organization [Hebrew].

Nunberg, H., & Federn, E., (Eds.) (1979). *Protokolle der Wiener Psychoanalytischen Vereinigung in 4 Baende*. Frankfurt: S. Fischer.

Nur, O. (2004). Sex, eros, and physical labor: HaShomer HaTzair and psychoanalysis, 1918–1924. *Zmanim*, 88: 64–73 [Hebrew].

Oberndorf, C. P. (1926). The Berlin Psychoanalytic Policlinic. *International Journal of Psychoanalysis*, 7: 318–322.

O'Doherty, P. (2001). Zionism bad, Zionists . . . good? Two GDR historical novels as journalism: Arnold Zweig's *Traum ist Teuer* and Rudolf Hirsch's *Patria Israel*. *Amsterdamer Beiträge zur neueren Germanistik [Reisende durch Zeit und Raum, Der deutschsprachige historische Roman]*, 11: 167–177.

Ohana, D. (2010). *Political Thelogies in the Holy Land: Israeli Messianism and Its Critics*. London: Routledge.

Ornan, U. (1985). The Revival of Hebrew. *Cathedra: For the History of Eretz Israel and Its Yishuv*, 37: 83–94 [Hebrew].

Ornston, D. (Ed.) (1992). *Translating Freud*. New Haven, CT: Yale University Press.

Ovadyahu, M. (Ed.) (1969). *Bialik Speaks: Words from the Poet's Lips Clues to the Man*. New York: Herzl Press.

Oxaal, I. (1988). The Jewish origins of psychoanalysis reconsidered. In: E. Timms & N. Segal (Eds.), *Freud in Exile- Psychoanalysis and its Vicissitudes* (pp. 37–53). New Haven, CT: Yale University Press.

Oz, A. (2002). *A Tale of Love and Darkness*. London : Chatto & Windus.

Pappenheim, M. (1936). The aims of the psychic hygiene. *Harefuah*, 11: 511–516 [Hebrew].

Paris, J. B. (1994). *Karen Horney: A Psychoanalyst's Search for Self-Understanding*. New Haven, CT: Yale University Press.

Peled, R. (2002). *"The New Man" of the Zionist Revolution: HaShomer HaTzair and Its European Roots*. Tel Aviv: Am Oved [Hebrew].

Peters, U. (1992). *Psychiatrie im Exil-Die Emigration der Dynamischen Psychiatrie aus Deutschland 1933–1939*. Düsseldorf: Kupka.

Pick, D. (1993). *Faces of Degeneration: A European Disorder, 1848-1918.* Cambridge: Cambridge University Press.

Plotkin, M. B. (2001). *Freud in the Pampas: The Emergence and Development of a Psychoanalytic Culture in Argentina*. Stanford: Stanford University Press

Pomer, S. (1965). Max Eitingon 1881–1943. In: F. Alexander, S. Eisenstein, & M. Grotjhan (Eds.), *Psychoanalytic Pioneers* (pp. 51–62), New York: Basic Books.

Rabin, A. I. (1965). *Growing up in the Kibbutz*. New York: Springer.

Rangel, L., & Moses-Harushovski, R. (Eds.) (1996). *Psychoanalysis at the Political Border: Essays in Honor of Rafael Moses*. Madison, CT: International Universities Press.

Rapaport, D. (1958). The study of Kibbutz education and its bearing on the theory of development. *The American Journal of Orthopsychiatry*, 28: 587–597.

Razi, T. (2009). *Forsaken Children: the Backyard of Mandate Tel Aviv*. Tel Aviv: Am-Oved [Hebrew].

Razi, T. (2010). "The family is worthy of being rebuilt": perceptions of the Jewish family in mandate Palestine, 1918–1948. *Journal of Family History*, 35: 395–415.

Rechter, D. (2001). *The Jews of Vienna and the First World War*. London: Littman Library of Jewish Civilization.

Reich, W. (1970[1931]). *The Invasion of Compulsory Sex-Morality*. New York: Farrar Straus Giroux.

Reichmayr, J., & Wiesbauer, E. (1979). Das Verhältnis vom Sozialdemo-kratie und Psychoanalyse in Österreich zwischen 1900 und 1938. In: W. Huber, (Ed.), *Beiträge zur Psychoanalyse in Österreich* (pp. 61–105). Wien: Geyer.

Reinharz, J. (1993). *Chaim Weizmann: the Making of a Statesman*. Oxford: Oxford University Press.

Reinharz, J., & Shapira, A. (Eds.) (1996). *Essential Papers on Zionism*. New York: New York University Press.

Reshef, Y., & Dror, S. (1999). *Hebrew Education in the Years of the National Homeland (1919–1948)*. Jerusalem: The Bialik Institute & The National Israeli Science Academy [Hebrew].

Rice, E. (1990). *Freud and Moses: The Long Journey Home*. New York: State University of New York Press.

Rice, J. (1993). *Freud's Russia: National Identity in the Evolution of Psychoanalysis*. New Brunswick, NJ: Transaction.

Richards, A. (Ed.) (2010). *The Jewish World of Sigmund Freud: Essays on Cultural Roots and the Problem of Religious Identity*. Jefferson, NC: MacFarland.

Roazen, P. (1968). *Freud's Political and Social Thought*. New York: Knopf.

Roazen, P. (1985). *Helene Deutsch: A Psychoanalyst's Life*. New York: Simon & Schuster.

Robert, M. (1976). *From Oedipus to Moses: Freud's Jewish Identity*. New York: Anchor.

Roith, E. (1987). *The Riddle of Freud*. London: Tavistock.

Roith, E. (2008). Hysteria, heredity and anti-Semitism: Freud's quiet rebellion. *Psychoanalytic History*, 10: 149–168.

Rolnik, E. J. (1998). Mit Freud nach Palästina: Zur Rezeptionsgeschichte der Psychoanalyse, *Tel-Aviver Jahrbuch für Deutsche Geschichte, XXVII*: 273–300.

Rolnik, E. J. (2001). Between memory and desire: from history to psychoanalysis and back. *Psychoanalysis and History*, 3: 129–151.

Rolnik, E. J. (2002). Between ideology and identity: psychoanalysis in Jewish Palestine (1918–1948). *Psychoanalysis and History*, 4: 203–224.

Rolnik, E. J. (2004). The migration of psychoanalysis from Central Europe and the reception of the Freudian paradigm in Jewish Palestine 1919–1950. Doctoral Dissertation, Tel Aviv University [Hebrew].

Rolnik, E. J. (2006). Final analysis: the psychoanalytic movement and its first encounter with National Socialism. *Dapim Studies on the Shoah, 20*: 7–38 [Hebrew].

Rolnik, E. J. (2007). *Osei Nefashot: Im Freud le'Eretz Yisrael 1918–1948*. Tel Aviv: Am Oved [Hebrew].

Rolnik, E. J. (2008a). "Why is it that I see everything differently?" Reading a 1933 letter from Paula Heimann to Theodor Reik. *Journal of the American Psychoanalytic Association, 56*: 409–430.

Rolnik, E. J. (2008b). ". . . wo sich die Intellektuellen gegenseitig im Wege stehen": Ein Beitrag zur Migration deutschprachiger Psychoanalyse und Ihre Schicksale. *Luzifer-Amor, Zeitschrift zur Geschichte der Psychoanalyse, 42*: 88–99.

Rolnik, E. J. (2008c). Berliner Empfindlichkeiten, Russische Bildwelten, und Jerusalemer Wirklichkeiten: Die Etablierung der Psychoanalyse im jüdischen Palästina/Israel. *Jahrbuch der Psychoanalyse, 57*: 57–77.

Rolnik, E. J. (2010). Therapy and ideology: psychoanalysis and its vicissitudes in pre-state Israel (including some hitherto unpublished letters by Sigmund Freud and Albert Einstein). *Science in Context, 23*(4): 473–506.

Rolnik, E. J., & Simkin, A. (2005). Throbbing between stars and abyss: a reconsideration of the mood swings in the life and work of the poet Chaim Nachman Bialik. *MEKAROV, December*: 13–31 [Hebrew].

Rose, J. (2005). *The Question of Zion*. Princeton, NJ: Princeton University Press.

Rose, L. (1998). *The Freudian Calling: Early Viennese Psychoanalysis and the Pursuit of Cultural Science*. Detroit: Wayne State University Press.

Rose, N. S. (1990). *Governing the Soul: The Shaping of the Private Self*. London: Routledge.

Rosenbaum, M. (1954). Freud–Eitingon–Magnes coresspondence: psychoanalysis at the Hebrew University. *Journal of the American Psychoanalytic Association, 2*: 311–317.

Rudnytsky, P. (2002). *Reading Psychoanalysis: Freud, Rank, Ferenczi, Groddeck*. Ithaca, NY: Cornell University Press.

Ruppin, A. (1971). *Arthur Ruppin: Memoirs, Diaries, Letters*. London: Weidenfeld & Nicolson.

Ruppin, A. (1985). *Tagebücher, Briefe Erinnerungen*, S. Krolik (Ed.). Königstein/Ts.: Jüdischer Verlag Athenäum.

Sadan, D. (1996). *A Psychoanalytic Midrash: Studies in Brenner's Psychology*. Jerusalem: The Magnes Press, The Hebrew University [Hebrew].

Safir, M. P. (1983). The kibbutz, an experiment in social and sexual equality? An historical perspective. In: M. Palgi, J. Blasi, M., Rosner, & M. P. Safir, (Eds.) *Sexual Equality: The Israeli Kibbutz Tests and Theories*. Philadelphia, PA: Norwood Press.

Said, E. (2003). *Freud and the Non-European*. London: Verso.

Salberg, J. (2010). Hidden in plain sight: Freud's Jewish identity revisited. In: A. Richards (Ed.), *The Jewish World of Sigmund Freud* (pp. 5–21). Jefferson: NC: McFarland.

Sand, S. (2000). *Intellectuals, Truth, and Power: From the Dreyfus Affair to the Gulf War*. Tel Aviv: Am Oved [Hebrew].

Santner, E. (2001). *On the Psychotheology of Everyday Life: Reflections on Freud and Rosenzweig*. Chicago, IL: University of Chicago Press.

Scharaf, M. (1983). *Fury on Earth: A Biography of Wilhelm Reich*. New York: St. Martin's Press.

Schatzker, C. (1992). The Jewish youth movements as an historical phenomenon. *Studies in Jewish Civilization*, 3: 149–165.

Schatzker, C. (1998). *Jewish Youth in Germany between Judaism and Germanism*. Jerusalem: The Zalman Shazar Center for Jewish History [Hebrew].

Scholem, G. (1982). *From Berlin to Jerusalem: Memoirs of my Youth*. New York: Schocken.

Schorske, C. E. (1981). *Fin-De-Siècle Vienna: Politics and Culture*, New York: Vintage Books.

Schreibaum, D. (1993). *Interpretation of Dreams in S. Y. Agnon's Literary Works*. Tel Aviv : Tel Aviv University Press [Hebrew].

Schröter, M. (1997). Max Eitingon ein Geheimagent Stalins? Erneuter Protest gegen ein Zählebige Legende. *Psyche*, 51: 457–470.

Schröter, M. (2002). Max Eitingon and the struggle to establish an international standard for psychoanalytic training (1925–1929). *International Journal of Psychoanalysis*, 83: 875–893.

Schröter, M. (2004). Der Steuermann: Max Eitingon und seine Rolle in der Geschichte der Psychoanalyse. In: M. Schröter (Ed.). *Sigmund Freud–Max Eitingon. Briefwechsel 1906–1939* (pp. 1–33). Tübingen: edition diskord.

Schröter, M. (2008). Psychoanalyse in Berlin: 1920–1936. *Jahrbuch der Psychoanalyse, 57*: 13–39.

Schröter, M. (2009). "Hier läuft alles zur Zufriedenheit, abgesehen von den Verlusten". Die Deutsche Psychoanalytische Gesellschaft 1933–1936. *Psyche, 63*: 1086–1130.

Schröter, M., Mühlleitner, E., & May, U. (2004). Edith Jacobson: forty years in Germany (1897–1938). *Annals of Psychoanalysis, 32*: 199–215.

Schweid, E. (1985). *The Land of Israel: National Home or Land of Destiny*. Rutherford, NJ: Fairleigh Dickinson University Press.

Schweid, E. (2008). *The Idea of Modern Jewish Culture*. Boston, MA: Academic Studies Press.

Segev, T. (2001). *One Palestine, Complete: Jews and Arabs Under the British Mandate*. New York: H. Holt.

Sela-Shefi, R. (2006). Integration through distinction: German–Jewish Palestine. *Journal of Historical Sociology, 19*: 34–59.

Sengoopta, C. (2000). *Otto Weininger: Sex, Science, and Self in Imperial Vienna*. Chicago, IL: University of Chicago Press.

Shafir, G. (1989). *Land, Labour and the Origins of the Israeli–Palestinian Conflict, 1882–1914*. Cambridge: Cambridge University Press.

Shaked, G. (1996). Shall all hopes be fulfilled? Genre and anti-genre in the Hebrew literature of Palestine. In: J. Reinharz & A. Shapira (Eds)., *Essential Papers on Zionism* (pp. 763–789). New York: New York University Press.

Shalom, Y. S. (1942). Freud's repressed Judaism. *Moznaim, 14*: 317–319 [Hebrew].

Shapira, A. (1992). *Land and Power: The Zionist Resort to Force, 1881–1948*. New York: Oxford University Press.

Shapira, A. (1996). Native sons. In: J. Reinharz & A. Shapira (Eds.), *Essential Papers on Zionism* (pp. 791–821). NewYork: New York University Press.

Shapira, A. (1997a). *New Jews, Old Jews*. Tel Aviv: Am Oved [Hebrew]

Shapira, A. (1997b). The origins of the myth of the 'New Jew': the Zionist variety. *Studies in Contemporary Jewry, 13*: 253–270.

Shavit, Y., & Reinharz, J. (2009). *Darwin and Some of His Kind: Evolution, Race, Environment & Culture—Jews Read Darwin, Spencer, Buckle & Renan*. Tel Aviv: Hakibutz Hameuchad [Hebrew].

Shavit, Z. (Ed.) (1998). *The History of the Jewish Community in Eretz Israel since 1882: The Construction of Hebrew Culture in Eretz Israel*. Jerusalem: The Israeli Academy for Sciences and Humanities and The Bialik Institute [Hebrew].

Sheffi, N. (1999). The Hebrew absorption of German literature. *Israel Affairs, 5*(4): 158–171.

Sheffi, N. (2011). *Vom Deutschen ins Hebräische: Übersetzungen aus dem Deutschen im jüdischen Palästina 1882–1948*. Göttingen: Vandenhoeck & Ruprecht.

Simon, A. E. (1998). *Sechzig Jahre gegen den Strom: Briefe von 1917–1984*. Tübingen: Mohr Siebeck.

Slavet, E. (2009). *Racial Fever: Freud and the Jewish Question*. New York: Fordham University Press.

Slezkine, Y. (2004). *The Jewish Century*. Princeton, NJ: Princeton University Press.

Smeliansky, A., & Nacht, A. (1941). Max Eitngon, von Freunden gesehen. In: Die Chewrah Psychoanalytith B'erez Israel gratuliert ihrem Praesidenten zum sechzigsten Geburtstag. Unpublished manuscript (ECI).

Spector, M., & Kitsuse, J. (2000). *Constructing Social Problems*. New York: Aldine de Gruyter.

Spiegel, R. (1975). The survival of psychoanalysis in Nazi Germany. *Contemporary Psychoanalysis*, 11: 479–491.

Spiegel, R. (1986). Freud's refutation of degenerationism: a contribution to humanism. *Contemporary Psychoanalysis, 22*: 4–24.

Spiro, M. (1958). *Children of the Kibbutz*. Cambridge: Harvard Univ. Press.

Stadler, F. (Ed.) (1987). *Vertriebe Vernunft: Emigration und Exil Oesterreichischr Wissenschaftler 1930–1940*. Wien München: Jugend und Volk.

Stanislawski, M. (2001). *Zionism and the Fin de Siècle: Cosmopolitanism and Nationalism from Nordau to Jabotinsky*. Berkeley, CA: University of California Press.

Steedman, C. (1995). *Strange Dislocations. Childhood and the Idea of Human Interiority, 1780–1930*. Cambridge, MA: Harvard University Press.

Stein, L. (1945). Eder as Zionist. In: J. B. Hobman (Ed.), *David Eder: Memoirs of a Modern Pioneer* (pp. 139–142). London: Victor Gollancz.

Stein, R. (2009). *For Love of the Father: A Psychoanalytic Study of Religious Terrorism*. Stanford, CT: Stanford University Press.

Steiner, R. (1989). It is a new kind of Diaspora ... *International Review of Psychoanalysis, 16*: 35–78.

Steiner, R. (2011). In all questions, my interest is not in the individual people but in the analytic movement as a whole. It will be hard enough here in Europe in the times to come to keep it going. After all, we are just a handful of people who really have that in mind ... *International Journal of Psychoanalysis, 92*: 505–591.

Stengel, E. (1939). On learning a new language. *International Journal of Psychoanalysis*, 20: 471–479.

Stepansky, P. (1988). *The Memoirs of Margaret S. Mahler*. New York: Free Press.

Sterba, R. F. (1985). *Errinerungen eines Wiener Psychoanalytikers*. Frankfurt: Fischer.

Stern, M. M. (1988). *Repetition and Trauma: Toward a Teleonomic Theory of Psychoanalysis*, L. B. Stern (Ed.). Hillsdale, NJ: The Analytic Press.

Sternhell, Z. (1998). *The Founding Myths of Israel: Nationalism, Socialism, and the Making of the Jewish State*. Princeton, NJ: Princeton University Press.

Stone, L. (1997). German Zionists in Palestine before 1933. *Journal of Contemporary History, 32*: 171–186.

Stonebridge, L. (1998). Anxiety at a time of crises. *History Workshop Journal, 45*: 171–182.

Straus, H. A. (Ed.) (1978–1988). *Jewish Immigrants of the Nazi Period in the U.S.A: Vols. 1–6*. New York: K. G. Saur.

Straus, H. A. (1980–1981). Jewish emigration from Germany. Nazi politics and Jewish responses. Part I. *LBI Year Book, XXV*: 313–363; Part II: *LBI Year Book, XXVI*: 343–411.

Straus, H. A., & Roeder, W. (Eds.) (1983). *International Biographical Dictionary of Central European Emigres 1933–1945*. Munich: K. G. Saur.

Strikovsky, Z. (1928). Review of Freud's *Group Psychology and the Analysis of the Ego*. *Shvilay Ha'chinuch*, 1928–1929: 475–479 [Hebrew].

Strozier, C. B. (2001). *Heinz Kohut: The Making of a Psychoanalyst*. New York: Farrar, Strauss and Giroux.

Taylor, C. (2007). *A Secular Age*. Cambridge, MA: Harvard University Press.

Thompson, N. (1987). Early women psychoanalysts. *International Review of Psychoanalysis, 14*: 391–407.

Thompson, N. (2010). The transformation of psychoanalysis in America: emigre analysts and the New York Psychoanalytic Society, 1935–1961. Unpublished lecture delivered as the 58th A. A. Brill Lecture at the NYPS, December 14, 2010.

Timms, E., & Segal, N. (Eds.) (1988). *Freud in Exile – Psychoanalysis and its Vicissitudes*. New Haven: Yale University Press.

Turkle, S. (1992). *Psychoanalytic Politics: Jacques Lacan and Freud's French Revolution* (2nd edn). New York: Guilford Press.

Ufaz, A. (1991). The world of symbols in Kehilateinu. *Cathedra: For the History of Eretz Israel and Its Yishuv, 59*: 126–143 [Hebrew].

Utley, P. (1979). Siegfried Bernfeld's Jewish Order of Youth, 1914–1922. *LBI Year Book, XXIV*: 349–369.

Velikovsky, I. (1933). Psychoanalytische Anschaunungen in der Traumdeutungskunst der alten Hebräer nach dem Traktat Brachoth. *Psychoanalytische Bewegung, 5*: 66–69.

Velikovsky, I. (1934). Kann eine neuerlernte Sprache zur Sprache des Unbewußten? Wortspiele in Träumen von Hebräisch denkenden, *Imago, 20*: 234–239.

Viest, A. (1977). *Identität und Integration: Dargestellt am Beispiel Mitteleuropäischer Einwanderer in Israel*. Bern, Frankfurt, Las Vegas: Peter Lang.

Vital, D. (1975). *The Origins of Zionism*. Oxford: Oxford University Press.

Vital, D. (1982). *Zionism: The Formative Years*. Oxford: Oxford University Press.

Vital, D. (1987). *Zionism: The Crucial Phase*. Oxford: Oxford University Press.

Volkov, S. (2006). *Germans, Jews and Antisemites. Trials in Emancipation*. Cambridge: Cambridge University Press.

Wallerstein, R. (1998). *Lay Analysis: Life Inside the Controversy*. Hillsdale, NJ: Analytic Press.

Wehr, G. (1991). *Martin Buber: Leben, Werk, Wirkung*. Zürich: Diogenes.

Weidemann, D. (1988). *Leben und Werk von Therese Benedek (1892–1977)*. Bern: Peter Lang.

Weiner, A. (1984). *Out of the Family. Placement of Children in the Land of Israel during the Mandate*. Tel Aviv: Hakibutz Hameuhad [Hebrew].

Will, H. (2001). Was ist Klassische Psychoanalyse? *Psyche, 7*: 685–717.

Willet, J. (1984). *The Weimar Years: A Culture Cut Short*. New York: Abbeville Press.

Williams, J. A. (2001). Ecstasies of the young: sexuality, the Youth Movement, and moral panic in Germany on the eve of the First World War. *Central European History, 34*(2): 163–189.

Wilmers, M. K. (2009). *The Eitingons: A Twentieth-Century Story*. London: Verso.

Windhager, G. (2002). *Leopold Weiss alias Muhammad Asad: Von Galizien nach Arabien 1900–1927*. Wien: Boehlau.

Winnicott, D. W. (1953). Transitional objects and transitional phenomena—a study of the first not-me possession. *International Journal of Psychoanalysis, 34*: 89–97.

Winnik, H. Z. (1977). Milestones in the development of psychoanalysis in Israel. *Israel Annals of Psychiatry and Related Disciplines, 15*: 85–91.

Winnik, H. Z., Moses, R., & Ostow, M. (Eds.) (1973). *Psychological Bases of War*. New York: Quadrangle Books & Jerusalem Academic Press.

Wistrich, R., & Ohana, D. (1995). The shaping of Israeli identity: myth, memory, and trauma. *Israel Affairs, 1/3*.

Wittels, F. (1933). *Set the Children Free*. New York: W. W. Norton.

Wittenberger, G., & Toegel, C., (Eds). (1999). *Die Rundbriefe des "Geheimen Komitees"*. Tübingen: edition diskord.

Witztum, E., & Margolin, J. (2004). Establishment of the "Ezrath Nashim" Psychiatric Hospital in Jerusalem: Selected Issues. *Harefuah, 143*: 382–385 [Hebrew].

Wolf, A. (1993). "Freund Eitingon" Geschichte einer "freudianischen" Freundschaft: Arnold Zweigs im Spiegel seiner Korrespondenz und seines literarischen Werkes. In: Arnold Zweig—Psyche, Politik und

Literatur. Akten des II. Internationalen Arnold-Zweig-Symposiums, Gent 1991. *Jb. Int. Germanistik*: 137–157.

Woolf, M. (1945). Prohibitions against the simultaneous consumption of milk and flesh in Orthodox Jewish Law. *International Journal of Psychoanalysis, 26*: 169–177.

Woolf, M. (1946). Joseph K. Friedjung (obituary). *International Journal of Psychoanalysis, 27*: 71–72.

Worman, K. (1970). German Jews in Israel: their cultural situation since 1933. *LBI Year Book, XV*: 73–103.

Wulff, M. (1926). Widerstand des Ichideals und Realitätsanpassung. *Interntionale Zeitschrift für Psychoanalyse, 12*: 436–443.

Wulff, M. (1928). Bemerkungen über einige Ergebnisse bei einer psychiatrisch-neurologischen Untersuchung von Chauffeuren. *Internationale Zeitschrift für Psychoanalyse, 14*: 237–242.

Wulff, M. (1942). A case of male homosexuality. *International Journal of Psychoanalysis, 23*: 112–120.

Wulff, M. (1946). Fetishism and object choice in early childhood. *Psychoanalytic Quarterly, 15*: 450–471.

Wulff, M. (1950). An appreciation of Freud's "Moses and Monotheism". In: M. Wulff (Ed.), *Max Eitingon: In Memoriam* (pp. 141–150). Jerusalem: Israel Psychoanalytic Society.

Wulff, M. (1953). Dr. Ilja Shalit Obituary. *International Journal of Psychoanalysis, 34*: 357.

Wulff, M. (1957). Revolution and drive. *Psychoanalytic Review, 44*: 410–432.

Wünschmann, K. (2012). The 'scientification' of the Nazi camps: the writings of Bruno Bettelheim, Curt W. Bondy, and Paul M. Neurath and their reception in the New World. *Naharaim: Journal of German-Jewish Literature and Cultural History* (in press).

Yaffe, E. (1934). Against the current consensus. *Gazit, 2*(X–XI): 25–26 [Hebrew].

Yaffe, E. (1947). *Collected Works of Eliezer Yaffe*. 2 Vols. Tel Aviv: Am Oved [Hebrew].

Yaron, K. (2000). Martin Buber. *Prospects: The Quarterly Review of Comparative Education*. Paris: UNESCO: International Bureau of Education.

Yehoshua, A.B. (2005). An attempt to comprehend the infrastructure of anti-semitism [Hebrew]. *Alpayyim, 28*: 11–30.

Yerushalmi, Y. H. (1991). *Freud's Moses: Judaism Terminable and Interminable*. New Haven, CT: Yale University Press.

Yitzhaki, S. (1989). Psychoanalysis in the communal education of Ha'Shomer Ha'Tzair. *Hachinuch HaMeshutaf, 133*: 84–70; *134*: 56–66 [Hebrew].

Young-Bruehl, E. (1994). *Anna Freud: A Biography*. New York: W. W. Norton.

Zakim, E. (2006). *To Build and Be Built: Landscape, Literature, and the Construction of Zionist Identity*. Philadelphia, PA: University of Pennsylvania Press.

Zalashik, R. (2005). Psychiatry, ethnicity and migration: the case of Palestine, 1920–1948. *DYNAMIS*, 25: 403–422.

Zalashik, R. (2008). *Ad Nafesh: Refugees, Immigrants, Newcomers and the Israeli Psychiatric Establishment*. Tel Aviv: Hakibutz Hameukhad [Hebrew].

Zalashik, R., & Davidovitch, N. (2009). Professional identity across the borders: refugee psychiatrists in Palestine, 1933–1945. *Social History of Medicine*, 22(3): 569–587.

Zerubavel, Y. (1995). *Recovered Roots: Collective Memory and the Making of Israeli National Tradition*. Chicago, IL: University of Chicago Press.

Zimmerman, M. (1992). German Jews and the Jewish Emigration from Russia. In: I. Toren & B. Pinkus (Eds.), *Organizing Rescue: Jewish National Solidarity in the Modern Period*. London: F. Cass.

Zimmerman, M. (2003). Muscular Judaism: the remedy for Jewish nervousness. *Zmanim, 83*: 56–65 [Hebrew].

Zimmerman, M. (2006). Muscle Jews vs. nervous Jews. In: M. Brenner, & G. Reuveni (Eds.), *Emancipation through Muscles. Jews and Sports in Europe* (pp. 13–26). London: Lincoln.

Zipperstein, S. (1993). *Elusive Prophet: Ahad Ha'am and the Origins of Zionism*. Berkeley, CA: University of California Press.

Zohar, T. (1940). Amongst ourselves. *Hachinuch Hameshutaf, 11*: 17 [Hebrew].

Zohar, T., & Golan, S. (1941). *Sex Education*. Merhavia: Sifriat Poalim [Hebrew].

Zweig, A. (1937). Emigration und Neurose. Paper presented to the Psychoanalytic Institute of Jerusalem: AZA.

Zweig, A. (1989). *Traum ist Teuer*. Frankfurt: Fischer.

INDEX